RAILWAYS OF THE WORLD

1   Railways of Southern Africa

RAILWAYS OF THE WORLD

South African Railways

The 'Blue Train' ascending the Hex River Pass, in the days when this section
was steam worked. The engine is a '15F' class 4-8-2

RAILWAYS OF THE WORLD

1 *Railways of Southern Africa*

O. S. NOCK

B.SC., C.ENG., F.I.C.E., F.I. MECH. E.
PAST PRESIDENT, INSTITUTION OF
RAILWAY SIGNAL ENGINEERS

WITH 105 PHOTOGRAPHS
AND 8 COLOUR PLATES

ADAM & CHARLES BLACK · LONDON

FIRST PUBLISHED 1971
A. AND C. BLACK LIMITED
4, 5 AND 6 SOHO SQUARE LONDON W1V 6AD

© 1971 O. S. NOCK

ISBN 0 7136 1106 5

MADE AND PRINTED
IN GREAT BRITAIN
BY BUTLER AND TANNER LTD
FROME AND LONDON

Contents

Illustrations

7

Acknowledgements

The Author and Publishers wish to thank the following for permission to use photographs:

The South African Railways for plates 1, 2, 3, 4b, 6, 10, 12, 26a.

The Rhodesia Railways for plates 30, 31a, 33.

The East African Railways for plates 42, 44, 47.

To Messrs. Beyer, Peacock & Co. Ltd. for plates 15b, c, and d, 16c, 31b, 36, 39b, c and d, 41, 43, 46.

To the English Electric Co. Ltd. for plate 26c.

To the North British Locomotive Co. Ltd. for plates 9, 11, 13, 15a, 16b, 18, 19, 32a, 32b, 32d, 39b.

To Robert Stephenson & Hawthorns Ltd. for plate 32c.

To Westinghouse Brake and Signal Co. Ltd. for plates 22, 23, 28b, 40.

To the Cleveland Bridge and Engineering Co. Ltd. for plates 34, 35.

To K. Austin Esq., for plate 48.

To D. H. Constable Esq., for plate 38b.

To O. S. Nock Esq., for plates 4a, 5, 7, 8, 14, 17, 20a, 21, 26b, 27, 28a, 38a, 45.

To R. G. Pattison Esq., for plate 29.

To P. Ransome-Wallis Esq. for plate 20b.

To A. R. Walwyn Esq., for plate 25.

To *The Railway Magazine* for plate 37.

The colour plates A, B, C, G and H are from original paintings by Jack Hill.

Colour plates D, E and F are from colour transparencies by O. S. Nock.

When, following the publication of my previous books *British Steam Railways* and *Steam Railways in Retrospect*, Mr. Black asked me to consider extending the same kind of treatment to railways the world over I was somewhat taken aback. It was one thing to write of railways I had known from my childhood, but quite another to write of far places I had never visited. It is true that my life-time's work as a signal contractor had made me familiar with operating conditions in many parts of the world; but it was experience gained as a designer, and at the time Mr. Black first broached the matter my personal acquaintance with railways beyond Europe was confined to a few lines in South-East Asia. There were, however, vague prospects of some more distant travels, and so I agreed to 'have a go'.

Opportunity, and not a little extra-mural planning, have enabled me to write of Southern Africa first in the new series. The geographical term needs a little explaining, because the area sometimes referred to as 'Southern Africa' is not always considered to extend as far north as Kenya and Uganda. On the other hand I have not been able to visit all the railways in Africa south of the Equator. Tanzania, Moçambique, Angola and South-West Africa all lie beyond my particular pale. Elsewhere I have had the good fortune to travel extensively, and to supplement my technical knowledge of the engineering work with first-hand experience on the lines concerned.

The old saying 'Who runs may read' takes on a new and compelling significance in Southern Africa, for to appreciate the railways as they are today one must know something of their history, and indeed the history of the country itself. When travelling in Southern Africa I did not do much reading; there was too much to see from the train windows. But I certainly laid up literature to absorb when I returned home, and I found Lennox van Onselen's *Heads of Steel*, and George Pauling's *Chronicles of a Contractor* fascinating books. I read several biographies of Cecil Rhodes, while one can marvel at the measured prose and modest air of such great civil engineers as W. G. Brounger and G. A. Hobson, when describing their magnificent railway constructional achievements in papers read before the Institution of Civil Engineers.

In my travels I made many new friends, both in the railway service and among outside enthusiasts. Obviously I cannot mention all of them by name, but among those who have helped directly and indirectly towards the preparation of this book I must mention particularly Messrs. J. H. Jackson and F. J. Kent of the East African Railways, Mr. D. H. Constable of the Rhodesia Railways, and the splendid co-operation I have had from the General Manager's Department of the South African Railways. When I was in Johannesburg I became a member of the Railway Society of Southern Africa, and this, of course, opened the way to many new friendships, not to mention the data contained in the admirable journal of that Society.

Quite apart from the books already mentioned, and John Day's excellent *Railways of Southern Africa*, there is a wealth of historical matter in the early volumes of our old favourite *The Railway Magazine*, while locomotive and rolling stock developments are comprehensively documented in *The Locomotive*. A further source of information on latter day developments have been the papers of the late Edward Cecil Poultney, who was concerned with valve gear design for some of the largest locomotives of the 1930s. Lastly I am indebted to Mr. M. A. Crane, formerly Sales Director of Messrs. Beyer Peacock & Co. Ltd., for much valuable information about Garratt locomotive working.

To Olivia, my wife, I am, as always, much indebted for her help. Although all the journeys made in this book were made alone, before it even reaches proof stage we shall have journeyed to Africa together, and I shall have been able to show her some of the scenes that have gripped her imagination during the typing of the book.

Silver Cedars,   O. S. NOCK
High Bannerdown,
Batheaston,
BATH

July 1969

CHAPTER ONE

Introduction

In studying the railways of any country, or group of countries, one cannot go very far without dipping into history. There will be peculiarities of equipment-design or track layout that cannot be explained by an examination of the situation as it exists today. In Southern Africa however the history of railways is to a remarkable extent the history of the sub-continent itself. Only in Cape Province does the history of the country extend back to more than a century before the coming of railways, and history in all the countries of Southern Africa is dramatic and compelling to the last degree. Nevertheless the very wonder and facility of modern world communications can tend to make a present-day traveller's exploration of the railways of Southern Africa a process in reverse, and in so doing to lose something of the immense significance of pioneer railway development. To follow in the footsteps of history one should undoubtedly start at Cape Town, and from there make the arduous ascent of the Hex River Pass to De Aar, and on to Kimberley similarly in Kenya one should undoubtedly start at Mombasa.

It would, of course, be delightful if one had the time to sail in stately ships from Southampton to Cape Town, or in normal times through the Mediterranean and the Suez Canal to East African ports. In these breathless days however one must travel by air, to save time, and the great turbo-jets bring us to the goals of railway enterprise in Africa: to Nairobi, rather than Mombasa; to Johannesburg, rather than the Cape. Those who would trace the tracks of the great pioneers find themselves doing it in reverse. When all is said and done however it would be graceless to plant this modest indictment on the doorstep of B.O.A.C.; for it is only through their magnificent services that I, for one, in the midst of many other duties could see a great deal of the railways of Southern Africa in a very short time. Those services of B.O.A.C. do indeed make nonsense of great distances, when I could take a late afternoon tea in my own home at Bath and keep an appointment with the Deputy Chief Engineer of the East African Railways in his office at Nairobi at 10.30 a.m. next morning.

While the speed of transit between the United Kingdom and Southern Africa is now so fast the general tempo of railway operation in Africa itself is infinitely slower than anything to which we are now accustomed at home. A connoisseur of locomotive performance familiar with present standards on the electrified lines from Euston to Crewe might at first glance be inclined to write off, as of no consequence, the working of a long-distance through train equipped with dining and sleeping cars which took just over four hours to cover the first 100 miles out of Cape Town, albeit with electric haulage. But such a mental 'write-off' would be to miss the whole significance of railway working in South Africa. Riding such a train, and having passed on to a non-electrified line, I peered out from the open platform at the end of a vintage dining car and just listened to the huge Beyer-Garratt engine working steam hard in the stillness of the African night. It was cloudy, and although the moon was obscured it was making enough light to throw up the outline of a lofty mountain range, while ahead the track was floodlit from the powerful headlight of our engine.

The establishment of railway communication in Southern Africa can be likened, on a gigantic scale, to the policy adopted by those who built railways through the Highlands of Scotland. Here was no case of making rapid communication such as Brunel set out to do between London and Bristol, or Robert Stephenson did between London and Birmingham. In Southern Africa, as in the Highlands, the task was to secure some form of railways. However slow it might be in comparison with the railways already operating in other parts of the world, any journey by rail would be an immeasurable improvement upon the hazards, privations, and outright dangers of travelling the uncharted tracks of Africa by horse-drawn vehicles. In South Africa railway development began, as nearly everywhere else in the world, as a series of individual and unconnected enterprises, and those pioneers who carried the rails inland from Cape Town and from Port Elizabeth were heading into the unknown almost as completely as the intrepid band of men, women, and children who some twenty years earlier had set out from the Cape of Good Hope in the Great Trek that took them eventually into the land north of the Vaal River,

As in many other countries the pattern of railway development in South Africa, as distinct from the entire continent south of the Equator, underwent considerable changes, as major industrial, political, and strategic circumstances eventuated; but never so dramatically as when into the arena of independent, and at times hesitant, local endeavour came that colossus of Imperial development Cecil John Rhodes. How he formed the magnificent, yet stillborn, conception of the 'Cape to Cairo Railway', is one of the greatest romances of the British Empire. The first link had already been forged before Rhodes had ever set foot in Africa; but it had been a purely local affair within the Cape Colony— The Cape Town and Wellington Railway, a line no more than 58 miles long. This was completed in November 1863; but no more than six years later the whole direction and purpose of railways in South Africa was changed by the momentous discovery of diamonds at Kimberley. At that time the only other railway in existence was a short local line in Durban; but the prospect of immense wealth led to a certain rivalry between the established ports of Cape Town, Durban, and Port Elizabeth to secure railway communication with the diamond fields. At the end of 1869 it was only Cape Town that had a railway worth the name, and its railhead at Wellington was a long and hazardous distance from what became known as the 'diggings'.

It must, nevertheless, not be imagined that a breakneck race in construction ensued. Despite the need, and the promise of a fabulous reward, events moved slowly at first, and it was not until May 1872 that the Cape House passed legislation to enable the Government to acquire the railways, and extend the line from Wellington farther inland. On 1 January 1873 the transfer was effected, and the first plans began to be made for the continuation of the line northward from Wellington. In the meantime the journey from Cape Town to the diamond fields remained an exceedingly long and unpleasant one. The run of 58 miles by train to Wellington usually took between $3\frac{1}{2}$ and 4 hours, and then one transferred to a semi-covered wagon drawn maybe by eight horses, with a Hottentot driver. The journey northwards could take anything up to a fortnight, according to whether the wagon held together or not on the wild tracks across the mountain and desert country that had to be traversed. Yet despite the urgent need, such were the difficulties faced by the constructional parties that a full eleven years elapsed before the tracks

19

of the Cape Government Railway, as it became in 1873, reached the south bank of the Orange River.

By that time Cecil Rhodes, although no more than thirty-one years of age, was already a mighty power in the land. In 1880 he had founded the world-famous de Beers Mining Company in Kimberley, and in the same year he became a member of Parliament, in Cape Colony. More important still, in 1883, a year before the railway had reached the Orange River, he had visited Stellaland, and it was this visit that largely inspired his great vision of development in the north. The railway from the south had been constructed entirely in British colonial territory, though on its more northerly reaches it closely kirted the frontier between Cape Colony and the Orange Free State. The latter was a Boer republic, and like its neighbours to the north of the Vaal River, known then as the 'South African Republic', it was at that time entirely non-industrial. The discovery of gold in the Witwatersrand had not yet been made; Johannesburg literally did not exist, and these two pastoral countries were of no particular interest to Cecil Rhodes. In 1885, the year the railway reached Kimberley, Rhodes met President Kruger for the first time, and apparently neither was particularly impressed with the other. What was more important was the British Imperial development to the north-west of Kimberley, whereby the territory of Bechuanaland South became a Crown Colony, later to be absorbed into the Cape of Good Hope, while Bechuanaland North became a British Protectorate. The ground was clear for the northward extension of the railway from Kimberley.

In the meantime another route from the south had been completed, starting from Port Elizabeth, and making a way via Cookhouse and Cradock where the constructional work had been even more hazardous than on the route from the Cape. The two lines joined at that rather amazing outpost De Aar Junction. Nevertheless by the time the railway reached Kimberley the first great boom in diamond mining had passed, and with the numerous independent mines seeking ways in which the methods of digging could be improved, and their profits be maintained at something near the fantastic levels achieved when the precious stones were to be found near the surface, the stage was being set for Cecil Rhodes to engineer the biggest take-over bid of the nineteenth century by amalgamating *all* the diamond mines of Kimberley under his own control. That colossal merger took place in 1888.

20

Even before that, however, at the end of 1886, there had occurred the
event that was to change the entire economic and financial structure of
South Africa—the discovery of gold on the Witwatersrand. The foundations of Johannesburg were laid, and before the year 1887 was out
Rhodes had founded a Goldfields Company of his own, and was making
plans to extend the railway into the Transvaal. The difficulties here were
political rather than of engineering. The Republic was definitely hostile
to Great Britain. Prior to the war of 1877, after which the Transvaal
became a British Colony, there had been a scheme to build a railway
from Lourenço Marques, in Portuguese East Africa to the frontier of
the Transvaal. But the war put an end to any such prospects, and it was
not until the country had regained its independence in 1881 that any
further action was taken. Even so, the new President, the celebrated
Paul Kruger, faced immense opposition from his own countrymen,
particularly from those engaged in transport by trekking wagons. It was
the pioneer days of English railways all over again: the developers *versus*
vested interests. Before the dramatic revelation of the immense indigenous
wealth of the Transvaal, Kruger and those who supported him had the
greatest difficulty in raising funds for railway construction, and eventually
it was in Amsterdam rather than in London that investors were found in
sufficient numbers for a company to be formed in 1887. Naturally the
proposed railway took the shortest route from Pretoria to the sea, and it
was planned to run almost due east to the frontier of Portuguese East
Africa, and so to Lourenço Marques.

This line, known, by the initials on its rolling stock, familiarly as
the Z.A.S.M. (Zuid Afrikaansche Spoorweg Maatschappij), proved an
exceptionally difficult one to build, and long before it was completed
through to the coast Rhodes had taken advantage of the friendly attitude
of the other Boer Republic, the Orange Free State, to enterprise extensions of the Cape Government Railways towards the Transvaal border
from the south. Kruger viewed this development with much displeasure.
He considered it unfair to the bulk of his people to permit the extension
of the Cape railways to reach Johannesburg before the Z.A.S.M. was
completed, and positively maintained that until the latter line was
completed the railhead of the Cape Government Railway should not be
extended beyond Bloemfontein. To try and uphold such a position in the
face of a man like Cecil Rhodes, however, was rather like Canute trying

to stop the incoming tide. Nevertheless he was a man with whom Rhodes was quite prepared to negotiate. In any case, although head of no more than a small country it was one that had suddenly become fabulously rich. At the same time the wealth of the Witwatersrand was rapidly becoming no more than one factor in the immense prospect of Southern African development that Rhodes now envisaged. If the geological formation of the sub-continent could include a gold-bearing reef stretching for 30 miles across the high veldt of the Transvaal, might there not equally be rich mineral deposits elsewhere, and interest began to centre upon the country still farther north, which could be reached through all-British territory.

North of the Bechuanaland Protectorate lay the country of the wild and warlike Matabele. It was there that mineral wealth was suspected. Paul Kruger sent emissaries to Lobengula, King of the Matabele, but in this he was out-manœuvred by Cecil Rhodes, who engineered a Treaty of Peace of Amity between this powerful African potentate and Great Britain. A concession having been obtained, the British South Africa Company was granted a Royal Charter by the Imperial Government in 1889. It was in the subsequent opening up of the great tracts of Mashonaland and Matabeleland that Rhodes made his ever-famous statement: 'The railway is my right hand, and the telegraph my voice.'

The course did not always run smoothly, and at one time Rhodes, nettled by the attitude of the Imperial Government, was regretting the projected extension of the Cape Government Railway northward from Vryburg along the western border of the Transvaal to Mafeking. Subsequent events made further extension a more urgent necessity, and through the great energy and organising ability of the contractor George Pauling the line reached Bulawayo in October 1897. How the romantic 'Cape to Cairo' dream was brought a little nearer to fruition, by the construction of the line northward from Bulawayo to Wankie and the Victoria Falls, is told in a later chapter. At this stage the very important link-up between the Cape Government system and the Transvaal must be briefly recorded. Kruger's attempt to delay the completion of this line until the one from Delagoa Bay was through to Pretoria, was circumvented by Cecil Rhodes who carried a measure through the Cape Parliament lending the Z.A.S.M. £600,000 to do the work. In face of this Kruger relaxed his opposition. A temporary wooden bridge over the Vaal River was opened

22

jointly by himself and President Reitz of the Orange Free State in May 1892, and the first train from the south steamed into Johannesburg on 15 September 1892. This was another great triumph for Rhodes, for this line, which completed through communications to the Cape, was finished nearly three years ahead of the Z.A.S.M. line to the east coast. Somewhat naturally however the arrival of the first through train at Pretoria on New Year's Day 1893 received scant official attention, in view of the anticipated completion of the indigenously sponsored line from Delagoa Bay, which was completed and opened for traffic in January 1895. The Republic had to wait until July 1895 before the grand ceremonial opening of the Z.A.S.M. took place, and then festivities were somewhat clouded through thieves breaking in beforehand and making away with most of the victuals for the banquet.

By the last years of the nineteenth century the framework of the South African Railway system was virtually completed, with the great trunk line from the Cape to Bulawayo, and its vital offshoot to Bloemfontein and Johannesburg; the line from Port Elizabeth up to De Aar, and the Z.A.S.M. from Delagoa Bay. Lastly, of course, there was the developing Natal Government Railway system, striking northwards from Durban to Ladysmith, 203 miles. This section was opened in 1886, and was a vital artery for the export of Natal coal. At Ladysmith the line forked, one prong heading for the Orange Free State to establish communication with Bloemfontein and Kimberley; the other headed for the Transvaal. The former line reached Harrismith just across the border in July 1892, while the Transvaal line had reached Charlestown by April 1891. There, however, the line of through communication ended for a matter of three years. As on the line from the Cape political issues held up developments. The Natal railways were the scene of some exciting episodes in the second Boer War, when the Boers invaded the country and laid siege to its vital key point in the railway system, Ladysmith.

Such therefore is a necessarily brief historical background to railway development in South Africa. North of the territory over which the British South Africa Company held sway, railway development, although vaguely conceived by Cecil Rhodes in an all-British African federation, eventually took different and quite independent forms, and the remarkable story of the Uganda Railway is told in a later chapter. So from this introduction we can retrace our steps to Cape Town.

23

CHAPTER TWO

Northbound from the Cape

The setting could not be more dramatic nor beautiful. All down the
years the situation of Cape Town, lying so close beneath the beetling
crags of Table Mountain looking across the exquisite sweep of Table Bay,
has had a compelling effect upon all travellers, whether they were the
earliest European explorers who discovered the Cape of Good Hope,
whether they were returning migrants, or travellers of fifty or sixty
years ago whose first sight of South Africa was through the porthole of a
Union Castle liner entering Table Bay at dawn. My own first visit was
fortuitous beyond measure. I had made the long journey from De Aar by
a night train, and on arrival found a day of the most heavenly and cloudless sunshine. My hosts urged an immediate trip, by cable car, to the
summit of Table Mountain, and so rapid were our subsequent movements,
that in recalling that arrival I can truly say that my first contemplation
of Cape Town was from the mountain top. And on that cloudless
October day what a prospect was laid out below!

I saw how the city had grown up on the narrow foreshore between the
mountain and the bay. The railway network, spreading from the fine
new terminal station, was clearly traceable. In the still, clear air, smoke was
rising from the big motive-power depot of Padarn Eiland; brightly coloured
trains were moving to and fro; a Union Castle liner lay alongside one
of the quays in the harbour. But while a connoisseur of railways naturally
had eyes for the railway complex, as seen from so magnificent a vantage
point, the prospect over mountain, sea, and distant landscape was certainly
such as to put the railway in its right perspective, and to show it as a tiny
thing against the tremendous background of the African terrain. Even so,
the immediate environs of Cape Town did not present any particular
difficulties to the railway engineers. The prospect would have been
infinitely more inspiring had I, at some later time, been able to look down
24

Cape Town 1897

The 'Johannesburg Mail' on the quay, between the Castle liner *Tantallon Castle* and the Union liner *Norman*. The engine is a standard Dübs-built 4-6-0 of Class 6

upon the railway from the heights bordering the Hex River Pass, or take a medium-level aerial view of the main line across the veldt, between De Aar and Kimberley.

To me, it was rather more than forty years ago that Cape Town became much more than a mere name on the map, and the place of origin of those fascinating and very expensive triangular postage stamps. The old station was then being modernised. The Westinghouse Brake and Signal Company was awarded a contract for the signalling work, and as a young draughtsman I worked on designs for the new signal gantries and apparatus for the modified track layouts. Wynberg and Salt River Junction became household words in the office for a few months; but then, inevitably with a constructing firm, new work came in to take their place, and it was not until more than a year later that we, who were then working 'inside', learned that the Cape Town installation had been successfully brought into service. Even at that stage in my life however a love of railway history was strongly developed, and during our pre-occupation with Cape Town I had found time to do some delving into the past. It was not difficult from the signalling point of view, because the environs of Cape Town had been one area where the most famous of our constituents, Saxby and Farmer Ltd., installed their celebrated hydraulic system of interlocking. Cape Town itself was a straightforward mechanical job, but Salt River Junction, two miles out, had one cabin with a 76-lever frame of the hydraulic type. Both signals and points were operated by water under pressure acting in small cylinders.

By the time I first visited Cape Town the installation for which I made drawings in 1927 had also been replaced by a very modern push-button interlocking and for this also I was responsible as Chief Mechanical Engineer of the Signal Division of the Company. So it was with a slight feeling of proprietory interest that I began my exploration of the railways around Cape Town. The entire layout in the neighbourhood of the station has changed greatly in the last seventy years. As it then existed it was almost on the foreshore, with the approach lines weaving a way round the precincts of Cape Town Castle. A branch line led to the docks, and the Johannesburg Mail started its long run from a pier alongside which the mail steamers from England berthed. The transference from ship to train was as intimate as with a Channel packet steamer on the Admiralty Pier at Dover. At that time, also, there were two steamship lines in competition for the traffic to and from England, the Union, and the Castle, before those two lines amalgamated to form the company that is world-known today. The Johannesburg Mail stood on the pier, with the rival steamers towering on either side of it. The express engines of those days were tough little 4-6-0s built by Dübs & Co. in Glasgow, and apart from their large cabs, cowcatchers and huge head-lamps, could easily have been mistaken for an English or a Scottish class. A fine example of one of them has been restored to its original condition and green livery, and stands on a pedestal on one of the platforms at Kimberley station. A locomotive enthusiast would immediately remark upon the very small coupled wheels, for a passenger engine; the reason for this will be amply apparent before we get very far on our journey to the north.

Since the turn of the century much has been done to reclaim land on the foreshore at Cape Town, to improve and extend the business area in the heart of the city, and the present station is built on a site formed on re-claimed land. All passenger trains on the main line to the north, and on the suburban line that encircles Table Mountain and runs to Wynberg and Simonstown, are now electrically hauled; but there are still many steam workings on subsidiary lines and the motive-power depot at Paardn Eiland is fascinating in the variety of locomotives to be seen. Despite electric haulage over a considerable part of the mileage long-distance travel from Cape Town is relatively slow. The very luxurious 'Blue Train', which runs no more than twice a week, makes an end-to-end average speed of only 37 m.p.h. over the 999 miles between Cape Town and Pretoria. The 'Trans-Karoo Express', which is the fastest train running daily, averages $34\frac{1}{2}$ m.p.h. over the 954 miles between Cape Town and Johannesburg. Looking up to see how present-day times compare with those of former days I was interested to find an old timetable of the Cape Government Railways which must have been one of the last issued before all the railways in South Africa were amalgamated, following the forma-tion of the Union, in 1910. The cover was similar in style and attractive-ness to many of the timetables issued by the British railways in pre-grouping days, and no less striking in its advertisement:

ROYAL MAIL DIRECT ROUTE

to and from the

GOLD & DIAMOND FIELDS OF SOUTH AFRICA

Below was displayed a map of South Africa, showing the route of the Union Castle Line steamships. The average sea passage was then quoted as 17 days, and the timetable cover then proudly announced: 'England to Johannesburg in 19 days: England to Bulawayo in 21 days.' The fastest of the so-called 'Dining and Sleeping Saloon trains' then took 44 hours to cover the distance of 999 miles from Cape Town to Pretoria, an average of only $22\frac{1}{2}$ m.p.h.

Modern though the present rolling stock and locomotives working into Cape Town are, the sheds at Padarn Eiland still house several examples of truly vintage classes. The majority are still in full working order, and I found many of them in steam. To anyone interested in locomotive history this is one of the most attractive features of the South African Railways; these engines are not merely in steam, but for the most part in a well-groomed and handsome condition. By this it must not be understood that I travelled round the country looking for railway antiques: far from it! But to find so many vintage specimens among the splendid modern electric and steam locomotives was an added treat. Moreover it was the same at every shed I visited. At Padarn Eiland I photographed one of the oldest of the passenger engines, a 4–6–0 of 1893 vintage, and stationed at the shed were fifteen others all built between 1896 and 1901, and all in Glasgow. Some came from Dübs, some from Neilson Reid, and some from Sharp Stewart. Everywhere one travelled in South Africa the products of the North British Locomotive Company and its three constituents were prominent, from these little 4–6–0s with their 17 in. by 24 in. cylinders and 4 ft. 6 in. coupled wheels, to the giant 4–8–4s of the '25' class, introduced within the last twenty years. We have, however, yet to meet these mighty engines. None were stationed at Padarn Eiland at the time of my visit. Reverting to the time when the old Scottish 4–6–0s were doing the main-line passenger work I saw two survivors of an even older class, still in active service—two examples of the class 7 4–8–0s of 1892. Of these No. 987 was completely unaltered in outline. These were the main-line freight type with even smaller wheels than the 4–6–0s.

At this stage I must not dwell upon details of steam locomotives, fascinating though the prospect may be, because Padarn Eiland is not one of the major centres of steam activity on the South African Railways. I nevertheless cannot resist mentioning two other classes. One is the

27

'16D' Pacific, built in the U.S.A. by Baldwins in 1925/6, which were used on the crack trains to the north for several years. These are most handsome engines—anything but 'American' in their general appearance. The other class is the comparatively modern '24', a lightweight 2-8-4 built by North British in 1948/9, of which I saw many under construction at the Hyde Park Works in Glasgow. These engines made history so far as the British locomotive-building industry was concerned in having one piece cast steel frames, in which frames, cross-stretchers, cylinders and smokebox saddles were included in a single casting. These latter were a remarkably fine job.

In Cape Town and its environs, the electric locomotives used on the main-line trains are mostly of British-build, to a design of great simplicity, and colourful appearance. Until quite recently South African electric locomotives were painted green, but now they are finished in a handsome livery of Tuscan red, with yellow lining. These locomotives are of 2000 horsepower and on the heavy dining and sleeping car trains to the north they are used in pairs. The standard carriage colour is a cherry red for bodies and cantrails, with cream panels for the area surrounding the windows. As with the locomotives there are many vintage coaches in first-class main-line service; but they are all splendidly maintained and most comfortable for both day and night travel. The multiple-unit electric trains used on the Cape Town suburban services are finished in the same colour scheme as the main-line stock. The latest of these suburban trains were built entirely in South Africa incorporating British-made electrical equipment.

Setting out for the north the train may well consist of sixteen or seventeen coaches, including some of the latest South African-built stock, with high elliptical roofs, and many clerestory roofed coaches of an earlier period, mostly British built. The sleeping cars are arranged as in Great Britain, easily convertible for day or night use, and providing a pleasant and spacious *coupé* for sightseeing, and all the privacy of a single-berth sleeper at night. To anyone making the complete journey from Cape Town to Johannesburg or Pretoria they provide the maximum of comfort. Completely separate accommodation is reserved for non-white passengers in another part of the train. At its head will be a pair of the fine '5E1' class electric locomotives. In joining such a train one could be completely oblivious of the fact that this is a sub-standard gauge railway.

The South African gauge is 3 ft. 6 in., but the loading gauge fortunately permits of locomotives and carriages that are relatively wide, in relation to the gauge, and the traveller from Great Britain would notice no difference between the interior proportions of a South African coach, and one running on the home railways. What can be done in the way of locomotives on the 3 ft. 6 in. gauge will be startlingly apparent when we pause in our journey at De Aar Junction.

Nevertheless the railway out of Cape Town was not always of the 3 ft. 6 in. gauge. The original line, the Cape Town and Wellington Railway, was built to the standard 4 ft. 8½ in., and it was only when the task began of carrying the railway northward through the mountains that a decision was made to use a narrower gauge. The railway to Wellington formed an important part of the journey to the diamond fields in the first hectic days of the 'diggings'. Through wagons could be hired, which would be conveyed on an open truck on the railway between Cape Town and Wellington, after which they would be drawn by horses or mules. A contemporary account of a journey to the diamond fields is contained in Lennox van Onselen's fascinating book *Head of Steel*, and that portion of the journey made by rail is worth quoting in full:

We are informed by a superior clerk that the passenger waggon leaves Cape Town at 7 a.m. on the morrow. We pay over our £12 each, receiving a pink voucher. This entitles us to travel by train to the terminus at Wellington on the first stage of our journey. Rations have to be taken along, and our baggage may not exceed thirty-five pounds in weight.

The following morning all is bustle and excitement at Cape Town Railway station. The buildings are of wood and iron. They have nothing to recommend them nor has the train that has just pulled up in the confines of the station. We display our vouchers and are allowed to fight for seats—plain wooden benches—inside the carriages. The train is crammed with people who have but one topic of conversation—diamonds.

The waggon on which we are to continue our journey from Wellington is trucked on an open bogey. Our pink voucher entitles us to travel second class. We are moved out of our first class compartment and told to find seats in the second class carriage. It is terribly crowded but after a few ticketless persons have been thrown out, we find seats just as the train groans out of the station. According to my timepiece, it is 7.25 a.m.

The novelty of travelling by train at this colossal speed somewhat compensates for the discomfort. We are travelling at no less a speed than thirty miles an hour. We sit back exhilarated by the swift passing of the landscape, contemplating this sixty-mile stretch of railway track in our mind's eye. The cost of it all was prodigious: the problems that had to be overcome before it all became a reality and the suspicion and distrust with which it is even now surrounded, were almost insurmountable.

The country through which we are now passing, is thinly wooded with flat stretches of fallow ground that does not give the impression of sterility. There are no houses to be seen.

In our compartment, on a seat opposite me there is a burly old farmer, shaggy in his rough country-man's clothes. I lean over and ask him why the countryside is so sparsely cultivated. He tells me that the farmers fear fire: that this hellish contraption of a locomotive, this work of the devil, has set fire to the country-side on more than one occasion.

I enquire why he travels by train if it displeases him so. He replies gruffly that he is in a hurry to get home where his cow is expected to calve at any moment. He rumbles in his beard that Mankind was not intended to be hurled over the good earth at speed. With an ox-waggon, he says, a person may still pull up in time before going over into the bottomless abyss that encompasses the flat earth. I remind him that the world is round, not flat as he surmises. The old Boer stares at me incredulously, then informs me indignantly that it does not behove a young man to make fun of his elders.

It seems that the farmers gave ground for the railway as far from their houses as possible. They did not only fear the incendiary effect of the locomotive but also deep within them, they harboured a burning resentment towards all pro-gress: towards any new-fangled development that might interfere with their habitual way of life.

They referred to the Bible, pointing out that Man was intended to rely upon beasts of burden for transport and the garnering of his harvest. Engines are not mentioned in the Bible, therefore no provision was made for them: that they exist in reality is a sin in itself and a fact to be ignored.

The train chugs through Klapmuts and Paarl. The stations are deserted. Few people leave the train during the short stop it makes. We reach Wellington at 11 a.m. It is a pretty village snuggling at the foot of a lofty mountain range, protected by green railings. Rows of fine trees overshadow the streets and luxuriant foliage tumbles over garden walls. Apples, figs, apricots and quinces flourish together with fruits like loquats and Cape gooseberries that have been adopted as native fruits but which really originate from the American continent.

Today the modern electrically hauled train gathers speed smoothly, and soon we are speeding through a level and richly cultivated countryside. I first travelled that way in the African spring, and the fact of my having arrived in the Transvaal and seen the veldt before I came to Cape Town made me all the more appreciative of the intense green of the landscape, of the profusion of wild flowers, and of the miles and miles of yellow acacias on both sides of the railway, loaded with yellow blossom. If I had arrived in Cape Town straight from England I should no doubt have delighted in the flora, but perhaps not found the whole prospect so entrancing as after a fortnight in the arid north. The main line at first heads direct towards the mountains, to Paarl, in the heart of the fruit-farming country, and then turns to the north, running parallel with the rather forbidding range, until Wellington is reached. The country appeared easy enough for a continuation northwards; but a direct northerly course from Wellington was not the way the pioneers wanted to go. The way to the diamond fields lay to the north-east, and at the end of the 1860s no one could see a way of breaking through the mountain barrier.

Many of the local men in Cape Colony had no desire to see it broken through. Every farmer who had a wagon that would hold together, and oxen that would haul it, was engaged in transport to and from the 'diggings'. They felt that the mountain range was their best insurance against competition. Following the discovery of diamonds in the area that eventually became Kimberley the Cape Colony was granted responsible government; but even this did not provide the urge to set out on further railway construction beyond Wellington. It was the Cape Chamber of Commerce that eventually took the initiative, and they engaged a relatively old engineer, Thomas Hall by name, and commissioned him to find a route from Wellington to Worcester. Now the latter settlement is only 30 miles to the north-east of Paarl as the crow flies. The mountains lay between, and when this elderly but dedicated man set about his task the entire farming community impressed upon him the hopelessness of the task. It was not a case of forcible obstruction as encountered by the early pioneers in England; he was for the most part striking out amid rocky virgin country. It was a case of intimidation by sympathy! But Hall was completely undaunted, and by making a long detour to the north he found a way through to the Breede River. If his advice were followed

31

the distance from Paarl to Worcester by rail would be nearly 70 miles, but a more serious point in his report was that he considered this route practicable only if the gauge was no more than 2 ft. 6 in.

In skirting the mountains, he considered, there would be so much difficulty in providing the 4 ft. 8½ in. gauge of the Cape Town–Wellington Railway as to render it completely impracticable. There were no 'ifs and buts' in Hall's report to the Cape Chamber of Commerce. It had to be 2 ft. 6 in. The fat was now fairly in the fire. To reduce the gauge from Cape Town to Wellington would be very expensive, and quite undesirable. Furthermore, although little surveying for railway purposes had been done up on the High Veldt it was evident that the wide gauge was desirable to permit of steadiness of travel and eventually high speed. The Chamber of Commerce in its dilemma laid the report before Parliament and the Government called in an eminent civil engineer, William G. Brounger. He simply split the difference between the accomplished fact of the Cape Town–Wellington Railway and Hall's proposal: 4 ft. 8½ in. against 2 ft. 6 in. Brounger recommended 3 ft. 6 in. Parliament would not make up its mind, and referred the problem to a Select Committee. So the matter dragged on into 1873, and suddenly there came the realisation that a decision must be made, in order to get a railway through to the diamond fields. Brounger's compromise was accepted; he was instructed not only to commence construction of the Wellington–Worcester line, over the route discovered by Thomas Hall, but to find a route for the continuation of the line from Worcester up to the plateau of the Great Karoo Desert, across which it was expected the line would progress towards Kimberley.

Through this characteristic British compromise South Africa had her rail gauge settled. The extent of the 4 ft. 8½ in. gauge was at that time relatively small, and conversion was not an expensive matter. Although this line in the Cape was not the first railway in South Africa it was the first to make any progress, and fortunately when lines from other ports were constructed the same gauge was adopted. From this early date although independent railways were constructed in Natal and Portuguese East Africa this sub-continent did not develop the muddled situation that grew up in Australia, and which is even now no more than partially resolved. The railway reached Worcester in 1875—a soundly engineered, and well-built stretch of line, albeit one with a great deal of

32

severe curvature. Even today, with modern electric haulage, the crack trains take between $3\frac{1}{2}$ and 4 hours to traverse the 100 miles of track between Worcester and Cape Town. It was no mean achievement to get the line through to Worcester from Wellington in such a short time; but on reaching Worcester, Brounger's problems were only just beginning.

CHAPTER THREE

Hex River and the Karoo

Ten years after the railway first came to Worcester, William George Brounger was awarded the Telford Medal of the Institution of Civil Engineers for a paper modestly titled 'The Cape Government Railways'. In a scholarly factual survey, richly meriting the Institution's highest award, that great engineer barely mentions the appalling difficulties he encountered in building the railways he describes in such matter-of-fact detail. There appeared to be no alternative but to find a way up the Hex River Pass. In the 36 miles between Worcester and Matroosburg however there is a difference in altitude of approximately 2350 ft., and even if one reduces the problem to plain arithmetic it means an average rate of ascent of 1 in 80 throughout. But the natural ascent of the river valley is quite moderate at first and in the first 20 miles from Worcester the altitude has increased only from 794 ft. to 1570 ft. at De Doorns. It is beyond this latter point that a truly terrific ascent begins.

The country between Worcester and De Doorns is very fine, much of it strongly reminiscent of the West Highlands of Scotland. The railway makes its way into a narrow glen, with great crags towering on both sides, and it is only the vineyards, planted on every available acre of level ground that destroy the Scottish illusion. Shacks of the coloured people are seen along some of the roads, and each small township has its rugby-football ground. Brounger was a splendid organiser. He imported trained railwaymen and experienced contractors, and as the line progressed the running of it was entrusted to men with the British railway background, and British traditions of safety and service. With the labour force it was another matter. It was one thing to import a force of herculean, hard-working navvies, but quite another to secure fully experienced brick-layers and stonemasons for building bridges and other structures along

34

the line. From De Doorns however the first problem was to find a route at all. The difference in altitude was so great that at one time Brounger was thinking in terms of a rack section, and asked if he had any alternative plan he remarked with a smile that if he could not get over the mountain he would go through it.

His aim was to keep the gradient down to 1 in 40. As a man of international reputation he would doubtless have been aware that in Europe gradients as steep as 1 in 32 had been included in the approach lines to the Mont Cenis tunnel, which was completed a few years before he began to strike out from Worcester; but anything in the way of a direct line up the Pass from De Doorns would have involved gradients steeper by far. On the right hand side, while ascending, the mountainsides are deeply indented by numerous small glens, and out-jetting bluffs, and with the two-fold purpose of easing the gradients and minimising the earthworks the line was taken uphill on a bewildering succession of twists and curves, like a stupendously vaster edition of the West Highland line in Glen Falloch or in climbing from Loch nan Uamh to Beasdale. In 1886 the House of Assembly at Cape Town had this report:

From the town of Worcester (750 feet above sea level) the line proceeds up the beautiful Hex River valley and then begins to climb the mountains by curves and zig-zags along their sides, piercing some of the mountain spurs by tunnels and crossing gullies spanned by viaducts, until within a distance of 36 miles, it attains an altitude of 3193 ft.

Looking down from the top of the mountain, there is a magnificent view of the valley some 2,000 ft. below; and the stupendous character of the engineering works by which the ascent has been accomplished, can be appreciated. The highest point, however, is at Pieter Meintjiesfontein, seventy-seven miles from Worcester, where the height of 3588 ft. is attained—a little higher than the summit of Table Mountain.

On a long train there are times when the rear coaches are running almost parallel to the locomotives, but in opposite directions. Of the track itself Brounger remarks:

With a view to check the tendency to spread of gauge round the sharp curves of the Hex River Mountain on the Western system, bowl sleepers of Livesey's pattern for a few miles of road were ordered for the sake of the wrought-iron tie; all the different kinds of fastenings employed being found to yield in the case

35

of wooden sleepers, even where hard wood was employed, though the latter checks the tendency to some extent. This piece of road has answered well under a very trying traffic. Most of the sleepers are of cast iron, but a length of 1 mile is laid with wrought iron, and of the latter not a single sleeper has had to be replaced; many of the former, however, are broken in the process of packing.

Ascending the pass, on a practically continuous gradient of 1 in 40, the line is single-tracked, and at one point there is an ingeniously laid out crossing place. Any easing of the gradient to provide a crossing loop of the normal kind would be impracticable, and so lengthy head-end shunting necks have been engineered, on level track. If an ascending train has to be cleared for a train of higher priority it is drawn ahead till its rear is clear of the points and then it is set back, on level track into the refuge. When it is ready to proceed once more it has the advantage of starting on a short length of level track before entering upon the 1 in 40 gradient of the main line. A second siding extends in the opposite direction, so that two trains may be simultaneously berthed clear of the main line. So far as the bridges are concerned, Brounger remarks:

Owing to the difficulty in procuring good bricks, the importance of time, and the scarcity of skilled labour, iron superstructures, even in the case of bridges of small span and open culverts, have been largely employed. Arches, however, have been resorted to more extensively on the Eastern system. The character of masonry employed has varied between fitted and course rubble, and block-in-course, according to the nature of the stone available, ashlar having, as a rule, been avoided. Cement has been largely employed instead of lime for mortar, owing, not only to the difficulty in obtaining the latter of good quality, but to the saving of cost of carriage consequent upon the much larger admixture of sand which the former will bear.

In some cases of rivers which bring down trees and heavy drift during floods, a plate-diaphragm stiffened by T or L iron between the two cylinders forming each of the piers, has been adopted in lieu of open bracing; this gives the effect of solid piers, and saves them from the strain which might result from large accumulations of heavy drift.

In this paper he was writing of the Cape Government Railways as a whole, and the Eastern system, to which he refers, was the line from East London up to Sterkstrom.

Despite the extreme difficulty of the terrain, of the intricacies of surveying accurately a route of such bewildering curvature, the progress

PLATE 1. Cape Town Station in 1893

PLATE 2. Cape Town New Station

(*above*) The exterior

(*below*) The spacious concourse

of construction was remarkably rapid. In three years, 1875–8, the line had been carried up the Hex River Pass and on to the Karoo to reach Matjiesfontein. At that time it was a staging point on the coach route from Cape Town to the diamond diggings, but it was never more than a collection of shacks. It was after leaving Matjiesfontein, in building the line across the Great Karoo Desert that major troubles with the labour force began to develop. The bulk of the navvies were of the typical British type, capable of prodigious feats of physical work, possessed of enormous appetites, and still more enormous thirsts. Working round from Wellington to Worcester, and then up the Hex River Pass they were on a familiar type of ground. It was like the Highlands of Scotland, and that they worked with a will is shown by the speed with which construction of the line was carried up the pass. Then, having reached roughly level ground, they came into glens as bleak and desolate as the wilds of Sutherlandshire—and far more lonely; and after that came the Karoo.

Much has been written of the more colourful and humanly dramatic side of railway construction at home. The invasion of the quiet English countryside by hordes of rough, hard-working, highly paid navvies; of the disturbances on their pay-nights, of their turbulent codes of behaviour. Even on the most violent occasions however incidents at home were mild in the extreme compared with the events in the Karoo, and out on the Veldt, when the main line of the Cape Government Railway was under construction. Brounger as engineer was responsible for planning the route, but as in England in pioneer days much depended upon the individual contractors, and so I come to that amazing character George Pauling. He came to South Africa at the age of twenty, with the backing of an engineering training, and the fact that his father was already in the service of the Cape Government Railways. However he quickly decided that Government service did not offer the excitement or rewards that he sought, and at once he began seeking contract work. He obtained it for construction of a tunnel on the Grahamstown line in the Eastern Province. What manner of man he was, revealed itself very quickly by the energy with which he threw himself into this work. Although reference to the Grahamstown line is a digression from the main subject of this chapter, it is necessary for one to introduce the character of the man who was to do so much later in building the line to the north.

37

Fifty years later he was persuaded by many friends to write his auto-biography, and although *Chronicles of a Contractor* has no pretence to a work of literature it gives a vivid picture of life on the railways of Africa in their earliest days. Of his work on the Waai Nek tunnel he writes:

I write it, not in any spirit of vanity but more of thankfulness for the strength and endurance given to me, that these were really strenuous days. By four o'clock in the morning I was generally out of bed and away on horseback to inspect the work that was in progress beyond Ross's camp. I then visited practically every bit of work that was being carried on and was back at my camp at Waai Nek tunnel before breakfast. After a bath and a morning meal I super-vised my own work in the tunnel until the middle of the day. Then a snack and on horse again to ride right through the work and back to my camp. But I was not indifferent to the enjoyment of ordinary pleasures and, considering myself entitled to a little recreation, it was my habit to go into Grahamstown to the Masonic Hotel, enjoy a good dinner, drink freely with congenial spirits, and play billiards till the hotel closed. Riding back to camp I usually arrived there before midnight. Whenever a favourable opportunity occurred I put in an hour or so sleeping in the daytime, but generally speaking I was at work at least thirteen or fourteen hours a day.

From a very early stage in his African life he was indulging in sidelines, and even before Waai Nek tunnel was completed he had become owner of the Masonic Hotel. Being a man of immense physical strength he was frequently tempted by his patrons into attempting 'strong tricks', and one of his favourite exploits was to pick up a Basuto pony tethered in the yard, and carry it round the bar parlour. One day he was wagered to carry the pony upstairs. He took the bet immediately, but when half-way up he slipped, and the pony came crashing down. Railway construction in South Africa, needed men with the courage, 'guts', and sheer enter-prise of George Pauling, for very often the very circumstances were daunting in the extreme.

J. O. P. Bland, who edited his autobiography, wrote in 1926: 'George Pauling was staunchly and squarely British, of the breed of the Captains Courageous whose traffics and discoveries made by sea and overland, to the remote and farthest distant quarters of the earth have established and held the far-flung frontiers of the Empire. With the frame of an athlete, the solid commonsense of a practical engineer, and an inordinate

38

capacity for hard work he was able to hold his own in the rough and tumble of the pioneer days of the Rand and many other fields of outpost enterprise.'

'Rough and tumble' . . . 'Outpost enterprise . . .': the railway constructors learned a new meaning of those phrases when the construction of the line across the Karoo began. The men who had built the line up the Hex River Pass had hitherto found places of recreation for their off-duty hours, in the village taverns; but once on to the Karoo the incredible expanse was something none of them had experienced before. Their camps were the only human habitations in the vast panorama of desert extending in every direction. The line of railway certainly followed the coach route to the 'diggings'; but an occasional ox-wagon, trek-cart, or even a passenger coach was a mere nothing in such a completely depopulated region. Soon however the enterprising farming community of the valleys on the south side of the Hex River Pass began to realise that there was potential business in supplying the constructional gangs with the 'luxuries' they had enjoyed, particularly brandy.

The navvies could not wait for the liquor to arrive in orderly fashion. In their free time they took to roaming the countryside, raiding coloured and Hottentot settlements, and carrying away whatever they could find. Here and there these gangs would come across a Boer farmstead, where they would instantly demand brandy. Those exceedingly tough characters usually resisted and kept the navvies at gun point, even though such defence could result in the house being stoned and every window broken! The transport drivers coming up from the Cape usually brought a liberal supply of brandy with them, and as they came to where the gangs were working they advertised their wares. If the navvies had ready cash they did good business; if they had not these lawless men had a way of pelting the wagon driver with anything they had to hand. Coal was a favourite missile, but after the barrage was over and the wagon had passed on its way, the intrepid Boer drivers would return under shadow of night and collect as much of the coal as they could find! If wagons arrived when the navvies were off duty, and no money was available, attempts were sometimes made to take the kegs of brandy by force. Then some of the navvies discovered that their hulking strength was fully matched by the Boer transport drivers! To lessen the chances of attack however the wagons began organising themselves into convoys.

39

Today, as the electrically hauled express trains of the South African Railways make their way across the forbidding countryside it is not at all difficult to imagine what things were like in the constructional days. There is no doubt the gangs suffered privations from both heat and cold; they experienced the sudden changes of temperature between night and day, and the awe-inspiring fury of South African thunderstorms. The Karoo is nevertheless not a desert in the ordinary sense. Although it extends in one sheet of barrenness from one horizon to another, it is not entirely a sandy waste. There is much low scrub. No shade; the sun pours down, and more often than not the air is breathless. Time and again one sees the phenomenon of a mirage. The electrified line continues across the Karoo. The power of two '5E1' locomotives was invaluable in climbing the 1 in 40 gradients in the Hex River Pass, but now, at an altitude of more than 3000 ft. they are merely trundling along over this near-level track across the desert for much of the distance.

Electric traction now ends at Beaufort West; but the changeover to steam usually takes place at night. It is indeed significant of the many difficulties experienced on the Karoo, that although it took less then three years to build the line from Worcester, up the Hex River Pass and on to Matjiesfontein, another four years elapsed before the next 140 miles were completed and the first train steamed into Beaufort West. This was in 1882, and the event was made the occasion of a special celebration. Beaufort West was a little town that had grown up on the coach route from Cape Town to the 'diggings'. It was favoured as a staging point by the more affluent passengers, and there was, even before the arrival of the railway, at least one comfortable inn. More than this, it was a centre for the wool trade, and many farmers from outlying districts owned houses that they occupied at the time of sheep shearing. Here the railway was welcomed, and the whole population turned out to witness the arrival of the first train. The excitement was something akin to that displayed by present-day enthusiasts on steam farewell occasions in Britain, crowds swarming on to the track and being restrained only with difficulty by the *one* village constable! In more decorum, but in scarcely less feeling of excitement, stood railway officials and local dignitaries along the station platform. The ladies of the party were in their most extravagant finery.

Suddenly there was a shout: 'Here comes the train', and then the shout-

40

ing, waving of hats and handkerchiefs were suddenly punctuated by a series of loud explosions. The cheers gave place to screams, and then while the startled officials and police were wondering what on earth had happened there was a deafening roar from one of the nearby kopjes, and a great mass of rock shot in the air like the eruption of some volcano. It was not surprising that something like a major panic ensued. The great majority of the crowd had never seen a steam locomotive before. The frightful noises were inevitably associated with it, and the people fled in disorder. It was a little time before it was discovered that some enthusiasts, wishing to signal the arrival of the train with appropriate effect, had placed some detonators on the line, and the explosion of these by the oncoming train had been the signal for some fellow enthusiasts to light a fuse to ignite a hidden store of dynamite on the hill-top. The effect was more sensational than ever they hoped, and the Mayor was still quivering when he mounted the rostrum to make a traditional speech of welcome. Equanimity soon returned. The guests sat down to an official lunch that lasted four hours.

Beaufort West may have welcomed the railway, but it did not welcome the construction gangs that came with it. This once pretty little village soon found its inns frequented by the wild men of the railway. Canteens were erected for their refreshment, but at the same time a new factor began to enter into the problem of railway construction labour. Beaufort West is on the borders of Kaffir country, where the natives were altogether wilder and more primitive than the Hottentots of the Cape. Before the extension of the railway northward towards the Orange Free State the transport drivers, even of passenger coaches, were stark-naked savages, who seem nevertheless to have managed their complex mule teams very competently. The railway contractors began to seek ways of using this prolific source of labour, and to dispense with the troublesome and highly paid European navvies. This subtle change brings to an end the account of constructional days on the Hex River and on the Karoo. The problems awaiting men like George Pauling were quite different when the line came to cross the high veldt.

Before leaving this fascinating line, in its early days, we can turn again from the 'Wild West' atmosphere of the construction camps, to the rarefied atmosphere of the Institution of Civil Engineers, and the prize-winning paper of W. G. Brounger. In it he describes the original types of locomotives, and also the carriages. There were three orthodox locomotive classes of 4-4-0, 4-6-0, and 2-6-0 types, of which the Western line had 30, 30, and 28 respectively. They were for the most part tiny little things, none weighing more than 30 tons. It is not surprising that speeds were not high, and on this Brounger comments appropriately:

The small amount of passenger traffic renders it necessary, as a rule, to run 'mixed' trains, and for the sake of economy a low rate of speed was adopted, namely, 15 miles on an average per hour, including stoppages, for mixed goods and passenger trains. Where the gradients are long and steep, and the curves severe, it has been the practice to limit the speed to from 10 to 12 miles per hour, which still admits, on long lines, of the average speed being maintained without strain; but on lines where a large portion of their length consists of such gradients and curves, it is a question whether this average rate of speed is not too great for the economical working of goods traffic.

One passenger and mail train without goods is run each way per week between Port Elizabeth and Cape Town in connection with the ocean steamers. The distance, 838 miles, is covered in forty-three and a quarter hours, or at an average of 19.38 miles per hour, including stoppages, and there are suburban passenger trains which travel at a considerably greater speed.

The fastest long journey on record was that of a special train between Beaufort West and Cape Town, a distance of 339 miles in ten hours, exclusive of stoppages, or an average of nearly 34 miles per hour.

The original carriages were all four-wheelers, and for the first five years of operating the line north of Wellington nothing else was used. Then, however, public opinion demanded higher speeds, and it was therefore decided to import bogie carriages. Brounger comments thus:

There is no doubt about the bogie stock being more steady than the shorter carriages, both as regards vertical and horizontal oscillation, and its advantages in respect to stability in passing round sharp curves are very marked. This would naturally be supposed, the angle which the bogie frames make with the centre line of the carriage being increasingly great in proportion to the sharpness of the curves; thus giving a greater lateral width of base. On one occasion this was practically illustrated in a marked degree, when on a damp morning a train got beyond control on a long incline of 1 in 40; the result being that all the short vehicles were capsized at a curve of five chains radius and the one bogie carriage in the train kept the rails, although the drawbar was bent to a right angle by the derailing of the adjoining vehicle.

42

The bogie coach was subsequently developed very rapidly in South Africa, and before many years were out the Cape Government Railways had some of the most comfortable long-distance trains to be found anywhere in the world.

CHAPTER FOUR

Steam locomotives: early days to 1920

In studying the development of steam locomotive practice in South Africa one has to consider, at first, the running conditions on what were three quite distinct and independent railway systems. Of these the Cape Government and the Natal were organised and equipped largely on British lines, with the bulk of the equipment purchased from the United Kingdom. The Transvaal line was essentially Dutch. After the Boer War, and the brief period when the railways of the Transvaal were under military administration, the old Z.A.S.M. became the Central South African Railway, and it was re-organised largely to British standards. It was however, not until the formation of the Union of South Africa, in 1910, when the railways themselves were amalgamated under Government ownership, that a unified policy of locomotive development was adopted. The Cape Government Railway had been able to pursue a policy of continuity, from the nineties of last century, while in Natal and the Transvaal the nineteenth and twentieth centuries marked distinct periods of divergent practice.

The Z.A.S.M. had a very short existence. The through line from Lourenço Marques to Pretoria was not opened until 1895, and the war broke out in 1899. In that short period however the Z.A.S.M. established a highly distinctive type of tank locomotive, of which a fine example is preserved and on display in the present station in Pretoria. These engines were of the 0–6–4 type with outside cylinders, outside frames, and under-hung springs for all the coupled wheels. They were unusual for that period in having Walschaerts valve gear. Their most distinctive external feature was however the height and length of the side tanks; they extended from the cab to the smokebox, and their tops were level with the top of the boiler. They had huge steam domes, and the tall chimney tapered

44

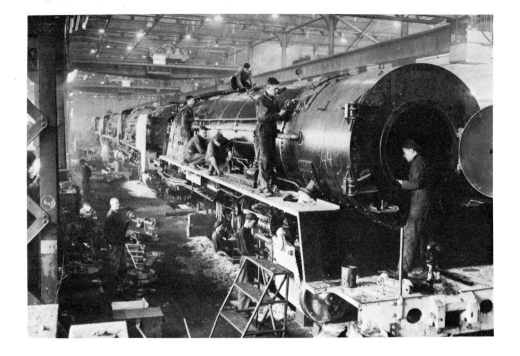

PLATE 3. Salt River Works

(*above*) Engine repairing
(*below*) The carriage shops

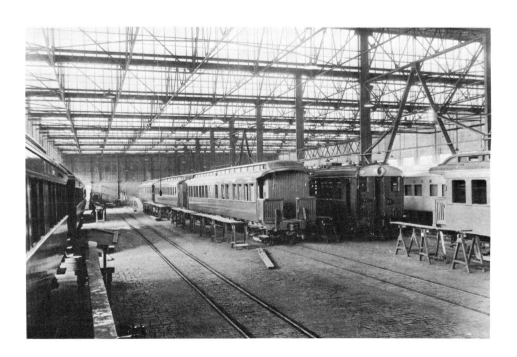

PLATE 4

(*above*) Cape Town New Signal Box
(*below*) 3000 volt d.c. surburban electric train leaving Cape Town

sharply outwards from the base. They were all named, and the engine now preserved at Pretoria is appropriately the *President Kruger*. These engines were built in Holland, by Kessler, of Esslingen, and their external finish was extremely plain. The colour was a very dark green, almost black, and they were quite devoid of any lining or polished fittings. What they lacked in this respect they more than regained in the most elaborate arrays of headlamps. Before the outbreak of war they worked the through mail trains up from the Cape, over the Z.A.S.M., but in the development of the railways afterwards they passed into secondary duty. In the circumstances it is fortunate that one of them should have been preserved, and so well cared for.

The Natal Government Railway was also a considerable user of tank engines. The main line out of Durban is very heavily graded, and the first 44 miles to Cato Ridge includes 38 miles of almost continuous ascent at 1 in 66. Having regard to the severity of this main line, traversed by passenger, mail, and freight trains working between Durban and Johannesburg, the railway had standardised the 4–8–2 type, and at the turn of the century there were no fewer than 120 of these engines at work. The design originated in the 1880s and the majority of the engines concerned were built by Dübs and Co. in Glasgow. It is remarkable that some of them are still at work in South Africa, though not on the South African Railways themselves. While in the neighbourhood of Johannesburg I was able to visit the Grootvlei Proprietary Mines, and to see two of these veteran locomotives in service. They now carry larger boilers than originally fitted, the former having been supplied by Borsig of Berlin, in 1930. But the 'engine' remains unchanged, with two cylinders 17 in. diameter by 21 in. stroke, and 3 ft. 9 in. coupled wheels. In contrast to the very sombre finish of the locomotives of the Z.A.S.M. the standard colour scheme in Natal was highly decorative in a rich dark green, with tanks having a broad chocolate border. I saw two of these engines working at the Grootvlei mines, one was plain black, very nicely polished up, and the other was in a livery that could be best described as 'milk chocolate' lined out in black and white.

At the turn of the century the need was felt for considerably larger engines for working on the mountain sections, and the locomotive superintendent, Mr. G. Reid, prepared designs for a remarkable 4–10–2 tank engine. After a prototype had been built and thoroughly tested a

45

further 25 were built by Dübs & Co. and supplied in 1901. They were enormous engines for that period, especially running on the 3 ft. 6 in. gauge. The cylinders were 19 in. diameter by 27 in. stroke, and in combination with relative small-diametered coupled wheels the nominal tractive effort was no less than 29,500 lb. This was far greater than any contemporary British goods engines, and running on the 3 ft. 6 in. gauge into the bargain. The new engines had no sooner arrived and been put into service when the design was adopted by, and 35 further engines built for, the Imperial Military Railways for service in the Transvaal. Their great power made them invaluable for any kind of duty, but they were not normally used on the Cape mails, on which through service was restored after the war. When new locomotives for the Transvaal arrived from the United Kingdom some I.M.R. 4–10–2 tank engines were loaned to Natal. After a time some were altered to the 4–8–2 type, by removing the rearmost pair of coupled wheels. In their altered form some of these engines are still at work in the service of the East Rand Proprietary Mines. I saw one of them in the autumn of 1968, very smartly turned out in a bright green livery, with the initials E.R.P.M. on her tank sides in huge letters. The reputation of South African locomotives for longevity, which will be appreciated to a greater extent when I come to write of the Cape and later Transvaal engines, is certainly upheld by the continuance in service of these Natal engines in the goldmines of the Rand. There were at one time no fewer than 136 of these 4–10–2s at work: 101 of the original Reid design in Natal, and 35 of the Imperial Military Railways series, which had certain slight variations in design.

Locomotive development on the Cape Government Railways was to a large extent determined by the tremendous gradients in the Hex River Pass. In addition to this, however, the 'Cape to Cairo' route, with the northward extension from Mafeking into Rhodesia, was operated by C.G.R. motive power, and the earliest locomotives in Rhodesia itself were of the same design. It is interesting to find therefore that with the exception of a few American-built 'Atlantics' none of the earlier Cape locomotives had carrying wheels under the firebox. They were all of the 4–6–0 and 4–8–0 types. It is well known that such locomotives are much less likely to slip in adverse rail conditions than 4–6–2s or 4–8–2s and slipping could quickly bring a train to rest on such gradients as those of the Hex River Pass. A design that could well be called a 'standard' in

Southern Africa was the Cape '17 in.' 4-6-0; a very simple, straight-forward job with 17 in. by 26 in. stroke cylinders, and 4 ft. 6 in. diameter coupled wheels. Engines of this type were also used in the Orange Free State, and also in Rhodesia. On the South African Railways today they are known as Class 6, and there are several varieties relating to the extent, or otherwise, that the engines have been rebuilt from the original. The design dates back to the nineteenth century and yet when I was in South Africa in the autumn of 1968 no fewer than 29 of these veterans were still on the active list: 3 at Germiston (near Johannesburg); 13 at Cape Town, and 13 at Port Elizabeth.

Of course the most fascinating of them all is old 645, of the '6J' series, which has been restored to its original livery and general condition, and stands on a plinth at the south end of Kimberley station. This engine, while having slide valves, differs from the various engines of Class 6B which I saw at work elsewhere in having a high running plate and the coupled wheels completely exposed. The majority have a running plate level with the buffer beam, and quite sizeable wheel splashers, seeing that the wheels themselves are only 4 ft. 6 in. in diameter. Engine No. 645, enthroned in state at Kimberley, and kept in beautiful condition, is in a shade of green very similar to that of the Glasgow and South Western Railway. This is certainly appropriate for an engine built by Neilsons. She has the huge oil-lighted headlamp, whereas the working engines of the class have the modern two-lamp electric headlight. The Kimberley exhibition engine has the original size of dome, a rather tall, slender affair, but the working engines that I saw and photographed all had the large-diameter dome that was used on the Central South African classes introduced in the days of rehabilitation after the Boer War.

One interesting type of locomotive used on the Cape Government Railways stands out from the rest. In 1898 the British locomotive build-ing industry was so heavily booked with orders, and the workshops of home railways so busy, that it was necessary for such lines as the Great Northern and the Midland to purchase locomotives from America. At this same time the Cape Government Railways purchased some 'Atlantic' engines from Baldwins. They were, in fact, the only Atlantics ever to run in Southern Africa, though quite diminutive little things with cylin-ders only 16 in. diameter by 22 in. stroke, and having coupled wheels 4 ft. 8 in. diameter. They were put to work in 1898, and would ordinarily have been regarded as no more than stop-gaps until more of the power-ful Scottish-built 4–6–0s and 4–8–0s could be obtained; but it so happened that they came to fulfil a special function in the later stages of the Boer War.

After the major campaigns were concluded the country was contin-ually harassed by the activities of guerilla bands, who did a great deal of damage by surprise attacks, particularly upon railways. The main line between De Aar and Mafeking was constantly subject to this kind of attention, and arrangements were made for its patrolling by armoured trains. Speed was the essence of this activity, and the American-built 'Atlantics' were chosen because of their particular speedworthiness, as compared with the much heavier and more powerful standard 4–6–0s. The 'Atlantic' engine propelled the train with a 'dummy' open truck leading, so that if any explosives or other obstructions were placed on the line the damage to the 'inhabited' part of the train would be minimal. There were four of these armoured trains, and they were used for escort-ing the ordinary 'mixed' trains by day, and constantly patrolling the lines at night.

At both Cape Town and Port Elizabeth I saw old engines, of nine-teenth-century vintage, engaged in propelling loaded wagons on to the coaling stages. At the major sheds there are high galleries, from which coal is discharged into the tenders of locomotives positioned below, and the job of propelling wagons up on to these galleries reminded me very much of the similar operation in which I had participated, on the foot-plate, on the staithes at various coal-shipping ports on the north-east coast of England. In South Africa, as at Blyth and elsewhere, the coal stage pilot, with its load, retreats a fair distance along the level at the foot of the incline and then going 'flat-out', takes a flying run at it! The sight and sound of a Dübs 4–6–0 of 1896 tearing into it up the gallery at Padarn Eiland, Cape Town, was something to remember. As I watched old 444 on this job I wondered if the gallery vibrated and swayed as much as the wooden staithes at Blyth! At Sydenham shed, Port Elizabeth, a Class 7 4–8–0—a Neilson of even earlier vintage—was on the job, and I watched fascinated several times while she went blazing up the ramp with a column of black smoke shooting skywards and safety valves blowing off furiously.

These 4–8–0s were introduced from 1892 onwards for the freight

PLATE 5. Coaling Stages

(*above*) A Dübs 4–6–0 of 1896 No. 444 at Padard Eiland, Cape Town

(*below*) Giant engines on the stage at De Aar

PLATE 6. Hex River Pass: '4E' Locomotives

(*above*) Electrically hauled express train

(*below*) A freight train in the pass

traffic on the Cape Government lines, and the survivors remain very much in their original condition except for the substitution of electric lighting for the old oil headlamps. Although the Class 7 was originally a Cape Government design examples are now shedded at many other parts of the South African Railway system, including Germiston and Krugersdorp in the Transvaal, Kimberley in the Orange Free State, Mossel Bay, and Port Elizabeth. The Class 7 engines are typically 'nineteenth-century British', with straight running plates and as much as possible of 'the works' neatly concealed, a shapely chimney, and the tall slender dome as sported by the preserved 4–6–0 at Kimberley. The Class 8 4–8–0s were originally introduced in 1903 by H. M. Beatty, and showed many evidences of American influence, particularly in the use of bar frames. The earliest engines of this class, as supplied by the North British Locomotive Company, had slide-valves mounted above the cylinders, though actuated by inside Stephenson's link motion. All the examples of Class 8 I saw and photographed in the autumn of 1968 had piston valves, but still with inside valve gear. Thirty of these engines are still in service, mostly in splendid mechanical condition, and working from Germiston, Krugersdorp, Bloemfontein, Cape Town, Mossel Bay, Port Elizabeth, and Pietermaritzburg sheds. They are indeed light-duty maids of all work.

One of the most interesting duties allocated to these engines in their early days was the working of the Zambesi Express, throughout between Mafeking and the Victoria Falls. At the former station were then situated the workshops and running sheds of the Cape Government Railway division dealing with the Vryburg–Bulawayo section of the line. Cape engines worked through into Rhodesia, and one Class 8 4–8–0 worked over the 490 miles from Mafeking to Bulawayo, and a second continued over the 282 miles from Bulawayo to Victoria Falls. The locomotives were manned on the caboose system with the two crews allocated to each engine working in 8-hour alternate shifts. The speed was not high, and the Zambesi Express, leaving Kimberley on Wednesday evenings at 8.10 p.m., reached the Victoria Falls at 7.15 a.m. on Saturday morning. With the 223 miles between Kimberley and Mafeking added to the mileages worked by the Class 8 engines already mentioned, the total distance covered was 995 miles, in 59 hours inclusive of stops. The average speed was thus 17 m.p.h.

After the establishment of the Central South African Railways, in succession to the old Z.A.S.M., the immediate motive-power situation was to some extent relieved by the transfer of various older engines from both the Cape and the Natal systems, and a number of Class 6 4-6-0s and Class 7 4-8-0s were rebuilt with larger boilers at Pretoria Works, while some of the numerous Reid 4-8-2 tank engines from Natal were rebuilt as 4-8-0 tender engines. These, of course, could not be regarded as anything but stop-gap measures, and from 1903 onwards engines of new design began to arrive in South Africa from various British manu-facturers. It was noticeable at once that in contrast to the previous Cape designs all the new main line classes for the C.S.A.R. had carrying wheels under the fire-box: 4-6-2 for passenger, and 2-8-2 for freight. The 4-6-2s were of two varieties, known as Class 9 and Class 10. The former was a relatively small-power job, though ornately and beautifully finished. They had comparatively short boilers and fireboxes having a grate area of $21\frac{3}{4}$ sq. ft. While this, and their total weight with tender of 109 tons, could be considered ample enough for a railway working on the 3 ft. 6 in. gauge, these engines were designed for secondary duties. Although finished in plain black, no London and North Western engine of the day could have outshone them in the gloss and polish of their turn-out, which was set off by copper-capped chimneys and large polished brass domes.

The Class 10 'Pacifics' were a remarkable job. They were designed for heavy main-line work, and the contract for the first 15 engines of the class was awarded to the North British Locomotive Company, not long previously formed by the amalgamation of Neilson Reid, Dübs, and Sharp Stewart & Co. The production of these engines was considered a great event in Glasgow, and the directors of the new company were photographed in front of engine No. 660: the four Reid brothers, William Lorimer and his son, from Dübs, and J. H. Sharp and J. F. Robinson, from Sharp Stewart & Co. The principal difference between the Class 9 and Class 10 'Pacifics' on the C.S.A.R. lay in the use, on the latter, of large-diameter piston valves with outside Walschaerts gear, and an immensely large boiler and firebox. The barrel was 18 ft. 1 in., against 12 ft. 10, in., and the grate area, on the Class 10, was no less than 35 sq. ft. The coupled-wheel diameter, of 5 ft. 2 in., suggested that considerably faster running was contemplated than on previous train services in South Africa. As originally built they were impressive engines in their great size, for the 3 ft. 6 in. gauge, and they are highly significant in representing the first move, by South African locomotive engineers, to eliminate the disadvantage of the narrow gauge. Henceforth, gauge or no gauge, the motive power no less than the passenger and goods rolling stock was to be developed to maximum proportions.

The Class 10 eventually proved a remarkably good investment, and at the present time 31 of them are still in service. One of the most handsome that I saw personally in 1968 was No. 772 beautifully groomed outside Bloemfontein shed. Apart from her huge dome, and the electric headlight, she seemed to be in original condition even to the retention of the Ramsbottom type of safety valves. Another good example was No. 744, heavily coaled up and going off the shed at Sydenham, Port Elizabeth. To anyone interested in tracing the history of locomotives in South Africa the retention of the original numbers is a great help. The numbers are carried only on the cast plates on the cab sides. This makes it difficult sometimes to 'spot' individual engines, approaching or when no more than a fleeting glimpse is obtained; but when there is time to walk round the sheds the cab-side number plates are most useful. It was certainly an absorbing experience to be able to study South African locomotive history over more than sixty years from actual locomotives still in active service. In 1904 the *Locomotive Magazine* commented: '... the fifteen engines of this type now in course of shipment to South Africa should represent the high-water mark of tractive power on that system for some years to come.' Actually it was not until 1910, after the amalgamation of railways, following the establishment of the Union of South Africa, that any larger type was introduced and then it was H. M. Beatty, on the Cape Division, who put the first South African 4–8–2s on the road.

Reverting once again to the Transvaal, however, the immediate post-war years saw the introduction of the Class 11 2–8–2s for heavy freight work. These were the counterparts of the Class 10 'Pacifics', and with still larger boilers, having a total heating surface of 2278 sq. ft. against 1842 sq. ft., and a grate area of 37 sq. ft. These large engines, weighing 128 tons with their double-bogie tenders, had a tractive effort of no less than 34,667 lb. There were seven of them left in 1968, all stationed at Kimberley, and it was there I was able to photograph No. 932. The only change in appearance, apart from the inevitable headlight, is common to all the older South African locomotives, or rather to their tenders.

Originally they all had open rails; but in the course of the years these have been replaced by solid upward extensions of the tank side sheets. A further type of locomotive introduced after the conclusion of the Boer War was a handsome 4–6–4 tank, for suburban working on the Rand, and from Pretoria. These had the same boilers as the Class 9 'Pacifics' and similar cylinders and motion. They were designed for working passenger trains, running either chimney or bunker first, and as such had cowcatchers at both ends. The electrification of lines in the Johannesburg and Pretoria areas made these locomotives redundant, and they were scrapped some years ago.

Following the C.S.A.R. 'Pacifics' and 2–8–2s of 1904, the next major developments in South Africa motive power came in 1910 and 1913, with the introduction of large engines of the 4–8–2 type in the Cape and Natal respectively. As mentioned previously, the Cape engine of 1910 was designed by H. M. Beatty, and could be considered as a development of his Class 8 4–8–0. In any case, however, the advent of the 4–8–2 type for both passenger and freight working marked the beginning of an era that has extended to the production of locomotives that are, to a large extent, the mainstay of the main-line steam-worked services today. Beatty's 4–8–2 of 1910 was one of the largest then built for the 3 ft. 6 in. gauge, and was developed to provide greatly increased boiler capacity for the working of the heavy trains over the Hex River Pass section of the line. The boiler barrel was no less than 20 ft. 2 in. long and the grate area 37 sq. ft. The locomotive was a neat and handsome design, and although using the then-standard bar frames there was a notable concealment of 'the works', with inside Stephenson link motion actuating slide-valves mounted just above the cylinders. The nominal tractive effort was 37,000 lb. at 85 per cent boiler pressure. There was a later variant of this design, with piston valves and outside Walschaerts gear, and one of this series became the 20,000th locomotive to be completed by the North British Locomotive Company. The firm was always very proud of its work for South Africa, and a series of group photographs were taken with various grades of the staff, with this locomotive as a background.

Following the establishment of the South African Railways, Mr. D. A. Hendrie was appointed chief mechanical engineer, and in 1913 some very powerful engines of the 4–8–2 type were put into service on the Natal section. They were built by Robert Stephenson & Co. of Darlington, and despite the fact of their being for the 3 ft. 6 in. gauge they were the largest and heaviest locomotives which that firm had built, up to that time. They were designed for freight working on the most heavily graded section, where lengths of 1 in 30 exist, and are combined with curves of 300 ft. radius. They were known as Class 14, and no fewer than 86 of them are still at work today—50 at Greyville shed, Durban. This class was the first of three large and powerful varieties of 4–8–2 introduced by Mr. Hendrie within five years.

S.A.R. 4–8–2s: 1913–1918

Class	Cylinder		Coupled wheels diam. (ft. in.)	Total heating surface (sq. ft.)	Grate area (sq. ft.)	Total weight (tons)
	Diam. (in.)	Stroke (in.)				
12	$22\frac{1}{2}$	26	4 3	3139	40	143·2
14	22	26	4 0	2864	36	139·8
15A	22	28	4 9	2575	40	143

The '15A' class, of which many still remain in service, are very handsome engines. One of the very few that remain completely unrebuilt is stationed at Port Elizabeth, and like so many historic South African locomotives it is kept in immaculate condition. This particular engine, No. 1845, has been named, and carries the name *Uitenhage—The Garden Town* just below the electric headlight. I should mention that although he was introducing so many much larger engines Mr. Hendrie also put on the road, in the 1913–1918 period, a new series of 'Pacifics' known as Class 16, 22 of which were still at work during 1968.

The history of the locomotives so far discussed in this chapter can, with few exceptions, be followed up by seeing examples of the various classes still in service. Even the veteran tank engines of Natal are still to be seen in some of the gold-mine railways, while the Dutch-built 0–6–4 tank, *President Kruger*, standing on one of the platforms at Pretoria, represents early motive power in the Transvaal. One interesting phase of South African locomotive development is not now represented by 'living' examples, and that is the phase of the Mallet. In the period just prior to the outbreak of World War I and for some years afterwards, the Mallet type of articulated locomotive enjoyed great popularity in the U.S.A. For a line like the South African, having many of its heavily worked routes beset with much severe curvature in addition to steep gradients, the Mallet had many features of attraction. It had flexibility of wheelbase; it permitted of a large boiler, and the adhesion could spread over many axles, thus resulting in light individual axle loads. The Mallet principle also included compound expansion, the rear engine unit being driven by the high-pressure cylinders, and the leading unit driven by the low-pressure.

In 1914, the South African Railway took delivery of fifteen huge Mallet engines of the 2–6–6–0 type. They were designed for heavy freight service and had coupled wheels no larger than 3 ft. 9 in. diameter. The high-pressure cylinders were 18 in. diameter, and the big low-pressure ones driving the leading engine unit 28½ in. diameter. Both sets of cylinders had a common stroke of 26 in. Curiously enough the 'all-up' weight of this notable engine design was not significantly greater than that of the '15A' class 4–8–2s, being 146 tons, as against 143. It had, of course, the advantage of much greater flexibility of wheelbase, thus taking more kindly to the most severely curved stretches of line. That the Mallet type of locomotive achieved a degree of success is evident from the fact of further designs being prepared, for specialist duties elsewhere in South Africa. Hendrie introduced a rather lighter version of the 2–6–6–0 type primarily for banking duties on heavily graded sections of line. Eight of these handsome engines were built by the North British Locomotive Company, but the climax, so far as the Mallet principle was concerned in South Africa, was reached in the 'MH' class, of the 2–6–6–2 type, of which five were built, also by the North British, in 1915.

I find it rather difficult to write of these amazing engines. I have seen them only in photographs, and a broadside view gives the most vivid impression of immense length. The boiler was 6 ft. diameter, with a length of 22 ft. between tube plates; the grate area was 53 sq. ft., and the total heating surface, including superheater, 3827 sq. ft. The high-pressure cylinders driving the rear engine unit were almost exactly in line with the dome; they were 20 in. diameter by 26 in. stroke. The low-pressure cylinders were no less than 31½ in. diameter, also with a stroke of 26 in. These engines were a heavy main-line job designed for working coal trains over the steep gradients of the Natal line, and the maximum

54

axle load was as much as 18 tons. These grand engines weighed 128¼ tons without their tenders, and the total weight of engine and tender in working order was 179½ tons. One would dearly have liked to see them at work, but unlike many of the locomotives already described in this chapter they, and all the other South African Mallets, are now scrapped. They undoubtedly filled an important niche in history, but while one would like to have seen one of them preserved, an engine and tender measuring some 80 ft. from buffer to buffer and weighing nearly 180 tons is not exactly a thing to tuck neatly on to a pedestal on a station platform. It was the development of the Beyer–Garratt type of articulated loco- motive that sounded the death knell of the Mallet so far as South Africa was concerned, but the numerous tests following the experimental introduction of the Garratt had an even more widespread result. Until then it went almost without saying that all Mallet articulated locomotives were compounds. The Garratt, on the other hand, had four cylinders all taking live steam from the boiler. In view of the favourable test results obtained, and the fact that it made for a simpler layout, the majority of the engines subsequently built in the Mallet style, chiefly in the U.S.A., were simples and not compounds. Later chapters of this book will show to what an extent the Beyer–Garratt type was developed in South Africa; but with the end of World War I and the eclipse of the Mallets it is time to bring this particular chapter to a close.

CHAPTER FIVE

Lines across the Veldt

It is always interesting to try and trace the origin of towns that are 'out and out railway colonies'—as the *Railway Magazine* once described them. Crewe was created by the railway; so was new Swindon, and knowing the towns themselves one could indeed have wondered—in pre-grouping days in England—why so many important express trains called at stations like Hellifield and Carnforth. In South Africa there is what Lennox van Onselen has called 'the howling wilderness' of De Aar. By then, in the year 1881, Great Britain had already celebrated the Railway Jubilee; the Settle and Carlisle line had been opened, and the rivalry between the East and West Coast routes to Scotland was warming up towards the first great Race to the North; but then also, less than ninety years ago, De Aar was nothing more than the name of an isolated farmstead on the fringes of the Great Karoo. The farm had recently changed hands, and one day in 1881 the new owner, a man called Grundlingh, was surprised when a horse-drawn wagon stopped outside. The farmers in those outposts lived an incredibly isolated life, and travellers were exceedingly few and far between. The stranger introduced himself as a civil engineer who had been instructed to survey the land for a proposed extension of the Cape railway from Beaufort West towards Kimberley. At that time the railways from Cape Town and Port Elizabeth were in deadly rivalry as to which would reach the diggings of Kimberley first.

The surveys so far made had indicated that the two rival lines would converge somewhere near De Aar farm; but an examination of the proposed site revealed that the water supply was not adequate for a railway junction, and the point of convergence of the two lines was fixed a little distance away. In due course construction of the approach lines started, and then the lonely district began to experience something wilder and

PLATE C

South African Railways

The 'Union Limited' leaving Cape Town, around 1920, hauled by a '15A' class 4-8-2 locomotive

altogether more terrifying in the way of navvy disturbances than anything else that had previously occurred in South Africa, or anywhere
else for that matter. On the line from Port Elizabeth the gangs were
recruited from a community called Fingoes, who had been driven out of
Zululand in 1880, to make a servient existence across the Great Fish
River. These men proved good enough workers, but it was not surprising
that they nursed a burning resentment, and indeed hatred, against the
Zulus. And while the contractors on the Port Elizabeth line used the
Fingoes who had settled in the territory crossed by the new railway, the
Cape Government, for its extension from Beaufort West to De Aar,
began recruiting Zulus from Natal! As the two railheads drew nearer to
their eventual convergence the atmosphere grew steadily more tense,
though even if this was realised by the responsible contractors little
attempt was made to keep the two tribes apart.

It needed only the tiniest incident to set the Karoo ablaze. It came from
a mere triviality. Some dogs belonging to the Zulus found a small buck
and gave chase. It ran through the Fingoe encampments, and the Fingoes'
dogs joined in. Eventually it was the Fingoes' dogs and not the Zulus'
that caught the buck, and instantly pandemonium broke out. One of the
European engineers offered to mediate in what looked like becoming a
very ugly affair; but the Zulus, furious that their dogs had been robbed
of their quarry, set about the Fingoes without further ado. Both sides
were spoiling for a fight, and in a very short time nearly 1400 men were
involved. This was no ordinary game of fisticuffs; no large-scale 'rough-
house'. It was a savage, pitched battle between two native tribes, and a
large number of men on both sides were killed. Neither could claim
victory, and for a short time afterwards there was an uneasy truce,
watched with ever-increasing anxiety by the small white population
encamped around De Aar. Then on Christmas Day 1883, just before
sunrise, some 400 picked men of the Fingoes attacked the Zulu encamp-
ment with utter fury. This time the issue was not in doubt. The Zulus
were routed, and their once-proud warriors fled the place. Despite all
this, and despite the fact that armed reinforcements for the Europeans
were a long time in coming, construction of the converging lines of
railway went on, and only three months after the Christmas Day slaughter
the two lines were linked up, and De Aar became 'De Aar Junction'.
Then the projectors decided to rename it 'Broungers Junction', in honour

of the great civil engineer who had done so much to bring the railway up from the Cape; but this change caused much resentment among the inhabitants, and so it reverted to De Aar, which it has remained ever since.

I spent an afternoon and evening at De Aar and found both the railway and the town fascinating places. It still remains an outpost, a railway settlement; but the neat bungalows, wide streets, and simple shops are far removed from the sophisticated skyscraper atmosphere of the larger South African centres of population. De Aar is surrounded by wide open spaces, and its pleasant hotel in its homely atmosphere and warm hospitality has something of the air of a ranching community. Actually the great majority of the population of De Aar are connected with the railway. From the passenger point of view its importance as a junction is small; but as a locomotive staging point it is a centre of the first magnitude. The running sheds lie to the south of the junction itself, and at all times present a stupendous parade ground for some of the largest steam locomotives in Africa. There are few moderate-powered or vintage specimens to be seen here. De Aar is concerned with long-haul tasks with trains of caravan length across the waterless deserts of the Karoo, and hard runs northwards across the veldt to Kimberley. Great 4–8–4 engines with special tenders for conserving the water-supply tend to predominate. There are no small nineteenth-century 4–6–0s or 4–8–0s to propel the coal trucks up on the loading galleries; the big engines have to do the job themselves in between long main-line duties. For shunting passenger stock around the station massive vintage 4–8–2s blast their way to and fro.

Steam is nevertheless not entirely predominant at De Aar. The original junction was created by the convergence of two lines from the south, continuing north in a single main line of remarkable straightness over the veldt to Kimberley. Subsequently there came the line striking north-westwards from De Aar into the heart of what used to be German South-West Africa. I have never travelled by this route, and doubt nowadays if I should ever have the time to traverse it in a passenger train. It was a Saturday when I was at De Aar and at eight o'clock in the evening there was a train leaving for Windhoek, the capital of South-West Africa, some 800 miles away over remote, sparsely populated country. That train, we learned, was due to reach Windhoek some time on Monday. This is no disparagement to the splendid services of the South African Railways, but a commentary upon the conditions in which they have to

58

operate. The line into South-West Africa is now worked by diesel locomotives, and it is principally a freight route.

De Aar has been the first really large depot noted on our journey that is predominantly steam, since Cape Town has a high proportion of electrics, both locomotives and multiple-unit trains. A characteristic feature, which is common throughout the South African Railways, is an absence of turn-tables. With an abundance of space adjoining most of the depots triangles have been laid out where the engines may be turned. In most cases the head-shunt tracks are of sufficient length to accommodate a pair of the largest tender engines. Many of the main-line freights are of such weight as to require double heading, and the engines proceed round the triangles for reversing ready-coupled. A cloudless October day with the temperature in the eighties made tramping round the sheds and photographing the ceaseless procession of freight trains a hot task. Nightfall came early, and the warm day was succeeded by a cool brilliant night in which some of us, taking advantage of the broad sky-scapes of De Aar, unencumbered by any tall buildings, tried vainly to identify some of the unfamiliar star constellations of the southern hemisphere. Then back to the hotel to put on still warmer clothes for a final watch on the station platforms while we awaited the arrival of the 'Trans-Karoo Express'.

Now, however, our route is northward and not south from De Aar, and having observed the single-tracked line to Windhoek bearing away to the left it is thrilling to listen to the roaring exhaust of the great 4–8–4 engine as she is pounding up the long gradient to the high plateau of the veldt. It is now a splendid double-tracked railway, necessarily so in view of its heavy freight traffic, and almost from the moment of passing the end of the railway purlieus of De Aar we are out into the vast expanse of country that swells up to the high veldt. The soil is a vivid orange brown. For the most part it is sparsely covered by low scrub, and in the distance are occasional low, isolated hills whose slopes are steep escarpments and known hereabouts as kopjes. I remember once being very impressed with the utter isolation of the railway in the desolate moorland fastnesses on the borders of Sutherland and Caithness. It seems such a tiny thread of civilisation amid the limitless expanse of wild nature. I got the same impression, on an altogether vaster scale, as I once watched an enormous double-headed freight train slowly climbing the bank out of De Aar. The train itself soon became completely indiscernible, but above it was a slowly

59

moving cloud of black smoke as the two engines worked away, virtually all-out, and their mechanical stokers feeding coal as fast as machinery could on to those huge grates with an area of 70 sq. ft.

On this great trunk line, so finely engineered by the celebrated George Pauling, the intermediate stations are most spaciously laid out. All have four tracks between the platforms, and when passing through it is not unusual to see two freight trains berthed to be overtaken by a passenger train. One can certainly ponder upon why it was necessary to provide such long platforms, when surrounding the stations there are often no more than a dozen or so native dwellings and not another habitation in sight in the entire limitless expanse of the veldt. The names are intriguing: Perdevlei, Behrshoek, Hontkraal, Potfontein, Poupan, with some fine kopjes near at hand, and in the hot shimmering noonday there are frequent mirages. Then, at about 70 miles from De Aar, the line comes to the Orange River, where there is always a lengthy stop for watering and fire-cleaning. The non-stop expresses take between 110 and 115 minutes for the run from De Aar, and in view of the long uphill slogging, the heavy loads conveyed, and limitation of maximum speeds to 55 m.p.h., this entails some very hard work.

The main line to the north, although crossing the Orange River, does not actually enter the Orange Free State but keeps about five miles to the west along its western boundary. At the time of construction of the line Rhodes saw to it that his great strategic line to the north did not run through any part of the two Boer republics, although at that time the Orange Free State was quite friendly towards Great Britain. It was otherwise with the Transvaal, and President Kruger sought to contain the spread of British influence by a move into Bechuanaland. Dutch farmers were encouraged to settle there, and having arrived to proclaim a republic of their own. The Cape Government was quick enough to appreciate the significance of what was going on, and the presence of a third Boer republic to the west of the Orange Free State could have had most awkward consequences towards the northward advance of the railway. By this time Pauling's construction gangs had reached the Orange River, and he was in process of building a temporary bridge by which to carry materials to the north bank. After some delay a British expedition to Bechuanaland was launched under the command of Sir Charles Warren, and eventually its columns arrived at the Orange River. Pauling assisted

60

in transporting the troops to the north bank, where somewhat to his surprise the military commander soon found innumerable offers of horses, mules, and carts to carry the troops forward. It then became apparent that the very settlers who he had been sent to fight had hired themselves to transport the expedition. The army arrived in Bechuanaland to find no enemy! The Boer farmers who trekked over and settled in the country saw no reason to quarrel with the British, and in due course the Crown Colony of British Bechuanaland was established. And from this truly Gilbertian situation, Pauling ferried the army of Sir Charles Warren back again.

Today the station at Orange River can present a most animated scene during the 20 minutes or so that a long and heavy passenger train awaits the servicing of its locomotive. Gaily attired native passengers leave their own coaches, and form animated groups on the platforms; in the South African spring the station flower-beds are a blaze of colour, while the railway enthusiast will never cease to be impressed by the sheer volume of traffic passing now over this line. I was travelling on one occasion by the 8.55 a.m. southbound train from Kimberley, and as we entered Orange River, and turned into the platform line, a southbound freight standing on the through line was just leaving. We left after a twenty-minute stop, but before we got away yet another southbound freight had arrived and stopped on the through line for its engine to be serviced. We had five intermediate stops to make between Orange River and De Aar. The freight that was ahead of us was no doubt running non-stop, but we suffered only one slight delay by signals from it before we reached De Aar. To add to the interest, a northbound freight was running into Orange River just as we left. Three southbound and one northbound train all within twenty minutes!

The Orange River itself, as seen from the railway viaduct, is an interesting spectacle. I was there in September, and throughout the South African winter there had been a long drought. The trees lining the banks of the river, in their fresh foliage, were a vivid green, altogether contrasting with the arid slopes behind welling up to the high veldt. The river seemed sluggish, almost turgid, with the water level low, between golden yellow sandbanks. Starting northbound from Orange River the locomotives of heavy trains have a long continuous tug-of-war till the high plateau is reached. With mechanical stokers the exhaust from the great 4–8–4 engines is a continuous cloud of black smoke, which nevertheless disappears very quickly in the hot, dry air. There are shallow cuttings blasted out of the solid rock; one passes many a dried-up water course and eventually we attain the height of the plateau, and once again can see for score upon score of miles across the country. Ten miles of hard going has brought us to Witput, where there was a green 'oasis' surrounded by many cypress trees. Not far away one could see an enclave, with many fresh green trees and no fewer than seven windmills, pumping water.

Along a magnificently straight length of main line the names of the stations now become a mixture of English and Dutch: Chalk Farm, Belmont, Heuningneskloof, Klokfontein, Merton, Spytfontein, Wimbledon, and Beaconsfield. Perhaps the best-known name along this stretch, through its association with the Boer War, is Modder River. Observing at the stations, and seeing what traffic passed on the way, it was evident that the almost universal type of locomotive employed is the '25' class 4–8–4; and on the heaviest freights it seemed customary to run a condensing and a non-condensing engine in double harness. So the line begins to approach Kimberley, where on the through expresses from the Cape to Johannesburg and Pretoria steam traction ends. Kimberley is nevertheless a very important steam centre, and it is only on the main line into the Transvaal that electric haulage is used for the main-line trains. The eastwards connection to Bloemfontein, and the northward continuation of the 'Cape to Cairo' route to Mafeking and into Rhodesia, are still entirely steam-worked. Running into Kimberley one must on no account miss the restored and preserved Cape 4–6–0 No. 645, on its pedestal on the left-hand side as the train enters the station from the south.

Kimberley was the scene of one of George Pauling's more violent adventures. The specifications for the station layout had, one fears, been somewhat sketchily done, and when it came to the actual preparation for the site for the station Pauling discovered, to his consternation, that the stipulated levels required an excavation over much of the area, of a depth of 2 ft. to 4 ft. below the natural level of the ground. It was made infinitely worse in that this excavation meant blasting from the solid rock. This, of course, was going to increase the cost of the work far beyond the price estimated, and Pauling found that by making no more than a small deviation he could avoid all this excavation and save a great deal of money.

62

The Government inspector was quite adamant, however, and Pauling was forced to carry out the work strictly according to the specification, to which he had certainly quoted. This setback had not improved his temper or his attitude to those who were invigilating while the work was in progress, and on one occasion towards the completion there were high words over certain details of the work. An inspector of lower status was involved this time, and when this individual persisted Pauling took to his fists and floored the man like a ninepin. He then called upon him to get up and fight, and when the unfortunate inspector showed no inclination to do so Pauling picked him up, shook him, and then hurled him across the room! Such was the way contractors dealt with pernickety inspectors in the building of the Cape to Cairo Railway. Including the fracas at the finish it took Pauling nine months to build the 77 miles of main line from Orange River to Kimberley.

A very interesting cross-country line, 106 miles long, connects Kimberley with Bloemfontein. Today the latter place is not on the main route from the Cape to Johannesburg; but when the initial market for the Kimberley diamonds largely collapsed, and attention turned to gold-mining in the Transvaal, Rhodes saw to it that the Cape Government Railways were extended towards the Transvaal border, equally with the projection of his great project towards the north. The main line came up from Port Elizabeth, through Cookhouse and Cradock, and this was joined at Hamilton, two miles short of Bloemfontein, by the cross-country line from Kimberley. I travelled over this latter route on a stopping train, and a fascinating experience it was to observe all the points in operation on a single-line, but one conveying a heavy freight traffic. This line has little of a main-line character. For much of the way it follows the curves and contours of the land; the curves are often severe, and 'stations' as such are not frequent. The country is partly veldt and partly farmland and the progress of a stopping train, albeit worked by a large modern engine, had much the style of a traditional English branch train of the pre-1914 era. The train by which I travelled from Bloemfontein to Kimberley was actually worked by one of the very fine Class 16E Pacifics, built in Germany by Henschel in 1935. Detailed reference to these locomotives is made in Chapter Six.

On this line many of the stopping places for an intermediate passenger train are mere halts in the open country. Several times I saw groups of native passengers standing by the lineside, where there was no evidence of platforms, or of a station in any sense of the word. The train drew up, and many of those waiting clambered aboard. As often as not, however, there were as many to see the passengers off as those that were actually travelling. The larger intermediate places, where there were passing loops were nicely accommodated stations, with full-height platforms, station buildings, and the usual profusion of flowers. Occasionally the speed would rise to about 50 m.p.h. between stations, but for the most part progress was slow, and gave ample time to enjoy the passing scene and all the incidentals of travel. The countryside is more varied than ever over the almost uninterrupted veldt between Kimberley and De Aar. In places there is much ploughed land; there was an occasional sight of ostriches, and the soil, where cultivated, was of a rich chestnut-brown colour. The station names are varied: Sleepdam, Kelly's View, Olienhoutplaat, Reinhoidskoft—where one native woman was waiting, out in the middle of nowhere. Where she had come from, goodness knows, because this happened to be one of those halts right out on the veldt with no habitation anywhere to be seen on the broad horizons!

At the stations proper, water was taken, and we were usually standing for about ten minutes. Progress was leisurely as will be seen from our booked times on this westbound run.

Olienhoutplaat	17 miles	56 min.
De Brug	30 miles	83 min.
Petrusburg	54 miles	130 min.
Perdeberg	77 miles	180 min.
Kimberley	106 miles	255 min.

I travelled over this line in the reverse direction to the general trend of this book, and I was most impressed by the heavy freight traffic flowing over this single-tracked route. At the majority of the passing loops there was a freight train of the usual tremendous length characteristic of the South African Railways, though here not so heavy as to require double-heading. In all probability these trains were made up to the maximum length that could be accommodated in the passing loops. From my actual direction of travel however we must now turn about, and make the approach to Bloemfontein. Later in my travels in South Africa I did arrive from the south, by the main line up from Port Elizabeth, and the

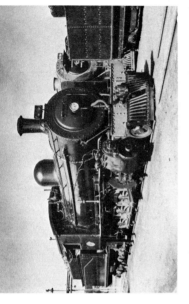

Class '8' 4-8-0 No. 1223 (1903 vintage), ex-Central South African Railway at Bloemfontein, 1968

Class '11' 2-8-2 No. 932 (1903 vintage) ex-Central South African Railway at Kimberley, 1968

Class '7' 4-8-0 No. 987 ex-Cape Government Railways built in Glasgow 1892—as running in 1968

Class '10' 4-6-2 No. 772 (1903 vintage) ex-Central South African Railway at Bloemfontein, 1968

PLATE 7. South African Locomotive Veterans

PLATE 8

American-built 4–6–2 No. 860, Class 16D, at Cape Town.

One of the handsome '16E' Pacifics built by Henschel—with decorated smokebox door: No. 854 *Harrismith*

A '25C' condensing 4–8–4, No. 3481 at De Aar Junction

last stage of this journey, from Springfontein was over another notable 'line across the veldt', of which I shall have a good deal more to say in Chapter Eight of this book, when I am discussing signalling methods.

The line from Kimberley joins the main line at Hamilton, about two miles short of Bloemfontein, but it is on leaving for the north that the traveller must look out on the left-hand side of the train to see Naval Hill, and the surprising apparition of a White Horse, fully in the tradition of the English downland. A battalion of the Wiltshire Regiment was stationed at Bloemfontein during the later stages of the Boer War, and having to hand so splendid an escarpment as the western face of Naval Hill they proceeded to cut a fine White Horse in the best traditions of their native land. They had no chalk to work on. It was a case of exposing and surfacing the rock, and the 'horse' is now maintained and kept gleaming white. The flat top of Naval Hill, near the crest of the escarpment where the White Horse is cut, is a magnificent vantage point for observing the whole railway complex of Bloemfontein. One can look down over the large running sheds and marshalling yards, and watch the biggest South African steam locomotives, frequently in pairs, moving on and off the shed. Bloemfontein is in fact one of the largest steam depots in the country, and at the time of my visit a total of 175 locomotives were stationed there. Although there are other sights to be seen on Naval Hill, including zebras so tame that one can photograph them at quarters as close as the New Forest ponies, a railway enthusiast is drawn like a magnet to the sheds, which provide an impressive parade ground of steam, modern, and vintage alike.

Although the '15F' class 4–8–2 engines are in such general use on both passenger and freight service in South Africa there are none of them stationed actually at Bloemfontein. The main strength of the heavy main-line motive power is provided by no fewer than 97 of the Class 23 4–8–2s, which look very similar in outward appearance to the '15F' class, but include a number of variations that are described in Chapter Six, following. All six of the special large-wheeled Pacifics of Class 16E are stationed at Bloemfontein, and the shedmaster took great pleasure in parading a gloriously clean specimen of this class alongside an old Central South African 'Pacific' of Class 10C, No. 772. It was inspiring to see the pride taken in the appearance of individual engines, with little touches of special adornment such as one saw long years ago on the Caledonian. Whereas the

'Dunalastair' drivers used to fit ornamental decorations to their smoke-box doors, one sees certain South African giants that are special favourites decorated with figures of leaping springbok, in sheet copper; the smoke-boxes themselves are treated with aluminium paint, and touches of colour are added to running plate edges, axle-ends, and anything that is copper is burnished to the utmost.

All the train workings from Bloemfontein are steam, and in addition to the stud of 97 huge 23 class 4–8–2s there are many jobs requiring engines of lesser power, and what is more important a lighter axleload. For this the depot is well provided with modern 4–8–2s of the '19D' class, and a few of the very interesting light-weight 2–8–4s of Class 24. Both of these, as will be discussed in more detail in the next chapter, are post-war products.

CHAPTER SIX

South African steam locomotive development: the big engines

Towards the end of the 1920s the engineering direction of the South African Railways threw off any lingerings of the attitude that they were operating a 'narrow-gauge' line, and were constrained by limitations of a gauge of only 3 ft. 6 in. The loading gauge, as distinct from the rail gauge, was ample, and there commenced a policy of building locomotives that would compare with the most *puissant* to be found anywhere in the world. At the same time the peculiar operating conditions existing in South Africa must be taken into consideration. There was no case for providing 60 m.p.h. services between important cities. Freight was the major source of revenue, and although internal air services had not then begun to supplement the railways as a means of transport for the man in a hurry, the need for really high-speed services between centres like Johannesburg and Kimberley, Johannesburg and Durban, and above all between the Transvaal and the Cape, had not arisen. The crack express trains were relatively few, but those that did run were provided with every luxury for the traveller and very heavy in consequence. Power had to be provided for climbing gradients like those of the Hex River Pass, while out on the veldt speeds were limited to 55 m.p.h. South African motive-power development thus partook of a character entirely its own, and all the more interesting in consequence. In this chapter I am primarily concerned with the huge tender engines for the main-line traffic between the Transvaal and the twin—and at one time rival—railheads of Cape Town and Port Elizabeth.

The era of the really big tender engine on the South African Railways began with the introduction of the '15CA' class 4–8–2 in 1926. Although the rail gauge is only 3 ft. 6 in., as compared to the standard 4 ft. 8½ in. in Great Britain, the height of the locomotives can be made 13 ft., as here; it is however in width that the South African loading gauge gives such advantage to a designer. Whereas the majority of British steam locomotives were limited to an overall width of about 8 ft. 9 in. the South Africans can be built up to 10 ft. wide, and this gives scope for the mounting of very large boilers. In addition the two-fold circumstances of very severe gradients and limitation of maximum speed—even on the fastest stretches—to 55 m.p.h., renders the use of large-diameter coupled wheels unnecessary. All these factors were used to the greatest advantage in the development of the very large engines introduced from 1926 onwards, commencing with the '15CA' class. This was a design of massive simplicity, arranged to give maximum accessibility to all the working parts. The very large boiler overhung the wheels to such an extent that it was absolutely essential to have all the running gear outside. Anything between the frames, for example the old-style Stephenson link motion would have been inaccessible except when over a pit.

These large engines, of which the first examples were built in Glasgow by the North British Locomotive Company, were designed for mixed traffic and have coupled wheels only 4 ft. 9 in. in diameter. The two cylinders are enormous, 24 in. diameter by 28 in. stroke, but the narrow rail gauge and the liberal overall width enabled them to be conveniently accommodated. The very maximum diameter of outside cylinder that could be used within the limits of the British loading gauge was 22 in. and that was possible only on certain routes. These new South African 4-8-2s, of which a total of 84 were built between 1926 and 1930 were not normally used on passenger trains. At that time the fastest passenger duties were undertaken by the '16D' class 'Pacifics', built in the U.S.A. by Baldwins, from 1925 onwards. But although the '15CA' were not a passenger design they certainly showed the shape of things to come, and in 1935 two new classes of remarkable appearance and enhanced power were introduced. These were the '16E' class 'Pacific' and the '15E' class 4-8-2.

When the entire journey between Cape Town and Johannesburg was worked by steam, 4-8-2 engines were used between Cape Town and Beaufort West, 339 miles, and the largest 'Pacifics' worked over the 'desert' and veldt sections between Beaufort West and Kimberley. The older

68

The '12A' class of 1929

PLATE 9. Development of the S.A.R. 4–8–2

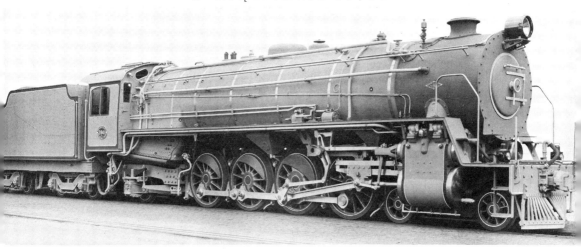

(*above*) The '15CA' class, also of 1929

(*below*) The '15F' class of 1939

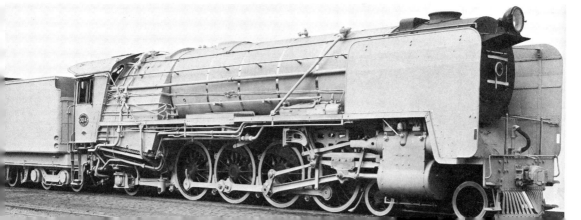

A Beyer–Peacock 2–6–0 tank of 1879

A main line train of 1899

A train of 1884

'Pacifics' undertook the most northerly section on the easier graded route between Kimberley and Johannesburg, 308½ miles. With loads of about 450 tons, rear-end banking assistance was necessary up the Hex River Pass, usually provided by one of the compound 'Mallets' described in Chapter Four. An enlargement of the '16D' class 'Pacific' had been made in 1930, in the handsome '16DA'; but these, like their predecessors, had coupled wheels of no more than 5 ft. diameter. In the early 1930s consideration was given to a substantial speed-up of the principal express train services, and a design was prepared for an entirely new 'Pacific' engine, having 6 ft. diameter coupled wheels. This was, however, no more than one unit in a programme for enhanced locomotive power that was to set the standards from 1935 to the present time. An important factor permitting the use of heavier engines was a notable improvement to the permanent way, including the easing of certain curves and gradients and the introduction of a stronger roadbed with rails weighing 96 lb. to the yard, instead of the previous standard size of 80 lb. The permanent way, wherever I travelled in South Africa, was certainly maintained in splendid condition and the riding of the trains was very smooth and comfortable.

To return however to the new engines, the '16E' class 'Pacifics' have boilers of maximum proportions, so much so that the chimney and dome have been reduced to almost negligible heights. The boiler is no less than 6 ft. 6 in. diameter, and the grate area is 62 sq. ft. Despite this however, these engines were designed for hand firing. Although the Belpaire type of firebox was common in earlier South African locomotives, all the latest and largest engines have had round-topped fireboxes, with the very deep, sloping grate spreading out almost to the full width permitted by the loading gauge. The boilers had certain features of design that were considerably in advance of current British practice. The ashpans, for example, were of the hopper type, permitting of very speedy removal of cinders and ash, without a lot of laborious hand raking, while the smokeboxes were fitted with a system of wire-net screens which rendered them self cleaning. The so-called 'self-cleaning' smokeboxes were not adopted on British railways until some ten years after the building of the '16E' class South African 'Pacifics'. Then they were most effective, and locomotives so fitted ran from one boiler-washout day to the next without any need for the smokebox door to be opened. Previous to the introduction of these self-cleaning screens a vast amount of ash had to be shovelled out of the smokebox after every run. The South African Railways certainly led the way in this respect.

The six engines of Class 16E are fitted with rotary-cam poppet valve gears, and although the locomotives themselves were built in Germany, by Henschel und Sohn, of Kassel, the valve gear as specified by the South African Railways was manufactured by the English firm of Associated Locomotive Equipment Ltd., of which that great enthusiast and historian, the late Edward Cecil Poultney, was the designer. From his lifelong study of locomotive design and performance Poultney was particularly careful to provide steam and exhaust passages to ensure an unrestricted flow of steam to the cylinders, and a free exhaust. The design throughout was a very advanced one, and it would have been highly interesting to see what one of these imposing engines could do in the way of speed, if really given her head. Unfortunately the accelerated services for which they were originally designed did not materialise, and with the 55 m.p.h. limit still prevailing their capacity for really high speed remains an unknown quantity. They were shipped, partially dismantled, from Germany to Cape Town, and then re-erected at Salt River Works.

The first engine, No. 854, was subjected to a test run from Cape Town to Wellington and back, shortly after its arrival, and for this the speed limit was temporarily relaxed. Speeds up to 70 m.p.h. were attained, but owing to the difficulties of the route and the need for various intermediate speed restrictions it was not possible to cover the $45\frac{3}{4}$ miles from Wellington back to Cape Town in less than $61\frac{3}{4}$ min. The 'crack' Union Limited express was then allowed 75 minutes for this particular section, and although that train usually conveyed a load of about 400 tons, as compared with the 280 tons of the special test train, it was evident from the intermediate details of the test that it was the restrictions of the road rather than the locomotive capacity that governed the overall time possible. It was this engine, now named *Harrismith* and kept in simply spanking condition, that hauled the train by which I travelled from Bloemfontein to Kimberley in the autumn of 1968. The photograph facing page 65 gives no more than a slight impression of this truly beautiful locomotive. She was indeed a classic example of what a black engine can look like. No London and North Western engine in the greatest days of Crewe could have had a *deeper* shine than this '16E'. With the project for higher speeds unrealised

70

no more than the six original engines of the class were ordered. Today all six of them are stationed at Bloemfontein.

While Henschels were building the '16E' 'Pacifics' the Darlington firm of Robert Stephenson and Hawthorn's Ltd., were building the first of the enormous '15E' 4-8-2s. These had cylinders and rotary-cam poppet valve gear interchangeable with the corresponding parts of the '16E' Pacifics; the boilers were of the same girth, but even longer, though the firebox remained the same. The coupled wheels were 5 ft. diameter, and this gave the high tractive effort of 47,980 lb. A total of 44 engines of this class was added to the stock in 1935–7. It was a time when poppet valve gears were very much in favour in Europe and in many overseas countries. It was generally considered that they made possible a more accurate distribution of steam, and by the facility of rapid opening and closing reduced wire-drawing to a minimum and made possible a very free-running locomotive. In Great Britain this was certainly the experience with both large and small engines of Sir Nigel Gresley's design on the London and North Eastern Railway, while the Caprotti valve gear was used to advantage on certain London Midland and Scottish types. On the other hand the comparison of similar locomotives with piston, as against poppet valve gave results in favour of piston valves, to such an extent in the case of the large 2-8-2 express locomotive *Cock o' the North* as to eventuate in its being rebuilt with piston valves, in keeping with the rest of the class.

Although I have never seen any figures to prove it one can infer that experience in South Africa was exactly the same. The '15E' as a motive power unit was ideal for general service on all main routes; but when further engines of this power class were required, in 1938, a modified design known as '15F' was specified having the same boiler and cylinder proportions as the '15E' but with piston valves actuated by Walschaerts gear. The '15F' has proved an outstanding success, and no fewer than 255 are now in service. They certainly rank as one of the really *great* engine designs of the steam era, and it was a deeply impressive experience to travel behind them, to note their tremendously rapid acceleration from rest, and the way their steaming remained rock-steady during long periods of severe 'hammering', at high power output, in climbing lengthy gradients with heavy trains. My personal experience of travel behind them was of course confined to passenger trains; but I saw them starting enormous freight trains out of the Germiston marshalling yard, on the Rand, and working in pairs on the freights entering and leaving Kimberley; whilst equally arduous duties that I observed were the freights out of Port Elizabeth, working up the north line to Cookhouse.

The general appearance of these engines, in hard common-user duty, was such as to underline the excellence in standards of maintenance that are sustained. Whether pounding away from Germiston yard with heavy freight trains, or working on crack passenger duties the engines were all clean, and more important still, showing no evidence of steam leakage from valves and glands. Some that were obviously star engines were, to use a popular slang phrase, gloriously 'tarted up', with whitened wheel rims, white cab-roofs and the usual touches of colour on axle-ends, number plate backgrounds, and running plate valances. It was not only the odd engine, like the specially resplendent 3150 at Capital Park depot, Pretoria, or 2958 with her prancing copper horses on the smokebox door, which worked the afternoon Johannesburg–Port Elizabeth express from Kroonstad to Bloemfontein. There were many engines only slightly less excellently turned out; and this pleasing situation was not only confined to the '15F' class. There was a magnificently arrayed '15E' on the shed at Bloemfontein, and a '16DA' Pacific that bid fair to rival the 'super-star', '16E' *Harrismith*. It was all the more exhilarating to one sadly familiar with the state of decrepitude that characterised the last days of steam on British Railways.

Next in the line of succession in this remarkable locomotive dynasty is the '23' class 4–8–2 introduced in 1938. Experience with the '15E' class in express passenger service had been so successful that a decision was taken to standardise on eight-coupled engines in future for the heaviest long-distance passenger workings. At the same time it was considered that a slightly larger driving wheel than 5 ft. was desirable for the faster stretches of line, and so the '23' class was given 5 ft. 3 in. coupled wheels. With the same sized cylinders, a higher boiler pressure of 225 lb. per sq. in. was used to maintain a nominal tractive effort equal to that of the '15E' and '15F' classes. All three classes have the same boiler, except that the higher working pressure is used on the '23' class. The '23' class have a general appearance very similar to that of the '15F', but the two classes may be easily distinguished by their tenders. The '15F' have 8-wheeled tenders, carried on two 4-wheeled bogies, whereas the '23' class have enormous 12-wheeled tenders. The respective capacities are 5940 and 9500 gallons of water, and 12 and 18 tons of coal. On the '23' class the tenders alone weigh 105 tons, while the engine weighs $111\frac{1}{4}$ tons. The '23' class, like the '15F' have piston valves actuated by the Walschaerts gear.

While the '15E' and '15F' classes were designed for mixed traffic, for rapid acceleration from rest with passenger trains, and an ability to start freight trains of exceptional tonnage, the '23' class was designed to develop a high proportion of their potential power at full running speeds, and to enable the steam raising capacity of their fine boilers to be sustained indefinitely, mechanical stokers were fitted. These permit of a firing rate in excess of that which it could be reasonable to expect a single fireman to maintain, by hand. Coal is conveyed from the tender by the revolving screw in the bunker conveyor unit, to a telescopic intermediate unit, located between the tender and the cab. From this point it passes up the fixed elevator pipe and is then fed to the distribution table. From this it is blown by steam jets to the desired points of the firebed. The conveyor screw is rotated by a small steam engine, and the speed of rotation, and thus the speed of firing is under the control of the fireman. It was to provide sufficient fuel for the higher rates of combustion on the '23' class that the huge 12-wheeled tenders were introduced. All the 136 engines of the '23' class were built in Germany, 98 by Henschel, and 38 by the Berlin Maschinenbau A.G. At the time I was in South Africa in 1968 no fewer than 97 of them were stationed at Bloemfontein; a further 25 were at De Aar, and the remaining 14 at Kimberley. They are essentially express engines, and although I awoke too late to begin any detailed recording I was most impressed with the performance of one of them on the overnight express from Port Elizabeth to Johannesburg, on the section between Springfontein and Bloemfontein.

Successful though the '23' class proved in heavy duty over the long stretches of the veldt and the Karoo desert, the steady increase in the loading of both passenger and freight trains suggested the need for still more powerful locomotives, and moreover of a design that could cover increased distances without taking water. One has only to travel across the veldt, not to mention the Karoo, to appreciate the scarcity of natural water supply in the rainless seasons. In producing a design for a locomotive of increased power the tenders even of the '23' class, with a water capacity of 9500 gallons, were not considered adequate, and so a large batch of the new engines were arranged to condense their exhaust steam, and thus use the same water over and over again. The locomotives themselves, known as Class 25, are of the 4–8–4 type, and have cylinders, coupled wheels, and running gear interchangeable with the '15F'; but the boiler is of a modified design, and the firebox with a grate area of 70 sq. ft. is fed by a mechanical stoker, as on the '23' class. The South African authorities placed orders for no less than 140 of these engines in 1951—50 with the orthodox type of exhaust, and conventional though very large tender, and 90 with the condensing apparatus. The work was divided between the North British Locomotive Company, and Henschels of Kassel, as follows:

Condensing engines	All 90 to N.B.L.
Condensing tenders	30 to N.B.L., 60 to Henschels
Non-condensing engines and tenders	10 to N.B.L., 40 to Henschels

It was interesting, and a matter for much gratification that the two firms worked together in the closest cooperation, and that much of the design work was done jointly.

Principal interest centres, of course, around the arrangements for condensing. Exhaust steam from the cylinders is passed into a turbine which drives a fan blower in the smokebox. This replaces the normal draught created by the action of the blastpipe. From the blower turbine the exhaust steam passes in a large pipe along the side of the locomotive, and then through an oil-separator to another turbine in the tender. This latter turbine drives a series of air-intake fans. Finally the steam passes to the condensing elements mounted on both sides of the tender, and the condensate is collected in a tank fitted underneath the tender frame, from which it is fed back to the boiler. It is claimed for these engines that they can run 700 miles without taking water. Technical details apart, they are some of the most remarkable-looking engines that have ever been produced anywhere. The condensing tenders are considerably longer than the engines: 60 ft. 5 in., against 49 ft. 7 in., and they are built practically to the limit of the loading gauge. At the front-end the condensing locomotives can be distinguished by the V-shaped casing leading the exhaust to the fan blower. A prominent feature of the running gear is the use of roller bearings for the connecting and coupling rods.

74

A very interesting feature of these engines, introduced on the South African Railways for only the second time, is the use of a one-piece steel casting incorporating the main frames, cylinders, and front buffer beam in a single entity. This principle, which by 1951 was virtually standard practice in the U.S.A., was first introduced in South Africa on the light-weight branch line 2–8–4s of the '24' class. It was a marked departure because hitherto South African locomotives had barframes machined from steel slabs, and the various cross-stretchers and other attachments were duly fabricated separately. The use of a one-piece steel casting permits of some considerable reduction in weight, and the castings themselves had to be imported from the U.S.A. The innovation was very successful, in the case of the '24' class. It was no less successful on the great '25' class. The complete onepiece 'frame' for the latter engine weighed 18 tons. Mention of these frames, or 'beds' as they were known in America, leads me naturally to the '24' class, which I saw under construction at the Hyde Park Works of the North British Locomotive Company. Although these could not be included under the classification of the 'giants', with which this chapter is mainly concerned, they, and the '19D' 4–8–2s, are essentially modern engines, and form an important part of the present locomotive stock. The esteem in which they are held can be judged from the fact that from their first introduction in 1937 no fewer than 235 of the '19D' class have been added to the stock, while the present strength of the '24' class, first introduced in 1949, is 100.

We make the acquaintance of the '19D' class of 4–8–2 more intimately at the end of Chapter Seven, after the journey through the 'Garratt country'. The '19D' is about the largest and heaviest engine of the non-articulated type that could be put on to a line where the maximum axle load is only 14 tons. They are finely proportioned engines with all modern aids to quick and efficient maintenance, and having a tractive effort roughly three-quarters that of the main line giants of the '15F' and '23' classes. A number of locomotives of this same design have been purchased by the Rhodesia Railways. The South African '24' class is even more of a lightweight, very cleverly designed to provide a maximum power locomotive running on rails as light as 45 lb. to the yard. This precluded any axle load of more than 11 tons. In superficial appearance the '24' is very similar to the '19D', but of the 2–8–4 wheel arrangement. Apart from the skill with which a boiler of high steaming capacity and a powerful engine unit has been designed against such rigid weight restrictions, the principal feature of these engines was the first use, in any locomotive manufactured in Great Britain of the one-piece cast-steel 'bed'. The tractive effort of these smart branch-line engines is roughly three quarters of that of a '19D': 27,600 lb. against 36,000 lb.

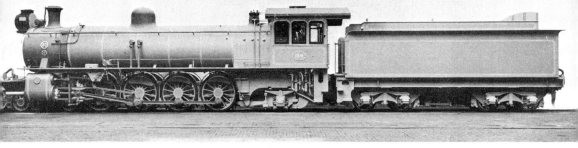

Rhodesia Railways 12th class 4–8–2 (1926)

South African Railways, '19C' class 4–8–2 (1934)

East African Railways '29' class 2–8–2

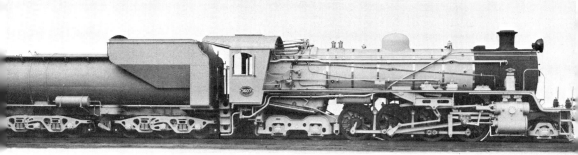

South African Railways '24' class 2–8–4 for light branch working

PLATE 11. Variety in Eight-coupled Locomotive

PLATE 12. On the Line in South Africa

(*above*) Express train crossing Little Fish River (Cape Province)

(*below*) An early Garratt locomotive leaving Kelso on the Durban–Port Shepstone line (Natal)

CHAPTER SEVEN

Garratt country

At 4 p.m. each day a train lavishly equipped with dining and sleeping cars leaves Cape Town for Port Elizabeth. Studying a map, and finding that the distance between the two cities is only 400 miles in a direct line, a British observer, with his mind running perhaps on the fast services from Euston and King's Cross that leave about the same time and reach Glasgow and Edinburgh before midnight, might ponder for a moment as to why sleeping cars were necessary; but a reference to the timetable then reveals that a through passenger on this South African journey would be spending not one but *two* nights on the train. In fact this train traverses one of the most difficult pieces of railway in all Africa. It diverges from the main line to the north at Worcester, and thenceforward steam haulage is the order of the day. Like most intermediate train services on the South African Railways the overall speed over the electrified part of the route is not high, and more than four hours are spent over the first 108 miles out of Cape Town.

By that time, with Worcester reached and change made from electric to steam haulage, it is dark; and although the acoustic effects from the front-end can be music in the ears of a steam locomotive enthusiast, after dinner the thoughts of most travellers are inclined more towards bed than to recording locomotive performance. In South Africa one needs to go to bed early to cope with the early rising habits of the entire population. Someone said there was a Garratt at the head of the train, and before turning in I watched, fascinated, from my sleeper window and listened to the big engine working steam. Rounding curve after curve I saw her powerful headlight penetrating far ahead into the still African night. The traveller by day is constantly on the look-out for signs of wild life; but it is at night that the more reluctant of the wild animals stray down to the railway, and it is then that the headlight is a boon. Apart from this reverie at the open window it was not until six next morning, when we changed engines at Riversdale that I really began to sit up and take notice. Then we were indeed in Garratt country, still only 240 miles by rail from Cape Town and already fourteen hours on our journey.

At a few wakeful moments during the night I had lain in bed listening to the heavy beat of the locomotive. On steep gradients there was an occasional slip, and I noticed how the forward and rear engines went temporarily out of synchronism, and also how quickly they got back into step. There is no mechanism for ensuring this synchronism; the exhausts from the two ends synchronised automatically. I dressed soon after day-break, and watched our long train winding round curve after curve. The weather was distinctly un-African—more like the West Highlands of Scotland indeed—and at Gouritz where we called at 7.45 a.m. the line was almost in the clouds, although at an altitude of only 208 ft. above sea level. We had a 12-coach train, and were being hauled by one of the 'G.E.A.' class Beyer–Garratt locomotives. These splendid engines, first introduced in 1946, have cylinders $18\frac{1}{2}$ in. diameter by 26 in. stroke, coupled wheels 4 ft. 0 in. diameter, and a nominal tractive effort of 63,030 lb. Their total weight in working order is 184 tons. Before coming to describe in detail the continuation of this most fascinating journey a word is necessary about the origin and development of the Beyer–Garratt type of locomotive, and the reasons for its outstanding success in country such as this.

This railway, like the main line through the Hex River Pass, was built to open up the country. There was never any question of operating high-speed services, and in wild mountain passes, deep valleys, and on precipitous hillsides great skill was displayed by the engineers in securing a route that would involve a minimum of earth works, of expensive bridges and of long tunnels. Gradients as steep as 1 in 40 were generally accepted, and the curves were frequent and severe. Again, to keep the cost of construction and maintenance to a minimum, a relatively light rail section was adopted, and proportionately light construction for underline bridges and viaducts. This in turn made necessary a strict limitation of maximum axle load. There were thus three factors that governed locomotive design;

1. An ability to climb heavy gradients.

78

2. Flexibility of wheelbase, to permit negotiation of sharp curves.
3. A relatively light axle load.

Stated categorically thus the three factors seem quite contradictory, in that one would appear to need a large and heavy engine to climb the steep gradients, and that in turn would necessitate a multiplicity of coupled axles, to provide the necessary adhesion.

The ingenious conception of the Garratt type of locomotive, remarkably developed over the years by Beyer, Peacock & Co. Ltd., provided a complete solution to this difficult problem—not only in South Africa but in many parts of the world where similar conditions prevail. The Beyer–Garratt is virtually two locomotives fed by one enormous boiler. The dividing of the 'engine' unit into two permits the use of a large number of coupled axles with consequent spreading of the adhesion weight and no excessive axle-loading, while the suspension of the boiler on a central frame, articulated to the two engine units, permits of a boiler and firebox of ideal proportions completely unhindered by the need of accommodating it over coupled wheels. In the 'G.E.A.' class the maximum axle load is only 15 tons, and that only on the driving axles of each engine unit. The axle loadings decrease towards the extremities of the unit. This weight distribution permits of this very powerful locomotive being used on routes laid with rails weighing no more than 60 lb. to the yard, compared with the 110 lb. rails now in general use on British main lines. The boiler is of the huge diameter of 7 ft., but with a length of only 11 ft. 8 in. These are ideal proportions for free steaming. These huge and handsome engines have an overall length of 88 ft., but can smoothly negotiate curves of 275 ft. radius. A further point about this excellent design was that the South African Railways placed a first order with Beyer, Peacock & Co. for fifty, straight off the drawing boards, and the locomotives took up the hardest duties immediately after arrival in Africa with little or nothing in the way of teething troubles.

The particular engine that had taken over haulage of our train at Riversdale was No. 4019, and the trailing load was about 480 tons. We left Gouritz at 7.45 a.m., and although not then at a high altitude we commenced immediately a brisk downhill run. The country is moorland in character, and I have a note in my travelling diary that it was rather like Ribblehead. It was bleak, with the hillsides seared by many a watercourse,

79

and after descending rapidly to a big viaduct a terrific ascent began, on 1 in 40 gradients. Although the line includes many sharp curves following the lie of the land numerous vertical-sided rock cuttings could not be avoided in construction, and on these rock walls the wild mountain flowers in the profusion of their spring blooming were a delight. There was plenty of time to observe them, because the tremendous gradients soon pulled the speed down to about 10 miles per hour. The incessant curvature reminded me of the upper stretches of the Vale of Rheidol line, in Central Wales, with the striking difference that we had a 184-ton locomotive with a tractive effort of 63,020 lb. at the head of the train.

In the passing loop at Kleinberg we 'crossed' a westbound freight train worked by engine No. 4018 of the same 'GEA' class. Shortly afterwards, now at 8.40 in the morning, we had our first glimpse of the sea from near Bartlesfontein, and continued over a fine moorland country, with frequent incidence of gradients such as 1 in 100, 1 in 71 and so on. Then we began to descend a long continuous bank, and so came into Hartenbos, junction for the short branch that runs down to its terminus at Mossel Bay. Through trains make the short detour to include this popular resort, and engine No. 4019 'ran round' the train at Hartenbos, and took the train down into Mossel Bay. I was due to ride on the footplate on the resumption from Hartenbos, and while the train went down the branch I took the opportunity of visiting Hartenbos running shed, and meeting the driver and fireman, and the engine, with which I was to ride. This proved to be another 'GEA', No. 4048. In this, the very heart of what I have called 'Garratt country', I found five engines of the 'GEA' class in steam in the shed, and two others under light repair. There were also the almost inevitable vintage steam locomotives, also in steam, including a couple of Neilson 4-8-0s of the 1896–1900 period. I met the crew of No. 4048, Driver Bekker and Fireman Van Zyl, and also Inspector Young who was to be my guide and philosopher on the footplate. The engine certainly looked a picture. Though in the plain black livery everything that could be was polished up splendidly, with stainless steel boiler bands, copper pipes, and coupling and side rods burnished in what seemed the traditional South African standards of engine cleaning.

We were to run with the rear engine leading, so as to have the cab preceding the chimney. I was soon to appreciate the wisdom of this. When we came to the first tunnel on a heavy rising gradient I heard the terrific

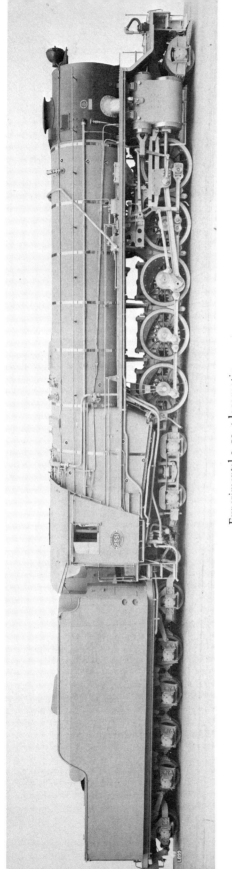

Experimental 2-10-4 locomotive

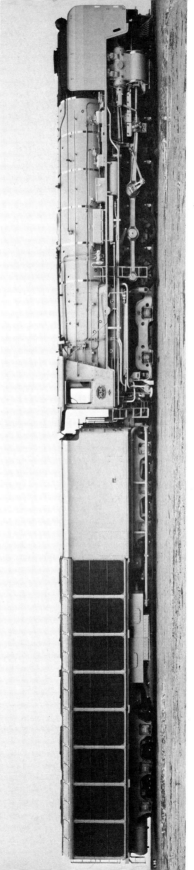

A '25' class with the enormous condensing tender

PLATE 13. Giant S.A.R. Locomotives

PLATE 14. On the Narrow Gauge

(*above*) Double-headed fruit train, Avontuur to Port Elizabeth, preparing to leave Lourie

(*below*) NG/G 13 Beyer–Garratt locomotive at Lourie

percussion of the exhaust, and realised how it would have been if the engine had been the other way round, and clouds of exhaust steam and smoke had poured into the cab, and much increased the already high ambient temperature. The load was now 484 tons tare, and about 515 tons gross behind the engine, and at 9.37 a.m. we got away. On this mountain route there is no block signalling, or tablet working at present. The working of trains is regulated by telegraph proceeding orders. Just before starting the driver was handed a 'chit' authorising him to proceed as far as Outeniekwa, where we were to cross a westbound goods train. If we arrived first it would be necessary to wait for the other train. With all my experience of signalling practice I must admit it seemed a little odd to head off on to a single line section, in remote country, without any definite authority from fixed signals; but of course the system is a long-established one in many countries of the world, and it has given eminently satisfactory results where traffic density does not justify the installation of any ordinary signalling.

On climbing into the cab I was at once impressed by the cleanliness, no less than the spaciousness of the layout. With the best will in the world the cab of a coal-fired steam locomotive is not the cleanest of places, especially —as in this case—if the firing is done by hand; but on No. 4048 everything was smart and tidy. Certainly with a cab nearly 10 ft. wide there was no suggestion of a 'narrow-gauge' locomotive in the ordinary sense. Almost from the start at Hartenbos we were coasting downhill, on a 1 in 40, to the crossing of the Little Brak River; but after a brief halt we had to go for it, hammer and tongs, up 1 in 40, and the engine was driven practically 'all-out' to make a speed of 15 m.p.h. The roar of the exhaust beat was thrilling to hear, and I noticed at once that on this engine, as on Garratts generally, the beats from the forward and rear engine units synchronised exactly. We were climbing into high moorland country, getting a magnificent view over the sea and of Mossel Bay. Not far from the shore two huge whales were disporting themselves. While the locomotive was giving almost of her utmost the young fireman stoked with care and precision, and I noted the excellent coal provided—hard, of uniform size, and looking as though it had been washed, so free was it from dust. We reached the top of the bank at Reebok, and after a few minutes of easy running stopped at Tergniet, three miles from Kleinbrakrivier in just eleven minutes.

F

From the restart we were coasting downhill at first, but from Groot-brakrivier there is a tremendous climb, not only on very severe grades but on a succession of positively hair-raising curves where the back of the train was frequently running parallel to the course of the engine, but in the opposite direction. To add to the difficulties there was a shower of rain just before we started. It was now that I saw the skill of the driver displayed in full measure. In these extremely arduous conditions one or other of the engine units would slip occasionally, and the driver eased the regulator back just enough to check the slip, but at the same time keeping the second engine developing high power. The one regulator valve supplies steam to both engine units. So we pounded away up the bank, with the speed often falling to less than 10 m.p.h. Slipping would send the exhaust from the two engine units out of synchronism, but once they were pulling hard they soon got back into step, and yielded a truly thunderous beat. In a short tunnel the percussion was terrific. For me the experience was thrilling beyond words. Here was a big Garratt fighting a tremendous gradient in a country for which the type was specially developed. Had I not seen it myself I could well have imagined that the fireman would have had difficulty in meeting the demands for steam; but no, he was working hard, but maintaining pressure just below the rated maximum for the boiler. He had plenty of time to keep the footplate free of dust and dirt, and when we drew into Outeniekwa, to cross that westbound goods, he was ready with a can of tea for us all.

The goods train was already in the loop waiting for us to cross, and with station duties and a new proceed order handed to us we were under way again in less than five minutes. We descended to cross a very high viaduct over the Maalgarten River and then went tearing into another stretch of 1 in 40 ascent. The line is straight on this incline, and with no slipping from either engine unit we held a speed of 13 to 14 m.p.h. So into Skimmelkrans, for a 'whistle stop' of only twenty seconds. Again we coasted down to a river viaduct, and again blasted our way up the subsequent 1 in 40 in the same competent style. All the time we were running parallel to the coast, with the Indian Ocean frequently in sight, crossing deep valleys, and climbing again on a line engineered to avoid expensive cuttings and tunnels. The huge locomotive rode the curves elegantly, though when the speed began to reach somewhere around 30 m.p.h. one was conscious of the rapidly revolving wheels, and the effect of the heavy running gear.

After all, 35 m.p.h. on this engine requires the same number of revolutions per minute as 60 m.p.h. on a British 'Pacific' with 6 ft. 9 in. coupled wheels. So in 36 miles from Hartenbos we came to George, where my own foot-plate authority ended—all but two hours of the most fascinating loco-motive performance I had ever witnessed at first hand.

George itself is a watering station on the railway, and we spent some twenty minutes there; but before going on to describe the awe-inspiring ascent of the Montagu Pass I must satisfy my readers' justifiable curiosity over the name of this very pleasant little town. In his book *In Search of South Africa*, H. V. Morton writes:

George takes its name from one of South Africa's mysteries, a man named George Rex, who arrived here in 1802, and was believed to be the son of the reigning monarch, George III, and the elusive Quakeress, Hannah Lightfoot. He moved from George to Knysna, where he bought a large estate and lived like an English country gentleman. Many people in South Africa are convinced that Mr. Rex had been sent out to the Cape to avoid political complications, but if this were so, surely he would have been persuaded to use a less provoking name?

Between Mossel Bay and George the line had been following a course parallel to the coast, and the tremendously steep gradients resulted from running athwart the courses of deep valleys running down to the sea. But from George the line turns inland, to make a precipitous way through the Outenigua Mountains. Even on paper, reduced to bare statistics, the details of the ensuing ascent are very impressive, but while we stood at George the smoke of another train could be seen slowly moving up the mountainside, far, far above us, and the thought that we were going to travel that way, in a 12-coach corridor, dining, and sleeping car train behind one *hand-fired* engine made one appreciate the unique character of the Beyer–Garratt type. When the gradient is mostly 1 in 40 one can climb to considerable heights, even in seven or eight miles, and the train I was watching was nearly 800 ft. above us! The range of hills inland from George are not in themselves dramatic, or precipitous; but the railway has to climb very steeply up their flanks to attain sufficient altitude to force a way through the Montagu Pass which, as yet, was hidden around the shoulder of one of the hills immediately ahead. I left the footplate as clean as when I climbed aboard and was immediately able to take a place in the dining car to enjoy lunch during the great ascent.

83

We were soon pounding our way up the 1 in 40. The alignment is fairly straight at first, and we made a steady 13 to 14 m.p.h. There were frequent glimpses of the engine, with the exhaust shooting skywards, and several of my fellow passengers were continually taking advantage of the slow speed to photograph and film the engine, from rearward stances in the train, and to take sound tracks of her splendid staccato exhaust. As we climbed, a magnificent panorama to seawards opened out, looking back over the town of George and the hilly country we had traversed in our run from Mossel Bay. It was a landscape strongly reminiscent, but on a much vaster scale, of the West Highlands of Scotland, as one climbs the hillside out of Crianlarich, for example, and looks down upon Strathfillan. In ascending towards the Montagu Pass the gradients vary, but are mostly 1 in 36, 1 in 41, 1 in 55 and so on. The average rate of ascent from George to the crossing station at Power is about 1 in 46. As we began to turn rightwards round the bluff where I had seen the preceding train making its way, our engine, despite occasional slipping, was going great guns at a steady 14 to $14\frac{1}{2}$ m.p.h. The hillsides, and occasionally the vertical sides of a rock-cutting flung back the roar of the exhaust in a thrilling echo, as we headed into a mountain *cul de sac*, and came to Power. This crossing station is nine miles from George, and 916 ft. above it. That nine miles had taken us forty-three minutes to climb—quite an excellent average of 14 m.p.h. throughout.

The crossing of two long trains in a desolate loop in 'Garratt country' can never be a rapid process. Train proceed orders have to be given up, new ones received, and here, 1656 ft. above sea level, at Power, we were crossing a heavy freight train hauled by another 'GEA' class, No. 4047. Water was taken, and then we started away up the bank, in scenery now changing rapidly from green uplands of a continuing Scottish character to fierce, barren mountainsides strewn with outcrops of the bare rock. The curves now became increasingly severe and, with the actual inclination becoming generally steeper, the task of the locomotive and its crew was still more arduous. There are one or two short strips of 1 in 36, and when such gradients occur on a line where the long train is so strung out as to find the engine running parallel to the rear coaches it was not surprising the speed dropped at times below 10 m.p.h. Even so, we were not conveying the maximum load permitted to these amazing Garratts on this bank. We had 'twelve'. The maximum allowed up the Montagu pass is 'fourteen'; this would rarely be taken. It is the section where I was on the footplate that governs the through load, as the maximum there is only 'thirteen'! It is that villainous bank from Grootbrakrivier up to Outeniekwa that is the critical section. Thus, unless an extra coach was added at George, it is unlikely that a Garratt would be called up to take maximum load up the Montagu Pass.

We hammered away, travelling frequently on the brink of tremendous escarpments. My speed readings, over successive half miles read $10\frac{1}{2}$, 9, 11, $12\frac{1}{2}$, $10\frac{1}{2}$, 13, $8\frac{1}{2}$—the engine was slipping here—$10\frac{1}{2}$, $13\frac{1}{2}$, and finally 11 m.p.h. In the meantime the scenery, in its wild profusion of rocky slopes, had become most sombre. Clouds were touching down upon the highest points; we had lost all of the intermittent sunshine that, between the showers, had made the passing scene so brilliant between Hartenbos and George, and on the farther slopes of this narrowing gorge the hillsides were newly scarred where a great new arterial road is being driven. Such signs of 'development' do not remain long in South Africa. A season's rain, and the vegetation quickly covers up all traces. So we came finally to the head of the pass, to the crossing loop appropriately named Topping, and stopped briefly there in a shade over 92 minutes from George—15 miles of railway and a clear lift of 1693 ft. The average speed over the 6 miles from Power to Topping was 10.3 m.p.h. against an average gradient of 1 in 41. It had been a thrilling experience. In that sustained, all-out slogging, seeing the engine snaking its way round those curves, disappearing behind vertical rock cuttings, going through short tunnels cut in the solid rock, one was conscious of a mighty tug-of-war, in which a misjudgment by the driver could result in slipping that could quickly stall the train. I had seen it on the footplate between Grootbrakrivier and Outeniekwa, and could well appreciate what was going on between George and Topping.

Now we were off again from our summit level of 2433 ft. in the Outeniekwa mountains, and coasting smoothly downhill, and as another writer has aptly expressed in crossing the watershed we had crossed from 'Scotland' into Africa. Even so, this was not the scenery of the Karoo, or even of the high veldt; we were running through a countryside alternating between lush vegetation and a fairly harsh arid character. The mountains were like those of the Hex River gorge south of De Doorns, and as so often happens in crossing a watershed we left the gloomy weather behind and continued in sunshine that highlighted the vivid colouring of the bare rocks on the upper slopes of the mountains. The station names were a rare mixture: Oupad, Camfer, Holgate—shades of race meetings at York!—Zebra, Blossoms, and Kandelaars. I did not see any zebra in this part of Africa, but we were certainly running into ostrich country. Many were to be seen in the intensely green fields on both sides of the line, but none obliged in giving a demonstration of racing the train. As everywhere else in South Africa the railway is fenced, not as a protection against the larger and wilder animals, but as an insurance against valuable cattle straying on to the line and paying the penalty. Although the line is on a gradually descending gradient, lowering the height above sea level from 2433 ft. at Topping to 1112 ft. at Kandelaars, we were making no speed records, and the 24 miles between these two points occupied $1\frac{1}{4}$ hours.

We were now approaching Oudtshoorn, famed for its ostrich farms, of which we saw many as we approached the town. But it is also a divisional point so far as the locomotive working is concerned. The time had now come for us to change from a Garratt to an orthodox tender locomotive. We were due into Oudtshoorn at 4 p.m.—exactly 24 hours after leaving Cape Town, and by a very nicely judged performance we clocked in just thirty seconds to the good. Driver Bekker and Fireman van Zyl had been on the job for a very strenuous $5\frac{1}{2}$ hours, during which we had covered no more than 72 miles. In that 72 miles nevertheless were packed operating conditions requiring highly expert enginemanship, and making the job a challenge in every mile—at any rate until the summit at Topping had been successfully negotiated. Engine No. 4048 coupled off at Oudtshoorn and went away to the shed, while in her place another gleaming black engine, a '19D' class 4–8–2 backed on. This is a much smaller type than the great '15F' and '25' class that run the main line expresses and freights over the high veldt; but a tremendous night's work was ahead of her, because our train had been increased in weight by some 70 tons, and we pulled out of Oudtshoorn with at least 590 tons behind the tender.

The '19D' class 4–8–2 is a clever design in which a locomotive with a nominal tractive effort of 36,000 lb. has been produced for working on lightly laid sections of line where the maximum axle load cannot exceed 14 tons. In Chapter Four of this book I referred to the first introduction

86

and early development of the 4–8–2 type; the '19D' represents one of its most modern examples. The earliest engines of this class were built by Robert Stephenson and Hawthorn's Ltd. in 1947; but the engine that took over from the Garratt No. 4048 at Oudtshoorn was No. 3323, one of a later batch fitted with an enormous Vanderbilt type of tender, as long and weighing nearly as much as the engine itself. It carried 12 tons of coal, and 6500 gallons of water. Although it is passing out of 'Garratt' country I must briefly mention the earlier part of our progress eastward, before night closed in. We left Oudtshoorn at 4.20 p.m. and ran through a countryside of hills and valleys where the railway largely followed the lie of the land. There were frequent stops; the intermediate gradients, though short, were often severe, and I heard from the exhaust beat that the engine was frequently being worked very hard to haul this long and heavy train. After nightfall the road seemed to get more severe, and there were times when the engine was frequently slipping. After dinner I stood for some time on the open platform at one of the coach ends, and watched her pegging away under the moon; and then for the second time in that sleeping car I turned in, and ultimately awoke next morning to find us running down to the coast near Port Elizabeth dead on time after our long run through from Cape Town.

CHAPTER EIGHT

Signalling in South Africa

In the preceding chapter I described a run on which we were travelling over a line with no signalling in the ordinary sense. The movement of trains was regulated by telegraphic proceed orders. The line eastwards from Worcester towards Port Elizabeth is of course not heavily used, but on other parts of the system some highly sophisticated methods of modern signalling are now to be seen. It is interesting nevertheless to go back to the turn of the century, because there were then some picturesque systems of mechanical signalling at work on the busiest lines. It was no more than natural that the plant and methods of working on the Cape Government Railways were based on British practice, with lower quadrant semaphore signals, and manual actuation of points. There was, of course, the notable exception of Salt River junction mentioned in Chapter Two, where the actuation was hydraulic. On the Central South African Railway, however, a surprising amount of Dutch-built equipment from the Alkmaar Iron and Foundry Works had survived the war, and the installations were repaired and continued in service in their old form until after the unification of the railways in South Africa.

Even as recently as the first decade of the twentieth century the railway system in the heart of the Transvaal was but little developed. Facing page 113 is a photograph of Johannesburg main station as it was in 1905; one can scarcely believe it to be the same locality as the teeming semi-underground station of today. And the signals were fairly primitive too. The main running signals were upper quadrant semaphores of a very angular design, as shown in the group at Park Halt in another of our pictures. This was a development of the original Dutch design, having a large rounded end, or disc, entirely in the Continental fashion. The semaphores illustrated had a white arm with a red disc. Beneath each of these main

88

Cape Government Railways

The preserved '6J' class 4-6-0 No. 645 on Kimberley station

arms was a shunt signal with a black diamond plate affixed. This diamond plate is reminiscent of London and South Western Railway practice though the latter company had a neater, if less striking, design. In addition, the posts themselves were painted in distinctive colours. Those for the starting and advanced starting signals were white; the home signals as shown in our picture were red and white in alternate bands; the outer home signals on single lines had green posts, and the 'through' or distant signals had posts with the top-half green and the bottom-half white. This system of painting the posts was devised to assist drivers in distinguishing the class of signal they were approaching. At night the colour of the posts could readily be picked out in the engine-headlight beam. In the signal-boxes the levers were painted in colours to correspond with the signal posts, and in addition black levers were used for points, blue for facing point locks and blue and black for economical facing point and lock.

At the turn of the century the Z.A.S.M. lines were virtually the only ones in South Africa to have any interlocking. The points, as well as the signals, were operated on the double-wire system greatly favoured on the continent of Europe, and the photograph of the signals at Park Halt shows something of the profusion of wires needed for working two semaphore arms on one post. The signal-boxes were picturesque affairs, and the signalmen produced some striking floral displays beneath the windows.

The Cape Government Railways standardised the Saxby and Farmer 1888 type locking frame, and although that firm subsequently introduced newer types of actuation, in 1905, 1914 and 1924, the South African Railways remained faithful to the '1888', and I remember examples of it being built new in the Chippenham works of Westinghouse in the 1930s. It was one of the earliest examples of the so-called duplex-plunger type of actuation. The nineteenth century in England was a time of intense competition between all the signal manufacturing firms. Every new idea was patented. At times litigation between the firms was fierce and costly, and it was literally a case of designing something different from everyone else, or going out of business. Of course Saxby and Farmer had a substantial lead on some of the later firms, with their celebrated 'rocker and grid' type. This was patented in 1871, and the 1888 design was no doubt developed to have something new ready for when the 1871 patent

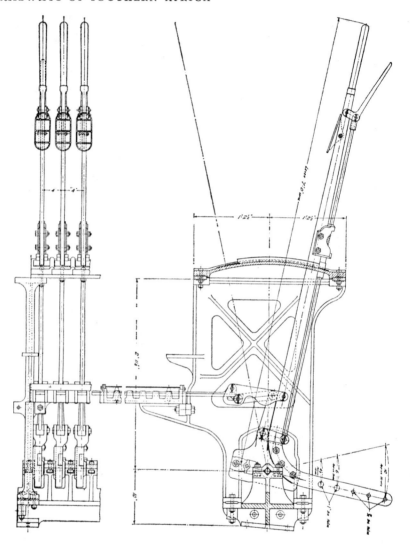

expired. Although the 'rocker and grid' pattern had been a money-spinner it was an expensive thing to make. The great Stevens' invention of single-tappet locking was anyone's property by that time, and the new Saxby idea was that of the duplex plunger.

Stevens had introduced the simplest possible form of actuation, with the locking tappet attached directly to the lever. The locking mechanism had to be very robust, because a signalman, using his full strength, had a very powerful leverage through which he could exert force upon the locking. The Saxby '1888' apparatus included a considerable refinement, in that the first movement of the locking tappet occurred when the signalman lifted the catch rod on the back of the lever. If the particular lever was locked he could not lift the catch rod, and he was thereby prevented from moving the lever itself from its latched back position. There was thus no chance of exerting a heavy pull, with the risk of 'forcing' a lever that was locked. The accompanying drawing shows a cross section of this interesting locking frame, which became standard for all mechanical installations in South Africa where rod-worked points were used. So far as the signals themselves were concerned, while all the original work in the Cape used lower-quadrant semaphores, in later years these have been changed to upper quadrant, and large numbers of these are still to be seen today in areas where colour light signalling has not yet been installed.

Before passing on to the era of modern colour light signalling I must not leave the mechanical age giving the impression that the lines were fully interlocked, and worked on the absolute block system, as in this country. In fact interlocking at the principal stations in the Cape and Natal was not commenced until after 1900, and then the progress was relatively slow. All this, of course, was directly related to the speed of traffic, and the methods of working unattended crossing places. There the practice of train crews working the points was accepted in view of the scarcity of much of the traffic, and the very slow speeds. Generally speaking signalling on the Natal railways was conducted by hand signal, and until the Boer War there was little or no signalling in the Orange Free State. It was the outbreak of war, and the additional traffic that the railways were required to handle, that compelled the introduction of more up-to-date methods. In Natal, for example, it was decided, in 1900 to introduce the electric train staff system for single lines. In the Transvaal under the Z.A.S.M. administration, all traffic was worked on the telegraph proceed order systems; but all the stations and crossing places were attended, and with relatively short distances between stations a fairly strict measure of control was maintained.

In the period between 1903 and 1910 when the Cape, Natal, and Central South African Railways were operated as independent units a measure of improvement was effected, particularly on main lines with the use of single-line staff instruments. But the train order system remained in use for unimportant main lines, as well as branch lines. In many places indeed it still remains today. In the Transvaal, as the industrial complex grew, faster train services were demanded, and on the line between Germiston and Pretoria, a trial was made of mechanical tablet exchanging apparatus, to speed up working through the passing places. But the apparatus was not considered suitable for general adoption, and hand exchange of tablets or staff continued, until the line in question was eventually doubled.

The establishment of the Union of South Africa in 1910, and the unification of the railways resulted in various decisions to standardise signalling equipment. Hitherto the electrical departments of the Cape and Transvaal railways had control of the electrical apparatus used for signalling; while in Natal this work had been carried out by the Post Office. In producing unified standards for the entire South African Railways system it was agreed that the Transvaal method of double wire operation of points was well suited to single-line crossing stations, of which there were very many, but as previously mentioned, where rod-operated points were desirable, as at the larger interlockings, the Saxby '1888' duplex frame was adopted as standard. So far as the signals themselves were concerned there was considerable difference of opinion as to whether the upper quadrant or lower quadrant semaphore should be standardised. The Cape and Natal railways used lower quadrant, and the Transvaal upper quadrant, and the quantities in use in 1910 were 1750 of the former and 900 of the latter. There was also a considerable difference of opinion among drivers. Eventually this particular point was referred to the General Manager, and his decision, to standardise on upper quadrant, anticipated the decision on the British home railways to do the same thing by at least fifteen years. All signal posts were to be painted white, and double-wire operation for signals was to be discontinued. Thus the South African mechanical signalling standards were established, and they have prevailed unbroken ever since.

After the formation of the South African Railways, in 1910, and the eventual retirement of the previous superintendents of the Cape and Transvaal lines, Sam Starkey was appointed signal engineer, and it was he who prepared the specifications for the first installation of colour light signals. This was occasioned by the electrification of the Cape Town suburban line to Wynberg, and the re-modelling of Cape Town station. Generally the signalling was based on contemporary British practice using three-aspect colour light signals and route indicators of the 'projector' type such as were being currently installed in England on the London suburban lines of the Southern Railway and on the London, Midland, and Scottish Railway at Manchester. But early installations of colour light signalling in England had revealed the considerable problem of the subsidiary signals, whether their function was that of a ground shunt, a calling-on, or a warning signal. The earliest British installations used miniature colour-lights, placed in correct juxtaposition to the main running signals. They had the disadvantage of being poorly visible by day, and providing the anomaly of a driver having to pass a red light in making a running movement. Confusion over this once caused a collision at London Bridge.

At Cape Town, Starkey, in collaboration with the contractors, pioneered an entirely new form of subsidiary light signal, in which there were no colours at all. It was a triangular-shaped device, in which two white lights horizontally meant stop, and two white lights diagonally meant shunt ahead. It was quite distinct from the running colour light signals with the usual red, yellow, and green indications. Where a subsidiary signal had to be used beneath a main signal, as in the old Z.A.S.M. arrangement at Johannesburg, a new so-called 'position-light' signal had only one aspect. The 'red' of the main signal indicated stop; a shunt ahead on to an occupied line was indicated by two white lights diagonally beneath the main red. This ingenious solution, incorporated in the new Cape Town signalling in 1928, was adopted for the remodelling of Leeds, London and North Eastern Railway, in 1936, and it is now standard on British Railways, with no more than a slight variation of the home railways adopting a principle pioneered in South Africa. As a young draughtsman I worked on the detailed design of these signals and for a time the track layout of Cape Town, on paper, became as familiar as the station yard at King's Cross!

The miniature-lever interlocking frame installed at Cape Town was of the standard Westinghouse pattern of that period. It was a direct development of the earliest type of power frame used in Great Britain in such large and busy interlockings as London Bridge, and the Southern Railway, and the group of interlockings in the approaches to Victoria and Exchange Stations at Manchester on the L.M.S.R. The interlocking between levers, as on the English examples, was by a miniature mechanical mechanism of great intricacy and precision. It was a period-piece of signalling history, so far as both British and South African development was concerned; because very soon afterwards electric interlocking between levers began to take the place of the intricate mechanism, and some fine examples of the newer techniques were introduced later on the South African Railways. Behind the locking frame, which had 143 levers, was a large illuminated diagram, and that also would now be regarded as a period piece.

The installations in the Cape Town area proved very successful, and when increased traffic in the heart of the Transvaal demanded some considerable extensions and improvements to the layout at Johannesburg it was decided to install power signalling, rather than extend and enlarge the existing mechanical installations. Johannesburg itself was regarded as a semi-terminal station. All trains from the coast, from Rhodesia, and from the north and eastern Transvaal terminated there. It was practically in the centre of the 'Reef' area, being 28 miles from Randfontein on the west, and 30 miles from Springs on the east, between which points a heavy inter-urban traffic was operated. At that time Johannesburg station, approached on both sides by quadruple-tracked lines, had seven through running lines. The general scheme of the new signalling was the same as at Cape Town except that by then the new Westinghouse miniature-lever power interlocking frame was in production, having electric lever interlocking, and one of these frames was selected, instead of the older type with mechanical interlocking, and used at Cape Town. This frame, with 129 levers, was commissioned in 1931. It was, however, unfortunately short-lived.

Electric traction was operating in the Reef area for some little time before the colour light signalling was completed. In April 1938, while a changeover was taking place, a leakage of the 3000-volt traction current started a fire at the Johannesburg signalbox after a heavy rainstorm. It was caused by the catenary carrying the contact wire coming in contact with the underside of a signal gantry during the passage of a train with four motor coaches. The cables to the signals on the gantry were in piping, but owing to the traction earthing system breaking down, the 3000-volt current which had 'charged' the gantry, caused the pipes to fuse and the current was taken up by the signal cables to the relay cabinets in the signal cabin. Unfortunately a short period elapsed before the breakers at the substation tripped, as the pantographs of the motor coaches, although fouling the overhead equipment, did not bring it to earth immediately. This period was sufficient to prevent the fire from being got under control, and practically the whole of the signal-box equipment was destroyed or severely damaged. Complete dislocation of traffic resulted and trains had to be signalled forward by hand. Steps were immediately taken to restore some signalling for through-working and essential shunting movements by using a 47-lever all-electric frame, imported for an installation at another station. All levers were made use of, and this temporary expedient was placed in service in the short space of 11 days; this was very satisfactory, seeing that another box had to be erected near to the old, new plans and circuit diagrams prepared, and frame electrically interlocked and all relay equipment installed. The frame comprised 32 levers controlling signal and route indicators and 15 levers working points (19 machines); there were 48 track circuits to be connected up. It remained in use until the end of 1939, when it was replaced.

By that time the trend of signalling practice in Great Britain was show-ing a very marked change. While certain administrations were retaining traditional methods the genius and forward-thinking philosophies of A. E. Tattersall on the London and North Eastern Railway were leading away from the orthodox locking frame, with positively locked levers towards the use of non-interlocked thumb switches with the interlocking effected through relays and interaction of the control circuits. Tattersall's work on the L.N.E.R. put Great Britain in the forefront of signalling development in the late nineteen-thirties—far in advance of anything that was then in contemplation in the U.S.A. or on the continent of Europe, and in replacing the burnt-out interlocking at Johannesburg on a permanent basis, Starkey decided to adopt relay interlocking. In so doing he chose the 'entrance–exit' rather than the 'one-control switch' type, and the new panel interlocking commissioned in 1938 was the largest in the world. It was not the first ever, nor yet the largest relay interlocking, because a small example of the entrance–exit type had been commissioned near Liverpool some years previously. But the new plant at Johannesburg, to a large extent, formed the pattern on which signalling development in years following World War II was based.

During the war years development was virtually at a standstill, because while planning for the future could proceed, it was not possible to obtain the specialised equipment from England, or from any other of the belligerent countries. Furthermore, the period of post-war austerity was experienced equally in South Africa and it was not until the year 1957 that any large-scale modernisation work was undertaken. By that time a very strong revival of electric-pneumatic working had taken place in England, and in addition to the North Eastern Region—which had always favoured the method—some large new installations were in process of commissioning on the London Midland Region of British Railways. In South Africa the system was chosen for the re-signalling of Bloemfontein station and yard. For this installation the miniature-lever type of power frame was used with electric interlocking between levers, as in the ill-fated mechanism at Johannesburg in pre-war days. The Bloemfontein plant, although giving excellent service, has remained the only one of its kind in South Africa.

When complete remodelling of the signalling in the Pretoria area was planned, relay interlocking panels of the entrance–exit type were specified, and a series of interesting and interconnected plant were installed at the main station, and at the outlying boxes. Principal interest in the latest plants, however, lies in the methods now being adopted for improvement of the train working on long stretches of open line. In previous chapters of this book, particularly that dealing with lines across the veldt, references have been made to the very heavy freight traffic. It has become a matter of the most urgent necessity to increase the carrying capacity of the lines in question, and a programme of large-scale signalling modernisation has recently been inaugurated. This work has taken two forms. In referring to the somewhat primitive methods of train working in existence before the unification of railways in South Africa in 1910, I mentioned the existence of many unattended passing loops on the Cape and Natal systems. One programme is providing for the more efficient control of these so-called 'interloops'; the larger and more comprehensive is for the full centralised traffic control of many of the more important sections of single-line route.

Taking the interloops first, the control of these is being placed at adjacent attended stations, and small desk-mounted control panels provided, on which there is an illuminated diagram, with the appropriate indication

The giant compound 'Mallet' class 'MH'

PLATE 15. Garratt Triumph in Natal

The competing 'GA' class Beyer-Garratt

(*above*) One outcome of the trials: the 'GL' Garratt for Natal, introduced 1929

(*below*) 2 ft. gauge 2–6–2+2–6–2 Garratt for light feeder lines in Natal

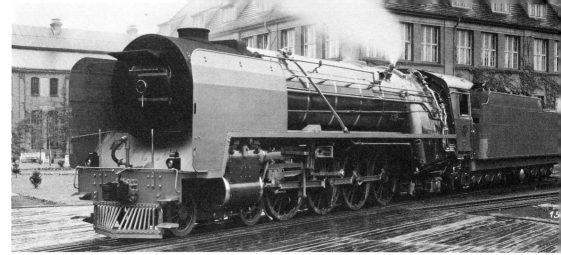

'23' class S.A.R. 4–8–2 at Henschel's Works, Germany

PLATE 16. Acceptance Tests in Europe

(*above*) '25' class S.A.R. 4–8–4 on curve trials, North British Locomotive Company

(*below*) 4–8–2 + 2–8–4 Beyer–Garratt on trial at Gorton Foundry, Manchester

lights and controlling thumb-switches. Each interloop layout consists of a single passing loop, and instead of compelling each train to stop for members of its crew to operate the points, as required, by hand, the points at each end of the loop are now electrically operated, and all train movements through the loops are controlled by colour light signals. This modernisation has permitted of a substantial speed-up on many single-tracked routes where there are many interloops. This method has been adopted on routes of what can be termed intermediate importance. It will be appreciated that the control applied to these interloops is to a large extent local, as the adjoining attended stations have to communicate with one another, and can have recourse, by telephone, to central control only as an emergency measure. The lines concerned are worked similarly to the English mechanical block system, on a box-to-box basis. On long stretches of line, especially when the workings become divergent from the schedule timetable paths, because of late running of one or more trains, the co-ordination possible on a box-to-box basis does not always produce the most effective working, or the quickest possible restoration of strict timetable punctuality, and it is in this respect that full centralised traffic control provides so admirable a remedy.

Reference to a particular installation, one which I saw in action on a busy evening, will help to make the principle involved clear. The job in question controlled the main line from Bloemfontein southwards to Springfontein, on the main line towards Port Elizabeth. The control panel covers 85 miles of single-tracked railway, with 27 intermediate stations or passing places, and the controller at Bloemfontein watches over train working on the entire line by means of the large illuminated diagram. He can see, from the appropriate indication lights, the position of all trains, and by the progress of the lights on the diagram can judge how the various trains are running. He is thus in an ideal position to decide at which loops opposite trains will pass, with a minimum of delay to each other and can regulate their approach to the loops by means of signal indication. To assist in the efficient control of traffic some of the passing loops are made long enough to accommodate two, and even three trains one behind the other, so that an express passenger can cross, or overtake two or more freight trains in the same loop. Having such long loops means also that with skilful manipulation two trains in opposite directions can pass without either stopping, making what is sometimes referred to as a 'flying crossing'. When I was able to visit the Bloem-fontein–Springfontein installation I saw that about 20 trains were on the panel simultaneously, at various points on the 85-mile stretch of line represented by the diagram. It was a remarkable example of how control of a complicated piece of railway may be centralised by modern signalling equipment.

During the 1930s the age-old problem of how to provide light-signal indications for a high-speed junction was at last resolved in England by the introduction of the so-called position-light junction indicator. Instead of having a series of signals, one for each route, a single colour light signal was installed with a direction indicator above it. If a train was required to make a divergence to the left the direction indicator showed a chain of white lights inclined upwards and diagonally to the left; similarly for a rightward divergence. No indication was shown if the train was to take the straight road ahead. This form of indicator was adopted as standard in South Africa, except that a chain of white lights pointing vertically upwards indicated the straight road ahead. Many of these indicators are now in use, particularly on the heavily worked lines around Johannesburg. Taken all round, the signalling on the South African Railways has developed in the past forty years from something that was extremely simple, if not primitive, to some of the most sophis-ticated layouts to be found anywhere. The centralised traffic control panels have revolutionised train working, and the punctuality of passenger train running is in itself a tribute to the success of the principles established and to the detailed carrying-out of the schemes.

CHAPTER NINE

Interlude on the narrow gauge

Before I begin this chapter I can almost hear some readers exclaiming: 'Well, but surely all the railways in Southern Africa are narrow gauge'. As compared with the European standard so they are, but as against the 13,250-odd route miles of 3 ft. 6 in. gauge on the South African Railways the administration also operates 440 miles of 2 ft. gauge, and a fascinating example of this 'still-narrower' gauge is provided by the line from Port Elizabeth to Avontuur. The railway geography of the region looks complicated and a trifle bewildering, because this tiny narrow gauge line takes us back within measurable distance of Oudtshoorn and George. One looks indeed at that extraordinarily roundabout route on the 3 ft. 6 in. gauge from George to Port Elizabeth that takes nearly 20 hours by a through express train, while the coastal highway by the supremely beautiful 'Garden route' is only 200 miles long. Then of course one recalls that in the early days of railways in the Cape of Good Hope nothing was farther from men's minds than the linking up of Cape Town and Port Elizabeth! The two ports were strongly rival jumping off points for railways to the diamond and gold diggings, and the more independent they could be of each other the better.

It was in the period of rehabilitation after the Boer War that new railways were projected, and just as the narrow gauge was used in both India and Ireland as a feeder to the standard gauge systems, in districts where the terrain was severe, and the construction of railways was undertaken to open up new districts rather than cope with an existing flow of traffic, so the 2 ft. gauge was chosen for the first line in South Africa to be Government-built on the 'still-narrower' gauge. The total absence of any large freight vehicles on the roads of South Africa results in a large volume of freight traffic being carried on the railways, and the successful opening up of the very hilly country west of Port Elizabeth as a highly productive fruit-growing area, certainly justified the original project of more than sixty years ago, of building a 2 ft. gauge line of 177 miles in length, to Avontuur. It was constructed as cheaply as possible, avoiding major earthworks by an exceedingly sinuous course, and by severe gradients. Avontuur, indeed, is no less than 2859 ft. above sea level. This little railway system of its own includes also a branch line of 17 miles, to Patensie. The 2 ft. gauge line was opened throughout on 1 January 1907, and at that time its passenger trains ran from a separate narrow-gauge platform in Port Elizabeth main station, and proceeded in the opposite direction to that of the standard gauge trains by a line through the dock area to a suburban station at Humewood Road. This latter is now the terminus of the narrow-gauge passenger service.

I have never met a true railway enthusiast who is not fascinated and charmed by routes operated on a sub-standard gauge. At home we have the preserved and privately owned Welsh railways; one recalls the narrow-gauge sections of the Northern Counties Committee section of the L.M.S. in Ireland, running to Ballycastle, and the 'boat express' from Larne to Ballymena. But those sections of the N.C.C. which I knew well, were, like other narrow-gauge lines in Ireland, fighting a rear-guard action against the onset of convenient road transport, and the continued existence of the Welsh lines is due to the devotion of enthusiasts rather than out of any economic justification. The Port Elizabeth–Avontuur line provides all the more interesting and exhilarating a ride, in that it is dealing with a substantial traffic, and one that is continually taxing the motive-power resources. The line is not alone in this respect in South Africa. There is an additional mileage of 206 on the 2 ft. gauge in Natal, and such is the traffic situation that new steam locomotives were purchased from England as recently as 1967 specially for this duty. These engines are of the Beyer–Garratt type, which has a particular significance so far as the 'still narrower' gauge railways of South Africa are concerned.

It was for these little narrow gauge railways that the Garratt was first suggested for service in Africa. The very first use, anywhere in the world, was in Tasmania in 1908, when a tiny little compound 0–4–0 + 0–4–0 was purchased from Beyer, Peacock & Co. The first South African examples were ordered in 1914 for the 2 ft. gauge lines in Natal. These

PLATE 17. En Route to the South

(*above*) Kimberley: a '25' class 4–8–4 preparing to leave for De Aar, beside the preserved Cape 4–6–0 No. 645

(*below*) A freight train double-headed with two 4–8–4s at De Aar Junction

L35.

PLATE 18. An impressive front view: a condensing '25' class 4–8–4

were of the 2–6–0 + 0–6–2 type, and were designed to run on rails weighing only 35 lb. to the yard, and limited to a maximum load per axle of only 6½ tons. The Beyer–Garratt type of locomotive made possible, within these physical limitations, a machine having a tractive effort of 18,000 lb. and capable of hauling a load of 150 tons up a 1 in 33 gradient. Because of the outbreak of war in 1914, however, work on these interesting engines was suspended, and they were not delivered until 1920. When they did take up their appointed duties, they did so well that not only was the type multiplied on the narrow gauge but the great development of the type on the 3 ft. 6 in. gauge began to lead to such magnificent modern examples as the G.E.A. class, used on the Worcester–Mossel Bay–Oudtshoorn section. And so, with this preamble on motive power for the 2 ft. gauge lines we can proceed past the dock area of Port Elizabeth, to the little station at Humewood Road to join a mixed train for Lourie. The locomotive sheds are alongside and there two classes are to be seen, the 'NG16' class of Beyer–Garratts, of 1937 vintage, and a number of 2–8–2 tender engines of the 'NG15' class.

A very long train had been made up, of 24 vehicles—12 covered freight cars and 12 passenger coaches. Such a load had to be hauled over some extremely steep gradients, and even a Garratt, with 21,300 lb. of tractive effort, could not comfortably handle such a tonnage. Instead we had two of the 'NG15' class 2–8–2s, having a tractive effort of 37,600 lb. between them. For the 2 ft. gauge, with a maximum permitted axle load of 6¾ tons, these are very powerful little engines. They were built in Belgium, at La Croyère, by the Société Anglo-Franco-Belge. The latest examples of this class were supplied in 1953, and were of a design originally prepared in the 1930s. The engine weighs 36¾ tons in working order, and the large double-bogie tender, 31¼ tons. The latter carries enough coal, 5½ tons, for a trip from Port Elizabeth to Avontuur and back. On the occasion of my trip the two engines, as always on the S.A.R., were very smartly turned out, and on the sharply curved route there was plenty of opportunity of seeing the pair of them slogging away on the hard gradients. The coaches, even the first class, were reminiscent of the Talyllyn and Festiniog Railways, in North Wales, with hard seats and straight-up backs. However, an enthusiast travelling on such a line does not look for Pullman comfort. Much of the time one is standing at the window, with camera at the ready, or dashing from one side of the carriage to the other to avoid missing points of interest, or features of the fascinating countryside.

Twice in the week when I was writing this chapter I heard fellow travellers on British Railways comment upon the inevitable dreariness of the prospect from a railway carriage window. The two days on which I heard this comment were, it is true, particularly cold and miserable examples of the weather experienced in the first few days of spring in 1969. But making due allowance for these climatic conditions I would never subscribe to such a view. I go to the extreme opposite and claim that a railway carriage is one of the finest grandstands from which to enjoy the scenery of *any* country. There are very few countries where the road offers a better alternative, and in these days few tourists have time to explore the by-ways, by car or any other means of transport. And when the scene is changed from a cold and inexpressibly dreary English day, which a cynical calendar is trying to make one believe is the beginning of spring, to the cloudless glory of early October in Cape Province, the prospect from a train window, and a slow narrow gauge at that, becomes a never-ending source of delight, from the moment we were bustled joggingly out of Humewood Road station.

Although the general line of the south coast of Cape Province lies roughly along the 34th latitude, the havens such as Port Elizabeth and Mossel Bay face eastwards, and at the start of our journey climbing steeply away from the coast the little narrow-gauge line swings round in a full right-angle, to the right, to attain a general direction of east to west. Gradient or no gradient the two engines are fairly lifting the train, high above the sea, through the eastern suburbs of 'P.E.', as it is affectionately known. Valley station is passed, and then having attained an altitude of about 500 ft. in a very short time the line continues on a fairly straight course through country that permits of a reasonably level railway. Once the plateau is attained the two little engines begin to show a fine turn of speed for such tiny coupled wheels. Those wheels are only 2 ft. 10 in. in diameter, and when the train speed reaches about 35 m.p.h. the revolutions per minute, and the frequency of reciprocation of the pistons and valve gear, are equal to those of a British steam express locomotive doing about 85 m.p.h. As one proceeds from one wayside station to another the colourful life of a less-frequented African countryside is brought vividly to life.

Go-carts waiting at the level crossings are drawn by a pair of donkeys. Cape-coloured people, young and old, throng the stations, and pile into the train, but one has not travelled far before realising that on every platform there are usually at least twice as many people there to see their friends and relatives away than those actually travelling. The children race about, and clap their hands in delight, while their elders, men and women alike, are clad in such a wealth of thick garments as to make the average visitor from Europe perspire at the very sight of them. Imagine English surfacemen, on days when the temperature is near 80 degrees in the shade, wearing not only shirts and trousers, but pull-overs! The women wear thick, brightly coloured shawls, wrapped around them like a Highland plaid. Beside the line there is much well-cultivated farmland, and a team of four donkeys ploughing makes a great sight. Acacias in the utmost profusion are in full bloom. While both engines carry a very ample supply of coal the water supply does not last long, and we are barely 15 miles out of Port Elizabeth before both engines are replenishing their tanks. Such stops are prolonged, and the French railway phrase is recalled: 'Tout le monde descend', because on the Avontuur line everybody does 'descend', to wander all over the tracks, and perhaps even leave the station and do some shopping in the local emporium. The railway enthusiast naturally makes for the locomotives, and makes an appraisal of their sturdy design. They are coal-fired, and the cabs, although wide in relation to the rail gauge, are cramped and the seats for the driver and fireman are arranged to swing outboard, so that these men may sit outside in the fresh air at times. In the hottest of African weather this must be a great boon, though when I was travelling the temperature was not greatly different from that of a fine mid-summer day in England.

Although this line, and the heavily graded line in Natal from Port Shepstone to Donnybrook are built on the 2 ft. gauge the engineering was carried out so as to permit of their conversion to the standard 3 ft. 6 in. gauge, if at some future time the traffic justified it. Along this pleasant upland stretch traversed from Valley onwards there are no striking physical features on the line; but soon we are drawing nearer to some rocky hills of considerable height, somewhat reminiscent of the wilder parts of the Scottish Highlands, and quite unlike the bare isolated kopjes of the veldt. The bare outcrops of rock towards the summits of these hills we are now approaching have a pleasant bluish tinge. Then quite suddenly and unexpectedly comes the big surprise of the journey: so surreptitiously, one might say, that even if a keen sightseer were letting his attention stray for a moment and was in conversation with a fellow traveller and looking inside the carriage, it could almost be missed. This supreme spectacle is the Van Stadens Gorge. The train threads an ordinary, and not very deep, vertical-sided rock-cutting and then in a trice you are out on the highest narrow-gauge railway viaduct in Africa, 254 ft. above the foot of the gorge. The gorge itself is an immensely deep cleft lying in the bottom of a Vee in the moorlands, but when I first crossed the bridge in a train it so happened that the sun was shining precisely at right angles to the railway, and the lighting in the gorge itself was in consequence completely 'flat'. There was little shadow, even in those depths, to pick out the grandeurs of the rocks on either side of the Van Stadens River.

The viaduct itself, built on slender latticed steel towers, reminds an Englishman of the once-celebrated Belau on the North Eastern line from Kirkby Stephen to Barnard Castle, now dismantled; but it is not so long —yet even so 642 ft. in length. Like the majority of famous bridges it reveals little of its character while the train is actually crossing, except that for a few minutes one seems to be floating across the gorge in mid-air; but immediately the line reaches the western bank of the gorge it swings round sharply to the left, and begins a steep climb up the hillside. From the passenger part of the train, at the rear, one can photograph the engines as they go swarming up the slope, and then as the rear of the train takes the curve, and one looks back there is a splendid sight of the bridge itself— a fairy thing, not very clearly discernible against the strong light and the green foliage of the banks. Frail though it might appear however the Van Stadens Viaduct was one of the structures on the line designed and built with a view to conversion to 3 ft. 6 in. gauge at some future time, and it is strong enough to carry standard South African locomotives and rolling stock. In writing this however it will be appreciated there would be a limit on what could be used. One could hardly picture the '25NC' class 4–8–4s pounding their way up to Sunnyside. The curves on this line would undoubtedly be the governing factor. One is barely out of sight of the Van Stadens Viaduct before the train is rounding a curve on which the engines were literally clean abreast of the coach in which I was travelling, but going in the opposite direction! Next came the stop at

Sunnyside, an aptly named halt, gay with flowers, and backed by a belt of acacias in full bloom. But the colourful costumes of the native passengers contributed even more than the flowers to the brilliance of the scene. So, on to Thornhill, where there was a lengthy stop for water, and a chance to walk away from the station and take a glimpse of the village. Most of the carriage doors in the train were open, first and third class alike, and those passengers who were not wandering about were sitting at the doors of their carriages, as they might be at the doors of beach huts. These narrow gauge carriages have very small wheels, and low footboards for entering with only a moderate step-up from track level.

On the re-start, climbing is continued briefly, but a different landscape is now beginning to open out, looking down towards a wide, deep valley of extensive cultivation. We reach Summit station, at 854 ft. above sea level, and then commence a steep and most spectacular descent, at an average of roughly 100 ft. in every mile. This is no replica of Hex River, with its Scottish-like mountain scenery; no Montague Pass, with its vicious rock cuttings and stark prospects. It is merely that our immediate destination, Lourie, lies only at the foot of the hill, within sight for most of the time, but a small matter of 750 ft. below! Marvellous ingenuity in the survey must have been shown in carrying the line down that hillside, with scarcely an embankment or a cutting worth the name. It contours on the slopes, taking advantage of every fold in the hills to double back and keep the line descending on an even gradient. The route was constructed at minimum cost. There was no cash available for the engineers to indulge in spiral tunnels in the Alpine style; they cut a simple track in the sandy soil, and our two engines coasted their long train down, curve after curve, each prospect opening up still more fascinating glimpses of the line wriggling its way down to Lourie. We were entering a country of orchards, and one could appreciate now why the trains on this line are known as the 'Apple Expresses'. Film after film is exposed, as the twists in the line bring ever-new glimpses of the engines in still stranger juxtaposition, till finally we reach the floor of the valley and draw slowly into Lourie.

There is something almost Mediterranean about this little town, shimmering in the noonday heat, with its elegant cypress trees motionless in the still air. The station becomes a scene of intense animation on arrival of the morning train from Port Elizabeth. The forty-five miles have

105

taken over four hours, and Lourie marks the end of regular passenger travel on this line. The front part of our train is going on to Avontuur, while the return service to Port Elizabeth is provided by attaching the string of coaches in which we have travelled to an eastbound goods from Avontuur which is expected shortly. Although no passenger service is advertised on the 133-mile section between Lourie and Avontuur the guard's vans used on the goods train have two third-class compartments frequently used by 'non-European' passengers. Should a first-class passenger wish to travel he must ride with the guard. As always in South Africa the locomotive yard is always a source of great attraction to the enthusiast, and at Lourie some of the 'NGG16' Garratts were on parade.

I was able to examine these splendid little engines in some detail. They certainly are small, compared with the giant engines of the Beyer-Garratt type in use on the 3 ft. 6 in. gauge sections of the line. They are of the 2–6–2+2–6–2 wheel arrangement, and yet weigh only 60½ tons in working order. Of course the limiting factor in their design is the maximum axle-load permitted, 6·875 tons. This is not due to the under-line bridges or to the Van Stadens Viaduct, but to the use of rails weighing no more than 35 lb. per yard. If at any time the line were converted to 3 ft. 6 in. gauge no doubt heavier rail would be used; but in the meantime the Garratts are doing a fine job on the 2 ft. gauge. The coupled wheel diameter is approximately the same as the 'NG15' 2–8–2 tender engines, 2 ft. 9 in., and the tractive effort is 21,360 lb. These engines are called upon for their hardest work on the Stuartstown branch in Natal where the ruling gradient is 1 in 33. Up this they work train loads of around 150 tons. Between Lourie and Port Elizabeth the worst gradients are around 1 in 40; but the performance of the Garratt engines, in hauling heavy trains single-handed, has provided such economies in operation as to postpone indefinitely any proposals to convert the route to 3 ft. 6 in. gauge. It is true that our train was beyond the unaided haulage capacity of a 'Garratt' and needed two 2–8–2 tender engines. A special party of some fifty first-class passengers making the trip from Port Elizabeth to Lourie and back necessitated the running of many extra coaches, so that on this day the load was an exceptional one.

On the return to Port Elizabeth we began with a fine demonstration of what a pair of 'NG15' class engines could do, with such a load as 250 tons. The climbing from Lourie to Summit, round that bewildering succession of curves, is continuous, and the 7¾ miles occupied exactly 24 minutes. In this time the train had been lifted a clear 750 ft., and on the steepest part of the ascent the speed was very steadily maintained at 20 m.p.h. In the last two miles the gradients are slightly easier and there was some quickening of the pace, so that we were able to average very nearly 20 m.p.h. from start to stop. Once Summit station was reached the technicalities of the engine performance ceased to have any particular interest, from the viewpoint of power output, and I gave myself up to enjoying once again the pleasant scenery, the vivid human pictures at the wayside stations, and the thrill of descending that steep gradient towards the Van Stadens Gorge with the bridge fully in view, till we swung round and entered upon it. So we jogged and bustled along, often touching 35 m.p.h. between stops till Valley was passed, and we came very cautiously down the steep descent into Port Elizabeth. Certainly an interlude to remember!

CHAPTER TEN

Railway complex on the Reef

I first arrived in Johannesburg, like the vast majority of present-day travellers, by air. Joining one of the big jets that had come overnight from England we had covered the 1800 miles from Nairobi comfortably between breakfast and lunchtime, and soon after seven next morning I was riding with my host in the ever-thickening stream of road traffic towards the Golden City. There is scarcely a top executive in Johannesburg who is not at his desk by eight o'clock. Later in the morning I had my first sight of the South African Railways. It might well have been from an aircraft, for I looked down upon the central station from one of the upper windows in the sky-scraping Paul Kruger building. As one who had come to South Africa very mindful of railway history I thought of those pictures of the old Park station which served all the needs of Johannesburg until less than sixty years ago: a single island platform, set amid parklands, and having just one through line on the up and down sides, outside the platform roads. It is one of the railway pictures that one never forgets, and yet, could this sylvan prospect really be the original site of the enormous station I now saw below me? Yet that old picture was dated 1903, almost within my own lifetime.

One reflects upon other great stations of the world. At home, Euston, Waterloo, Edinburgh Waverley, Manchester Victoria, were at that time teeming centres of traffic, and if not entirely in their present form certainly covering much of their present area, and dealing with vast numbers of passengers on highly complex track layouts and train movements. Abroad, Flinders Street in Melbourne was much as it is today, likewise Victoria Terminus in Bombay, though then of course entirely steam worked. One could move from country to country round the world, even to South Africa itself, at Cape Town, and not find so phenomenal a

108

PLATE 19. Condensing '25' class 4–8–4s

Cab view, showing the mechanical stoker

Front of the tender, showing the condensing pipe on right, and the screw of the mechanical stoker

The 'GEA' class Beyer–Garratt No. 4048 at Hartenbos

PLATE 20. Garratt Working

The author in the cab of No. 4048

transformation as at Johannesburg. My railway friends kindly allowed me to take some photographs out of their windows, pointing out some of the major landmarks the while. With the 'square' form of modern archi-

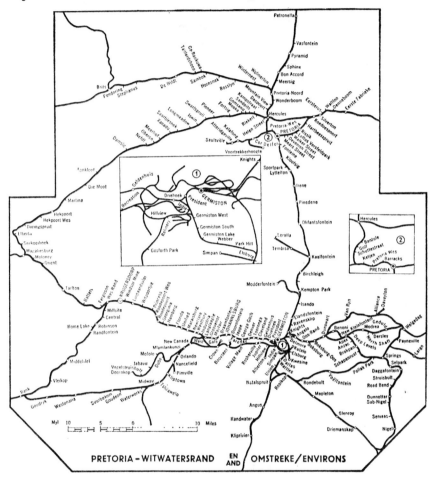

PRETORIA – WITWATERSRAND EN AND OMSTREKE/ENVIRONS

tecture and the great height to which many of the buildings attain it is sometimes said that all cities are now becoming to look alike; but this is not so at Johannesburg, where less than a mile from the central station, and clearly seen from where I looked out were huge golden cones of the refuse dumps of the mines on which the fortunes of the city has grown up. I watched the trains coming and going, mostly electrics, but steam is

109

not entirely excluded. My railway friends took me down into the station to see the Trans-Karoo Express, leaving for Cape Town at 10.30 a.m.; but our immediate concern was the lines on the Reef.

Studying a large-scale railway map of the area extending north from the Vaal river to Pretoria one is immediately surprised to see that Johannesburg does not lie at the very centre of things; in fact, on the 'Standard Railway Map of South Africa' contained in the Annual Report of the Administration one has to look hard to find it at all! Pretoria, Krugersdorp, and Germiston appear in large letters, and then half way between the latter two places one finds an unobtrusive 'J.H.B.', lying some little distance to the west of the main line from Pretoria into the Orange Free State. The fact is, of course, that after the country was being settled on a wholly agricultural basis the mineral riches were discovered almost by accident. Pretoria was the capital, and the railway configuration shows it even today. How Johannesburg came into being is picturesquely described by H. V. Morton in his charming book *In Search of South Africa*.

In remote ages to which no period can be given, a great river flowed southward through Africa into a lake which covered what is now the Rand . . . [or the Reef as it is generally known]. It carried with it particles of gold which had been washed out of rocks. These particles, settling down at the bottom of the sea, became covered with mud, sand and gravel, which in time turned to shales, quartzites and conglomerates. Then the sea dried up and its bed, containing the layer of gold, became warped and tilted in some geological disturbance so that, instead of lying flat, its rim became visible on the surface and then dipped down into the earth. So a golden sandwich was hidden in the Transvaal.

'Now here' we may imagine Fate saying, 'is a nice piece of trouble. This shall be concealed from the Chaldeans, the Babylonians, the Phoenicians, the Egyptians, the Greeks, and the Romans, and it shall lie there protected on the north by mosquitoes and everywhere else by mountains and sea until a remote and distant time . . .'

And of all places on earth this, the richest goldfield in the world, was the place chosen as grassland by simple farmers who were flying from the hated modern world and wished only to have nothing further to do with it!

So on the very site where the 'Rand Tram' used to stop, at the then Park Halt, is the great station round which I was being proudly shown. The present station is the fourth on the site. Park Halt gave place to Park, which was the station of the early 1900s referred to at the beginning of this chapter. This was enlarged piecemeal, in the way of many European stations one could name, until a general reconstruction took place in 1932. But such was the positively explosive increase in the suburban traffic that in 1940 it was decided to build a new ultra-modern station, with administrative head-offices for the railway, which it was hoped would prove adequate for at least fifty years. That was in 1940, but in view of what had transpired on the Reef in the previous fifty years, one can only comment: 'Who can tell?' It is perhaps not without significance that the Rand Tram made its first journey in March 1890, just fifty years before the decision was made to build the present station. It is a magnificent piece of modern planning, something like a vastly more spacious edition of the new Birmingham New Street, on the London Midland Region at home. The platforms are below street level and covered in for most of their length, while above them, as at Birmingham, there is a general shopping centre, with all facilities for travellers. An important feature just outside the main station buildings is the Rotunda, an attractive circular air-terminal building with the necessary facilities for arranging domestic, international and inter-continental flights.

The interdependence of all forms of travel in the heart of Johannesburg is provided for by fine new road bridges constructed across the station area, athwart the tracks. A most pleasing feature of the ensemble is that in the midst of all this modernity space has been found beneath one of the new bridges for the Railway Museum. Here there are no fewer than 1700 exhibits, most comprehensively depicting the history of the service, and including a beautiful collection of scale models of historic locomotives, carriages and wagons from all the constituent companies of the present administration. The scale of the rollingstock models appears to be 7 mm. to the foot, and one can study at leisure the locomotives of the Z.A.S.M., of Natal, and of the Cape alongside modern giants like the '15F'. While browsing among the exhibits I could not help feeling a little sad that the policy at home seems nowadays to be to expunge ruthlessly all relics of the past. How nice it would have been if space could have been found for a few historical models in the spectacular concourse in the new Euston!

The new station at Johannesburg is certainly designed for mass transportation of passengers. Each of the escalators between the platforms to the concourse is capable of conveying 8000 passengers an hour, while from one suburban branch line alone—to which I will refer later in more detail—more than 125,000 passengers are brought into Johannesburg by electric train each morning and a similar number taken home each evening. But referring once again to the map it will be seen that Johannesburg itself is not a focal point, or a junction; it is merely one station—admittedly a huge one—on the east–west line connecting Germiston and Krugers-dorp. By the very nature of its traffic, however, it is a terminal point for many trains, though some of the intense electric services in the Reef area work through from suburbs east to west of the city. The very heavy freight traffic passing between eastern and western extremities of the Reef, and beyond, is mostly routed via the parallel line to the south, from the complicated purlieus of Germiston to junctions with the main line to the south at New Canada and with the line to Mafeking and Rhodesia at Industria. Germiston was one of the first places I visited. From the freight point of view it is probably the most important centre in the whole of South Africa. It is not only a great junction, where lines from all points of the compass converge, but there is an immense amount of traffic originating in the area, from the gold mines and numerous other indus-trial activities. It could be likened to Crewe, with the staple traffics originating in Sheffield, the Black Country and the South Yorkshire coal field superimposed upon it!

On this first visit my immediate concern was signalling, and to get from box to box in the minimum of time I was taken by car. I must admit to losing all sense of direction and railway geography, and from a mere glance at the tangled conglomeration of lines in the enlarged map of the area reproduced herewith I fancy that most visiting railway enthusi-asts would extend me their sympathy! We saw the big freight marshalling yard, for which I had done some design work in the days before the war, and it was there that I first saw South African steam power in full action. Freight after freight was pulling out, each hauled by one of the incompar-able '15F' 4–8–2 engines. Coming, with only the slightest break, from our dieselised railways at home it was a joy to hear once again the fierce bark of high-pressure steam, but especially to see in what excellent condition those engines were, with the glands bottle-tight, and steam escaping only from where it should be—out of the chimney! But I have extolled the virtues of the '15Fs' in the earlier chapters, and Germiston provided my first introduction to another notable South African steam locomotive

112

The '15AR' class 4–8–2 at De Aar

PLATE 21. Shunting Engines

(*above*) An 'S2' at the dockside, Port Elizabeth

(*below*) An 'S1' in Germiston yards, Transvaal

PLATE 22. Johannesburg Park Station about 1905

class, the 'S1' 0-8-0 shunters. These imposing and very handsome tender engines are a wholly indigenous product of South Africa. Whereas other famous engines, like the '15F', the '16E', the '23', and the '25' classes, were designed in South Africa they were all built abroad, either in the United Kingdom or in Germany; but the first of the 'S1' class shunters were built at Salt River Works, near Cape Town.

They are tremendously massive and powerful engines. I have told earlier in this book how I saw them at Bloemfontein and Kimberley; but in point of time it was at Germiston yard that I saw them first and in the most strenuous service, drawing or propelling freight trains of caravan length. And if the '15Fs' had a healthy bark, the 'S1' class could certainly drown their efforts! They have a boiler of maximum physical dimensions, with a firebox rather smaller than that of the main line engines. This is good practice, because a shunting engine inevitably spends a certain amount of its time standing by, and during such time coal can be used merely keeping the firebars covered. The essential thing is to have a boiler than can provide a large reservoir for steam, ready for immediate use after a period of standing by. The coupled wheels, which are only 4 ft. in diameter, are spaced closely so as to permit of ready negotiation of sharp curves in marshalling yards; but even so, the wheels on the third axle on to which the connecting rods drive, are flangeless, to permit of even easier movement round sharp curves. The large bogie tenders, with a capacity of 6000 gallons of water and 11 tons of coal, are designed for long continuous periods of service without returning to a running shed. After the initial batch of 12 engines constructed at Salt River, an order for a further 25 was placed with the North British Locomotive Company.

The electrified suburban lines in the Reef area take the form of a slightly irregular inverted T, with the 'cross' extending from Springs in the east to Randfontein in the west, and the 'stroke' from Germiston to Pretoria. This was the extent of the great scheme brought into operation at the end of 1938. Since then railway electrification in South Africa has followed closely on the pattern set by the former Southern Railway in England, in that the electrified area has been gradually extended from the central complex of the Reef to the main lines running south and east of Johannesburg. Now the long-distance expresses for Cape Town are electrically hauled as far south as Kimberley; the trains for East London and Port

Elizabeth to Kroonstad, and into Natal the entire main line between Johannesburg and Durban is electrified. The Cape Town suburban lines, when first changed to electric traction were equipped on the 1500-volt d.c. system with overhead wires; but for the Reef electrification the system chosen was 3000-volt d.c., as in Belgium and Italy, and this has now been standardised throughout the South African Railways. In the Reef area, all passenger trains except the long distance main line expresses having dining and sleeping accommodation are of the multiple-unit type. Some of these convey both first- and third-class passengers, but a high proportion, as will be explained later, are confined to non-Europeans.

From the west three main lines converge upon the western suburbs of Johannesburg. There is first of all that from Mafeking and Rhodesia. This is joined at Krugersdorp, from a south-westerly direction, by the electrified main line from Kimberley, which is the principal route from Johannesburg to the south. From the junction of these two important routes the direction is roughly eastwards till at Langlaagte the line is joined by the main line from the Orange Free State, also electrified. The ensuing quadruple-tracked section from Langlaagte through Johannesburg to Germiston is the most intensively used passenger line in South Africa, though the more recent electrification of the Rand Mineral Line and the opening of a number of suburban stations on that line for the exclusive use of non-Europeans has considerably eased the pressure on the main line, and upon Johannesburg central station. Immediately to the west of Johannesburg is Braamfontein, where are situated the large shops for maintenance and repair of the electric stock, but immediately one passes to the east of the central station a mining area is entered. I made an inspection of signalling equipment on the line at Driehoek, a station just on the Johannesburg side of Germiston, and it was there that I became very much aware of certain conditions under which railways are operated on the Reef.

Beside the line were some enormous refuse dumps from the gold mines. In the sunshine they shone like gold indeed, and looked most picturesque; but there was a strong wind blowing and from the leeward side of another dump fine dust was being carried in a cloud that created something of a fog across the line. It was not so much that visibility was somewhat impaired—though the effect of this was minimised by the colour light signals—but that this driving dust has a way of penetrating into

114

any kind of lineside apparatus, and as much care has to be taken in design, particularly of miniature electrical gear, as if it were destined for installation in a waterless desert. The traffic passing was heavy: locomotive-hauled electric expresses, multiple-unit trains, and quite a few steam-hauled freights. I may add that many of the refuse dumps around Johannesburg are now being greatly reduced in height. The 'spoil' of which they are composed is much in demand for 'filling' in the construction of new arterial roads. It has been found to provide an impenetrable blanket against weeds, or any kind of vegetable growth from below. I am sure all concerned with the operation of railways on the Reef will welcome the reduction and ultimate removal of many of these 'landmarks'!

One of the most interesting junctions in the Reef lines west of Johannesburg is at New Canada where there is an intersection of *four* quadruple-tracked lines. The main line to the Orange Free State runs through the centre of the layout; to the west there diverges the purely passenger suburban line into the south-western townships, also quadruple-tracked, and eastwards there diverges a quadruple-tracked connection to what used to be called the Rand Mineral Line, which is now a teeming artery of commuter travel morning and evening, as well as relieving the main line through Johannesburg itself of practically all the through freight traffic. Through New Canada station, which is the centre of this complex system of junctions, there are no less than ten running lines, and to both east and west of the platforms a comprehensive system of 'flyovers' enables trains to be routed from any incoming to any outgoing lines without any opposing movements. At a busy period in the afternoon I watched the working from that supreme vantage point, the new panel signal box. The arrangement is one developed specially for their needs by the engineers of the South African Railway and consists of a relatively small desk, containing a reduced size diagram of all the tracks and the operating push buttons while displayed vertically on a large panel in rear are the tracks, with the various track-circuits delineated, and showing by the indication lights the position of every train in the area. In the morning and evening rush hour the number of multiple-unit trains passing through is enormous. A high proportion of these is routed to the quadruple-tracked branch line leading solely into the south-western townships. The number of passengers conveyed on this line alone now exceeds 125,000 in each direction morning and evening.

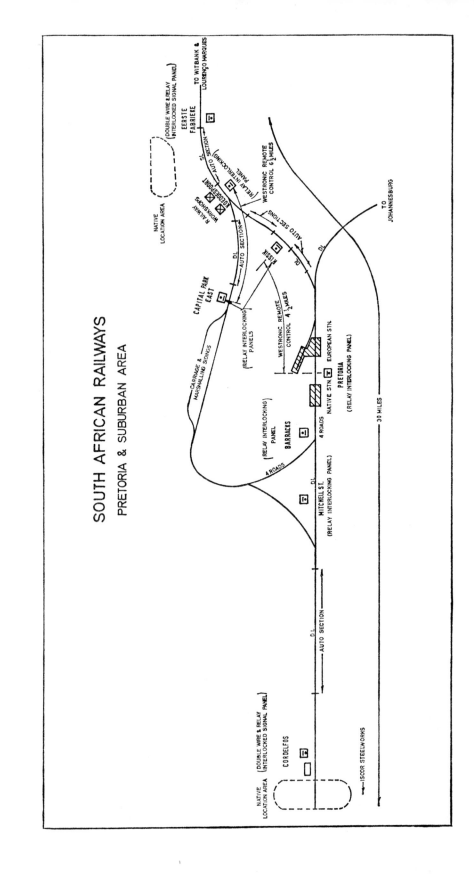

SOUTH AFRICAN RAILWAYS
PRETORIA & SUBURBAN AREA

Striking due north from Germiston is the electrified double-tracked main line to Pretoria. Except for one or two long-distance expresses the service is provided entirely by multiple-unit stock, both for the fast, and the all-stations stopping trains. Freight trains are also electrically hauled over this section. At Pretoria the working is naturally not so complicated as at Germiston, but there is an interesting network of lines, as shown in the accompanying sketch diagram. The main lines from Lourenço Marques and from Johannesburg form a converging junction to the east of the main station, though it is possible to work through without reversal by taking the triangle junction at Mitchell Street, passing the yards and locomotive sheds at Capital Park and rejoining the direct route at Koedoespoort. It is at the latter place that one of the largest repair shops for steam locomotives is located. This works is equipped for dealing with the very largest locomotives, and its overhead cranes can lift a 190-ton 'GMAM' Garratt in one piece. The junctions at Mitchell Street and Koedoespoort are signalled by relay interlocking panels of modern design, and the entire Pretoria area is equipped with colour light signalling. There is a large control panel at Pretoria itself, and one of the suburban stations, Rissik, is operated from Pretoria by electronic remote control methods. Mechanical interlocking frames of the double-wire type have been retained for point operation at some of the outlying stations but with these are combined relay interlocking panels from which the colour light signals are operated. The Pretoria area includes more than 30 route miles of continuous colour light signalling.

Before leaving Pretoria I must mention the important historical exhibits displayed on the main station platforms. One of these is the tiny little tank engine with the incredibly long chimney that worked the 'Rand Tram' service from March 1890. The other locomotive is one of the excellent Dutch-built 0–6–4 tanks of the Z.A.S.M. named *Paul Kruger*. The one locomotive is as important as the other in South African railway history, for while the tiny one hauled the very first train to operate in the Reef area, the other was one of the initial class of engines operating on the first independent line from the Transvaal to the sea. The design of these 0–6–4 tank engines is referred to in Chapter Four of this book.

While the working of the Reef area itself is largely electric there are three motive-power depots where large numbers of steam locomotives are stationed: Capital Park, near Pretoria; Germiston, with a sub-shed at

Springs; and Krugersdorp. The original Z.A.S.M. line from Lourenço Marques ran to Pretoria, and Capital Park shed provides some of the present-day power. But that shed has also to cover the workings northward from Pretoria, and when I was able to visit the shed in the autumn of 1968 there were no fewer than 101 engines of the 4–8–2 type allocated. Of these, 58 were of Class 15CA, representing the biggest concentration of that class on the South African Railways. They work the freights on the old Z.A.S.M. line, but of course the pride of the shed is the stud of 19 of the '15F' class. These latter engines are so generally popular everywhere one cares to go in South Africa that they could be likened to the Stanier Class 5 4–6–0s of the L.M.S.R. in Great Britain. At Capital Park there were several of them in spanking condition, but all the rest were outshone by No. 3150, which looked as if she had been given a positively exhibition finish. Of course the long periods of fine, dry weather must undoubtedly help in keeping locomotives looking smart. At busy sheds like Germiston and Capital Park, where the utilisation of important units like the '15CA' and '15F' classes is high, one could well imagine there would not be a great deal of time for cleaning if engines had regularly to take the road in the inclement weather associated with the United Kingdom. There is nothing like a stormy wet day to make a locomotive look shabby, especially if it is a black one. I visited Capital Park shed in September, and then there had been no rain on the Reef for nearly six months!

There were 43 of the '15F' class shedded at Germiston when I was there and also 21 of the big 'S1' shunters; but this shed also housed 50 diesel-electric locomotives, the characteristics of which are discussed in Chapter Eleven of this book. Germiston shed, situated in the midst of an intense railway complex, with a big marshalling yard nearby, is naturally not one of the cleanest of South African depots, and I was interested to see the care taken to keep the diesels and their servicing facilities well away from the steam area, and the diesel lines, like the locomotives themselves, were conspicuously clean. The adoption of a gay livery in red and cream is a natural inducement to keep the locomotives themselves in a smart condition. Of the 50 diesel-electrics on the strength a total of 43 are of Class 31. Even at Germiston, however, in the centre of an area in which modernisation in every sense is the watchword, there were a few old veterans still in active service.

Krugersdorp shed is a stronghold of Garratts and with good reason.

In the late 1930s there had been a rapid growth of traffic on the line to Zeerust and Mafeking. It is single-tracked, and includes much severe curvature and heavy gradients. From the high altitude of the Reef, 5700 ft. above sea level at Krugersdorp, the line descends about 2000 ft. in 105 miles, though this change in level does not represent the general inclination. There are some hard climbs in both directions of running, including long stretches of 1 in 40, compensated for curvature. Paradoxically, the heaviest loaded trains are worked in the eastbound direction, against the gradient. The traffic operation is made more difficult since some of the passing places are as much as 10 miles apart, on severe gradients, resulting in times of 30 minutes or more to clear the sections. One gradient alone involves more than $1\frac{1}{4}$ hours of continuous hard steaming. The rails are only 60 lb. to the yard, but the operating problem, as in so many other areas in Southern Africa, was solved by the production of a special class of Beyer–Garratt engine, having no axle load greater than 15 tons, and yet a tractive effort of 68,800 lb. These enormous engines are of the 'GM' and 'GMAM' classes, and have the 4-8-2+2-8-4 wheel arrangement. The leading tank is of rather smaller capacity than many large Garratts, and this, providing a less obstructive view of the smokebox, shows off the huge proportions of the boiler in most impressive style. This is not to suggest that these engines do not need much water. On the contrary, they have attached to them an auxiliary water-tank providing 6750 gallons, in addition to the 1600 carried on the engine itself.

I had the opportunity of examining and photographing these magnificent examples of British locomotive construction, not at Krugersdorp, which I was not able to visit, but at Capital Park. From the superb cleanliness of those I saw I should imagine they had just been through the Koedoespoort Works for repair, and were standing at Capital Park prior to returning to their normal shed. When first introduced on the Krugersdorp–Zeerust line it was usual for the locomotive to be worked chimney first, and to trail the auxiliary water tank at the cab end. It now seemed as though the reverse has become the normal practice, and on locomotives I saw at Capital Park, in 1968, the auxiliary tank was attached to the chimney end. When the 'GM' engines were first put into service the Reef electrification had not been completed, and they worked into the central area. Braamfontein depot, now entirely given over to electric stock, was a stronghold of these great engines. It is perhaps significant of

119

one's early allegiance that even in such a modern railway atmosphere one soon slips into the way of talking steam. But even in Johannesburg steam is never far away, and when it is steam of such quality as the '15Fs' and the 'GM' Garratts I think I can be forgiven my enthusiasm!

Though it hardly forms part of the Reef complex, mention can here be made of the former Z.A.S.M. line, which is one of the most important outlets from the Pretoria–Witbank–Middleburg area. It is now electrified throughout from Pretoria to the Moçambique frontier at Komatipoort. It is a fascinating route, especially where on steep gradients and heavy engineering works it climbs through the Drakensburg range to the high veldt. It is a route scarcely if ever heeded by the ordinary traveller by train, because the through express trains from the cities of the Reef to Lourenço Marques run at night. I have had the pleasure of travelling much of its length by car on the adjoining highway, and of seeing the lengthy electrically-hauled freight trains of today; and watching their progress in the rugged mountain country one could well appreciate the difficulties in construction faced by the pioneers of nearly eighty years ago, and how comparatively easily Cecil Rhodes won the 'race' for getting the first railway into Pretoria from the sea. One can also picture those sturdy little Dutch-built 0–6–4 tanks fighting their way up the gorge of the Crocodile River, beneath crags towering vertically on either side of the river.

Komatipoort is the junction for an important secondary line that makes its way north-westwards through almost virgin bush country to the Rhodesian border at Beitbridge. Soon after leaving Komatipoort this line comes to Crocodile Bridge and of this section I must tell a story against myself. On one of my visits to South Africa some Johannesburg friends took my wife and me to spend a few days in the Kruger National Park, spotting big game rather than locomotives; but one day in our leisurely perambulation of this wonderful nature reserve we came on to the road that runs parallel to the railway on the section where the latter runs through the 'reserve'. My host is also an engineer, and a railway enthusiast, and for a short time we were appraising the S.A.R. line, noting its splendid permanent way and the measures taken to protect items like telegraph-post guy wires from the attention of the animal population. In the meantime the ladies continued to scan the bush for lions, leopards and such like. We came to a small river, frequented by crocodile and

On the Narrow Gauge

Two 'NG15' class 2-8-2 engines on the run from Port Elizabeth to Lourie

hippopotamus, but it so happened that some 300 yards upstream there was also a railway bridge, and the approach of a lengthy freight train caused us to stop. Now cars are not plentiful in the game reserve, and if one comes upon a stationary one by the roadside it is usually the signal that something 'big' has been spotted. Oblivious of the snare we were setting we drew into a lay-by on the little road bridge and watched the passage of that train. Before it had passed from sight *three* other cars had drawn up behind us and their occupants were eagerly scanning the river banks for signs of wild life. We had not the heart to double back and tell them we were merely counting the number of wagons on that freight train!

CHAPTER ELEVEN

Natal: Classic locomotive tests

A reader making his way through this book, and studying details of loco-motive working in the three countries that I have covered will be in no doubt that the Beyer–Garratt type of articulated locomotive has proved an outstanding success in South Africa. The origin of the type itself, and its adoption as a standard product by Beyer, Peacock and Co., dates back to years well before World War I; but its introduction in South Africa did not come till more than ten years later, and then it received a rather lukewarm reception. The story of how that first reception gradu-ally turned into a great success story is quite one of the romances of British locomotive engineering history. Early in 1921 tests were commenced on one of the most severe 3 ft. 6 in. gauge lines in all Africa, the Natal main line between Durban and Ladysmith. In the first $44\frac{1}{2}$ miles, to Cato Ridge, the line climbs 2450 ft., but the vertical rise is 2400 ft. in the 27 miles from South Coast Junction and Botha's Hill, an average of 1 in 58 throughout. Because of a deviation built later this is now known as the 'Old Line', and it includes gradients of 1 in 30 on a 300 ft. radius curve!

It was on this fearsome stretch of line that a large Garratt engine, No. 1649, Class GA, was tested against one of D. A. Hendrie's standard Natal 4–8–2s, of Class 14, and against one of the giant 2–6–6–2 'Mallets' of Class MH. The leading features of the three engines were:

Class	'14'	'MH'	'GA'
Type	4–8–2	2–6–6–2	2–6–0+0–6–2
Tractive effort at 75% boiler pressure	37,360 lb.	65,000 lb.	47,385 lb.
Total wt. in working order	140 tons	$179\frac{1}{2}$	$133\frac{1}{2}$

The 'Mallet' was of course a compound, but was fitted with a change valve enabling the engine to be worked either compound or simple as desired or necessary. While one can be deeply impressed by the sheer length, and magnificent constructional engineering built into the 'Mallet' it does, on reflection, seem a most unlikely sort of engine to put on to a road with curves of 300 ft. radius! The stage was thus set, and the first tests were carried out by a young and very enthusiastic engineer attached to the staff of the Assistant General Manager at Durban; his name was W. Cyril Williams. His first report was forthright in the extreme:

COMPARATIVE TESTS—GA GARRATT, MH MALLET, AND 14TH (HENDRIE) ENGINES:

As requested by you I give in advance the chief facts deduced from above tests.

(1) As regards coal consumption per 100 ton miles the Garratt is the most economical, then the 14th class, then the Mallet.

(2) Although theoretically the Mallet should pull a 100 ton more than the Garratt it was found that the Garratt could take 1011 tons up the Estcourt–Stockton tunnel bank in 20 minutes less time than the MH Hendrie could take up 991 tons. Also that with these loads the MH was 'all out' while the Garratt was well within 'its limits'.

(3) By its very construction the Garratt is vastly superior to the Mallet. The chief factor in the Garratt's favour is the boiler. The Mallet boiler is 22 ft. long against the Garratt's 11 ft. $8\frac{1}{4}$ in. and the Mallet firebox is highly complicated while the Garratt is a simple distortion of the Belpaire.

(4) The Garratt is a comparatively simple engine and should be cheaper than the Mallet to maintain.

(5) The Garratt engine is $6\frac{1}{2}$ tons lighter than the fourteenth Class, yet will pull 350 tons more in the same time.

(6) The Mallet is 46 tons heavier than the Garratt and pulls less.

(7) The Garratt can go anywhere and has run passenger trains but the Mallet, owing to its length of boiler, has to be worked with the greatest care. It is unfit to run on a 1 in 30 grade and 300 ft. curve. It fouls the loading gauge and at speeds above 25 miles per hour is unpleasant.

(8) When I present my completed report all these points will be brought out and discussed. The tests have been conducted with the greatest care under similar conditions, using coal from the same *truck*, and with the same class of load.

123

This report was a great deal too enthusiastic for his superiors, and in October 1921 Hendrie himself, together with C. Lawson, the Mechanical Superintendent, made a number of tests between Ladysmith and Moor River, on the one hand, and over the fearsome stretch between Durban and Cato Ridge. Only the Garratt and the 'MH' Mallet were concerned in these tests. From the report of Mr. Lawson, which I quote in full, it would seem that his main concern was with the tracking of the wheels, and its effect on both tyre and rail wear. Hendrie seems to have been definitely antagonistic to the Garratt, even though the performance between Ladysmith and Estcourt was very much better. The Mallet got into trouble approaching Stockton Tunnel. When the driver attempted to change over briefly to simple working for this very heavy section the valve stuck, and the engine promptly sat down! At the conclusion of his report it is rather extraordinary to find Hendrie asserting that the Mallet was 'vastly superior' to the Garratt in regard to the design of the wheelbase. He then proposed a spell of three months' continuous running for the Garratt, between Durban and Cato Ridge.

By December 1921, after several months' experience of working the Garratts, the atmosphere was changing markedly, and the Acting Superintendent (Mechanical) reporting to the Assistant General Manager (Durban), is definitely favourable to the Garratt, thus:

10th December, 1921

Assistant General Manager,
DURBAN

Sir,

Tractive Force and Weight

In making comparisons between the GA Garratt locomotive and the MH Class of Mallet, it must be remembered that the former has a lower tractive force and less adhesion than the latter and is therefore a less powerful engine, yet it appears to have hauled as great a load very satisfactorily.

The Garratt engine has a much lower total weight than a Mallet of equal power and can therefore haul a corresponding greater load, its

Speed

ability to travel at greater speeds on the level and easy grades enables it to do a trip on most of our lines in considerably less time than the compound Mallet, an important factor. I have no doubt that a test on the Witbank line will demonstrate this.

The Mallet boiler is a compromise in design to meet difficulties which are peculiar to locomotives which carry their boilers over the coupled wheels.

Boiler

The Garratt boiler is free from these limitations and is designed with a simple deep firebox which is always aimed at, in fact it is the ideal locomotive type of boiler.

The tubes in the GA locomotive are much shorter, but in considering the efficiency of this boiler it must be noted that the flue area is 1/3 greater than that of the MH Mallet and that the gases of combustion flow at a correspondingly slower speed through the tubes and that a lower smokebox vacuum is required.

The Garratt firebox may be expected to give less stay trouble and to be less expensive in repairs.

Position taken by Garratt on Curves

The position taken up by the Garratt engines on curves is precisely that of two single engines, I do not think that the distance between the points of articulation are of much consequence nor the fact that the tractive force of the leading engine is transmitted through the cord formed by the frame carrying the boiler.

The Mallet system of articulation has proved very successful and I have an idea that similar results can be obtained in the Garratt without the introduction of additional guiding wheels.

Bissel Trucks

Our experience has proved that the bissel truck carefully designed and controlled is remarkably free from derailment, its flanges being always parallel with the high rail on a curve, a property which the four-wheeled bogie does not possess.

Flange Wear

The flange wear is what was to be expected and it must be remembered that the leading bogie wheels on single engines working the corridor train out of Durban require to be turned after 6 weeks work.

The longer life of the flanges on the smaller Garratt is due to the lower weight of these engines, and to the shorter wheel base. I do not think that the shorter distance between the points of articulation has much effect.

In a heavier engine the force required to guide the engine is correspondingly greater and consequently the flange wear is greater.

Suitable guiding wheels ahead of the inner coupled wheels undoubtedly save the wear on these wheels, but as I have suggested this object may possibly be attained by other means, which I wish to consider more fully.

Some form of articulated engine for hauling heavier loads is necessary, especially on light rails, and with the same axle load the Garratt can haul a greater load than the Mallet.

Test Loads   In making comparative hauling tests of Garratt and other loco-motives the test loads should be based on the tractive force of the respective engines in so far as speeds on grades are concerned.

The Garratt has less weight per 1000 lbs of tractive force than either the single engine or the Mallet, and if it can haul a correspondingly greater load or a similar load at a greater speed on grades, this should count in its favour and it should not be handicapped to neutralize this advantage.

The table below shows:

A. Booked load Bellair to Bothas Hill per 14th Class Engines.
B. Corresponding load based on the respective tractive forces, for the GA Garratt.
C. Load actually taken by latter.

It is clear that the Garratt was showing powers of haulage well beyond the predicted values.

Bellair–Bothas Hill: Loads (tons)

Axles	14th class booked	G.A. equivalent	Actual test load
30	288	391	427
40	275	378	415
50	263	366	402
60	250	354	389
80	225	341	377
90		338	365
100		329	352

The 'Garratt' equivalent was worked out on the basis of tractive effort, and in this respect the engine actually did very much better than this straight comparison would have suggested.

The three months' trial suggested by Mr. Hendrie was carried out in February, March, and April 1922 between Ladysmith and Glencoe Junction, and both Garratt and Mallet engines made 58 round trips, of 88 miles each. The average loads were roughly the same, 830 tons to the Garratt and 820 to the Mallet, but the Garratt showed a considerable saving in coal using 125 lb. per mile, against 143. Detailed timings were recorded on the three worst banks: Waschbank–Wallsend, and Glencoe Junction on the up journey, and Waschbank–Wessels Nek on the down. The aggregate time on 58 trips was 5358 minutes by the Mallet, but only 4130 minutes by the Garratt. As the report points out, the Garratt hauled a slightly greater load in 1228 minutes less time on the banks, and at the same time using some 12 per cent. less coal. Furthermore the Garratt was much freer in running than its rival, and on favourable stretches reached as much as 40 m.p.h. with these very heavy trains. Although no detailed timings were taken it was judged that the overall superiority in times was in the order of 2500 minutes. The saving in coal was roughly $\frac{3}{4}$ ton on every round trip.

In face of such results the Garratt type of locomotive could no longer be resisted, and by 1924 a further six were in service. Curiously enough it was not until 1929 when the first of the monster 'GL' class were purchased that any were specifically allocated to the Durban–Cato Ridge section. Several different designs of Garratt were made for a diversity of difficult sections on the South African Railways, but presumably the 'MH' Mallets were left to work out their lives on the Cato Ridge and Glencoe sections before new engines were purchased specially for those sections. The tests of 1921-2 were a triumph for the Garratt principle, and they were no less a triumph for the young man whose perception at the very outset had been a little too precipitate for his superiors. But his reports and his zeal did not pass unheeded in Manchester, and in 1923 he left the South African Railways to become London representative of Beyer, Peacock and Co. Before very long 'Garratt Williams', as he was affectionately known, became something of a legend in the British locomotive-building industry. The export orders he secured in nearly every continent, the world over, ran into many millions of pounds, and the type was never applied anywhere more successfully than in his native South Africa. It was my privilege to know him well, especially at the time when he was approaching the crowning honour of his career in the Presidency of the Institution of Locomotive Engineers.

Although he had been for so many years concerned with the commercial side of the business he never once lost his innate love of locomotives as such. It was not enough for him to secure large orders for very large Garratts; he must follow the engines into service, ride on their footplates, and then delight us all with his photographs, and accounts of his travels. It was a particular pleasure to him when the South African Railways ordered the monster 'GL' class engines with the 4-8-2 + 2-8-4 wheel arrangement, which were able to take loads of 1000 tons up the deviation line from Durban to Cato Ridge. Although the construction of this line eased the gradient very considerably from the terrors of the 1 in 30 stretches of the Old Line, the gradient is nevertheless 1 in 66 for more than 38 miles. When the 'GL' engines first arrived a number of tests were made on the great bank, beginning with 575 tons, a little more than the 500 tons taken by the Hendrie Class '14' 4-8-2s. This was on 8 October 1929. Day by day the load was increased, until finally on 21 October they sailed out of Durban with 1117 tons on. The engine performed triumphantly. Whereas the running time booked for the '14' class engines with a 500-ton load was 184 minutes for the 44¾ miles from Durban to Cato Ridge the 'GL' engine took this enormous load up in a running time of 163 minutes. As an all-weather figure, and to allow for that slight deterioration in performance that inevitably follows increase in total mileage run, the load was fixed at 1000 tons—a grand tribute to an outstanding locomotive development in a matter of only eight years.

PLATE 23. Semaphore Signals

Old Z.A.S.M. type at Park Halt, Johannesburg
about 1905

Bloemfontein: old semaphores with new
colour-light signals just before the commissioning of the latter in 1958

PLATE 24. Johannesburg—1905

(*above*) The old Z.A.S.M. cabin manned by Imperial Military Railways staff

(*below*) The approach to Park Station

CHAPTER TWELVE

Crack trains in South Africa: past and present

The early history of railways hardly suggests anything in the way of luxurious travel, and indeed on all the constituent systems of the national railways formed after the Union, in 1910, it was a case of providing some means of communication rather than any suggestion of fast comfortable trains such as were common enough at home by the turn of the century. None of the lines had much chance to develop passenger services before they were involved in war transport, while in Natal and the Eastern Transvaal operation came to include all the hazards of derailment by dynamite. After the war, with British administration in all four states, and ample supplies of new rolling stock coming in from manufacturers in the United Kingdom, some exceedingly fine long-distance passenger train services began to be built up, and it is with these that the story may well begin. Such a study is made all the more interesting in South Africa itself, because of the numerous main line coaches of an earlier period still in regular service, and finely maintained. To some extent it is the same with carriages as with locomotives; by no means all the veteran types have been scrapped. By this I am not suggesting that out-dated stock is still being used on the important trains. The older coaches are in such good condition and are so well appointed that it is a pleasure to travel in them.

No time was lost after the conclusion of the war in getting some magnificent new trains on to the through service between Pretoria and the Cape, and in 1903 the then Metropolitan Amalgamated Railway Carriage and Wagon Company supplied trains for this important service which were among the most luxurious to be found anywhere in the world at that time. Each train consisted of six clerestory-roofed bogie cars 60 ft. 3 in. over body, and details of the interior equipment make interesting reading today. These trains were built for the Central South

African Railway, and worked through to Cape Town via Johannesburg, Kimberley, and De Aar Junction. The C.S.A.R. worked the train between Pretoria and Kimberley after which haulage was taken over by the Cape Government Railway. Each train consisted of three day and sleeping saloons, one observation car, one dining and kitchen car, and a van for heavy baggage which also contained a refrigerator compartment and a private suite of compartments.

The observation saloon, which was placed at the rear of each train, was 15 ft. long. It had large glass windows, which could be taken out and curtains substituted if desired. The internal decorations were in mahogany and upholstered in green buffalo hide with embossed gold *fleur-de-lis*, the furniture consisting of a couch, two tables and easy chairs, all of which were removable. From this compartment a corridor led to five sleeping compartments all finished in wainscot oak, each of which had lavatory accommodation fitted with both hot and cold water service; and at the end of the corridor a bathroom was provided fitted with shower and needle bath for hot and cold water, and a small compartment alongside was used as a linen press. From this saloon a vestibule led to the day and sleeping saloons, of which there were two each having a bathroom and linen cupboard.

These saloons had large compartments in the centre with folding tables and upholstered easy chairs, which could be used as sitting rooms. A vestibule led on to the dining and kitchen car, and the dining portion afforded seating accommodation for 30 passengers. That car was decorated in polished mahogany relieved with mouldings and pilasters. The kitchen was fitted with an up-to-date cooking range and the pantry contained iceboxes. A vestibule led to another day and sleeping saloon designed more especially for the convenience of lady passengers travelling alone.

Next came a suite of compartments consisting of a bedroom, sitting-room, bath, and lavatory fitted with hot and cold water services. That suite was intended to accommodate four persons. The sitting-room contained a couch with a folding table and movable upholstered easy chairs, and the bedroom was fitted with spring mattress beds, wardrobes and upholstered easy chairs. The day and sleeping cars were furnished with buffalo hide cushions, and relieved with gold embossed *fleur-de-lis*. The remaining portion of that car was used for baggage accommodation and a refrigerator compartment.

The whole train was fitted with electric bell communication and lighted by electricity supplied by dynamos placed under the cars. Pullman vestibules, Janney couplers, vacuum brakes, and passenger communication were used, and the Gold system of heating was installed throughout the train. The underframes and bogie frames of all the cars were of steel. The exteriors were finished in mahogany, with the lettering in brass. The roofs were double, and gauze frames to keep out the dust and insects were fitted in the ventilators.

The original six-car formation did not suffice for long, and within a very few years additional coaches were added. The later standard clerestory roofed coaches were built to a standard body size with interior appointments to suit different purposes and classes of travellers. They were 8 ft. 9 in. wide over the body and 63 ft. long. The first-class saloons of the early 1920s had a balcony at each end, for observation and communication purposes; I have travelled in several of these carriages, and when ascending the steep gradients it was very pleasant to stand out on the balcony and obtain an even finer view of the passing scenery, and of the hard-working locomotives, than is possible from the large compartment windows. As originally built the balconies had folding seats, as though to encourage passengers to spend some time there. At one end of the coach, as originally laid out, three four-berth compartments and one two-berth *coupé* were provided, and at the other end there were two four-berth, and two *coupés*. The seats proper, as arranged for day use formed the lower berths, while the upper berths were provided by lifting up the upholstered backs, which engaged in special catches. The second-class saloons on the long distance expresses are similar to the first class, except that the compartments and *coupés* accommodate six and three berth respectively, instead of four and two.

The older dining cars, of which many are still in regular service, are exceedingly pleasant coaches to ride in, and in their homely interior appointments, panelled walls and ceilings are reminiscent of the East Coast, West Coast, and Midland Joint Stock in Great Britain in pre-grouping days. Like all South African coaching stock they ride well, and the interior is so spacious that one loses all impression of running on what, compared with the United Kingdom, is after all a narrow-gauge track. The dining cars are named, though not on the outside as with British Pullmans, and not with glamorous female Christian names. The South African 'diners'

131

are named after geographical features of the countryside such as mountains, rivers and lakes. The friendly crews were not always able to identify these names, but three typical ones I noted were UMGWEZI, which I was told meant a swamp, MABUSI, a little river, and UMVOTI, a river in Zululand. I found very pleasant the old-world courtesies of the dining car crews, and noted that other railway staff who had to pass through the dining cars during meal times, in the course of their duties always removed their caps. Shades of the grand old London and North Western!

But to revert to somewhat earlier days in South Africa, the luxury train introduced in 1903 in due time became the 'Union Limited', running in connection with the Union Castle mail steamer from England. The 'Union Limited', first class only, left Cape Town at 10.45 a.m. on Mondays and Fridays, and reached Johannesburg at 4.30 p.m. the following afternoon. The corresponding south-bound train ran on Sundays and Thursdays, leaving Johannesburg at 9.50 a.m. and reaching Cape Town at 2.13 p.m. on the following day. On the other five days of the week there was an all-classes express making the journey in 39 hours, with many more stops. The present-day equivalent of the 'Union Limited' is the celebrated 'Blue Train', which unlike all other South African expresses is composed of coaching stock that is actually painted blue. It is a very special train indeed, first class only, with supplementary fares on account of the extra degree of luxury. During the summer season, from November to March, it runs twice a week in each direction, leaving from both terminals on Mondays and Wednesdays, and for the rest of the year on one day a week only. It is by a considerable margin the fastest train on the service, taking 25 hours for the 956 miles from Johannesburg to Cape Town, against $27\frac{1}{2}$ hours by the Trans-Karoo Express. On the northbound run, made against the gradient, the 'Blue Train' takes 26 hours from Cape Town to Johannesburg. The vertical lift in the course of the journey is 5720 ft., but actually this does not adequately indicate the severity of the task set to the locomotive. One cannot take advantage of some sections of the steep falling gradient to increase the average speed, because on most sections the curves are so severe that the speed is little higher running downhill than it is climbing in the reverse direction.

It is no exaggeration to say that the 'Blue Train' today is one of the most luxurious trains to be found anywhere in the world. It is air-conditioned throughout, and while the accommodation is similar to that

132

PLATE 25. Johannesburg—1969

The 30th anniversary run of the 'Blue Train'—steam hauled throughout.
The '16E' Pacific engine surrounded by interested spectators

PLATE 26. Notable Non-steam Locomotives   South African Class 5El electric

(*above*) East African Railways '90' class diesel-electric   (*below*) Rhodesia Railways: Class DE4 diesel-electric

of the old 'Union Limited' of sixty years ago, in respect of the compartment and sleeping arrangements, the modern coaching stock provides noise-free vibration-free travel, with the amenities of a first-class hotel. I had an opportunity of seeing this train one day shortly before its departure from Cape Town, and very impressive it was. The compartments and dining car alike are upholstered in blue leather, and in the compartments one finds such things as loose cushions, writing tables and notepaper, and an excellent valet service always on hand. In addition to a really sumptuous dining car there is a beautiful observation lounge at the rear. The South African Railways set considerable store upon the 'public relations' rendered by staff on services such as the 'Blue Train', and all the staff are specially chosen.

In April 1969 the thirtieth anniversary of the inauguration of the 'Blue Train' occurred, and with the wholehearted co-operation of the railway authorities the Historic Transport Association of Johannesburg ran a special anniversary train from Johannesburg to Cape Town and back. The outward trip commenced at 10.15 a.m. on 11 April and the return arrived back in Johannesburg at 5.50 p.m. on 15 April. This special train, consisting of the usual twelve luxury coaches of the 'Blue Train', plus an additional lounge car, was steam-hauled throughout in both directions. This entailed quite a lot in the way of special arrangements, because express passenger workings into Johannesburg and Cape Town ceased some time ago. The railway authorities put up a magnificent show, and they must have felt well rewarded by the tremendous crowds that assembled at the stations to see the train. All the locomotives were beautifully prepared for the occasion and a trophy was awarded to the crew of the best prepared engine. The staging points for engine working were Klerksdorp, Kimberley, De Aar, Beaufort West, Touws River, and over the six successive stages the classes of locomotive used were Class 16E 'Pacific'; '23' class 4-8-2; '25' class non-condensing 4-8-4; '25' class condensing 4-8-4, and the same again on the penultimate stage; finally from Touws River to Cape Town a '23' class 4-8-2 was used.

A South African friend who witnessed a lot of the special working wrote to me as follows:

An estimated crowd of 3500 was on the platform to meet the train when she arrived at Kimberley around 9.00 p.m. It rivalled the crowd which had seen the train off in Johannesburg. Anyway, '23' No. 2559 was detached and taken

133

to loco. Pretty soon '25NC' No. 3444 backed slowly onto the train. This engine had her regular driver and the interior of her cab was a sensation! All the fittings, gauges and pipes, etc., therein had been polished to the limit. It was dazzling! I could hear gasps coming from the crowd around me and then cheers. Now these '25s' have quite a high cab floor (it is almost 6 ft. above rail level) and the driver was a big man. As he gazed down on the crowd while his engine was moving very slowly back into the train, I could see his face almost glowing with pride at the enthusiastic reception his mighty steed was receiving. '25NCs' might lack the height of American locomotives but they can look extremely massive and impressive nevertheless.

He and a friend chased the train by car, and his account becomes extremely vivid when they got south of Kimberley. Many of my English friends have 'chased' special trains by car, but never, so far as I am aware, through the whole of a night, and for most of the next day.

We were delayed leaving Kimberley and even when we did leave we got lost temporarily. The result was that the train got so far ahead of us that we never caught up with it all the way to De Aar. However, while we were racing along at about 70 m.p.h. we caught up with a southbound freight. This was a bit south of Modder River I think. Anyway, as we got closer I could see that the local was sending up a lot of sparks from her stack. Then as we drew level with the engine we were treated to the tremendous deafening roar of her exhaust. Normally all southbound freight trains over this section are on the full load (general freight and coal going south plus iron ore and manganese ore to Port Elizabeth) so I took it for granted that this train was on the full load (about 1450 tons) also. The engine was a '25NC' and her speed was a bit under 45 m.p.h. Not bad considering she was on the long climb out of the Modder River basin. Here was an ordinary old '25NC' doing an ordinary everyday chore as she battled through the night, her headlight beam piercing the darkness ahead. To me she was the unsung hero of the night (and not No. 3444 which was the engine receiving all the attention on this particular night) and I could have stayed with her hour after hour. However, my friend was in a hurry so we sped on ahead but not before we had noted that the '25NC' we were pacing was now going over 45 m.p.h.

South of Hopetown where the main highway veers away from the line, we cut across on a dirt road so that we could continue to follow the line. Soon we saw the lights of the 'Blue Train' some miles away, but we were still cutting across country prior to joining up with the line again. It was actually further ahead of us than we realized because of this. Then we began to run into trouble. Apparently there had been some storms in the area and water was lying across the road in a lot of places. It was only shallow but before long our windscreen was covered in muddy water and having no clean water or rags to clean it properly, our speed was greatly reduced.

When we had rejoined the line again I saw a powerful headlight behind us. It appeared to be gaining on us and I couldn't understand how a freight train could be travelling so rapidly. There were no other passenger trains scheduled for this time and the 'Blue Train' was definitely ahead of us. Finally when it had nearly caught up with us we stopped to watch it pass. It turned out to be the relief (standby) engine No. 3440. She was doing about 50 as she sped quietly past us.

Continuing on we passed several northbound freights (some were double-headers) before eventually reaching De Aar sometime after midnight.

Next highlight of the trip was chasing '25' No. 3496 from Beaufort West to Touws River next morning. This is very rough country. I think it must be the toughest mainline on the S.A.R. 3496 was often down to snail's pace on the long heavy grades and for once we had a fairly easy time keeping ahead of the train (necessary for taking frequent photos). The immaculate locomotive and train made an extremely picturesque sight as they traversed the equally picturesque terrain of this rugged area. The line is so hilly that several times I saw the front of the train going down grade while the rear of the train was still coming up grade.

All long distance expresses on the South African Railways involve lengthy periods of both day and night travel, and the first-class saloons have been designed specially to give maximum comfort at both times. From a wide experience of night travel in many parts of the world I have found the standard of British first-class 'sleepers' the finest of any for purely night travel; but if one's journey happens to be prolonged into the day time, or it begins well before bedtime, as it used to on the old 'Royal Highlander' at 4.15 p.m. from Inverness, that berth can put one well on the way to an attack of claustrophobia! The South African saloons are delightful for day travel, having all the spaciousness of an ordinary British compartment 'first', except that the seats are flat, instead of providing settee comfort. They are nicely padded, with carpets on the floor, and the windows are large and give an excellent look out. Furthermore, there is no 'sleeper' charge, as such. Bedding attendants travel on all long distance trains, and they prepare beds at night and take them up in the morning.

In a country like South Africa with such great distances to be covered, it is inevitable that a considerable part of every journey will be made by night, and so miss some of the most interesting scenery. The 'Blue Train' on its northbound journey climbs the Hex River Pass in the late afternoon, but in the reverse direction the descent is made soon after dawn. I have not travelled on this train myself, but the southbound Trans-Karoo Express which I joined one evening at De Aar runs several hours behind the 'Blue Train', and the sun is well up, and breakfast over by the time the descent of the pass is commenced. The 'Orange Express', running from Cape Town to Durban, climbs the Hex River Pass, and crosses the Great Karoo in the night, but has the compensation of crossing the Orange Free State in daylight—a notable run. But before referring further to the 'Orange Express' of today more than a passing mention must be made of the early years of the present century, when all trains leaving Durban had to face the tremendous gradients and curves of the 'Old Line' in climbing to Cato Ridge, and the justification for the Reid 4–10–2 tank engines is amply explained. After their temporary transfer to the Transvaal, under the administration of the Imperial Military Railways these engines were returned to Natal, and for a time were the most powerful passenger engines working on the line.

In 1903, at roughly the same time as the *de luxe* train was put on between Pretoria and Cape Town, a new corridor express was put on between Durban and Johannesburg. This consisted of four bogie coaches only— quite enough for the Cato Ridge climb—and was worked by a 4–10–2 tank engine. These engines were fairly soon superseded on the best trains by the earliest Hendrie tender locomotives, the 'B' class 4–8–0s, but the luxurious C.S.A.R. stock was not in general use for some years. Mr. J. P. Pearson, in his monumental work *Railways and Scenery*, has a description of a journey made in 1910 on the 9.5 a.m. train from Durban to Pieter-maritzburg—or plain Maritzburg as it was then known—and a load of eight small 8-wheelers, estimated at 140 tons, was taken by a Hendrie 4–8–0 with great competence up the 1 in 30 gradients, with speed at no time falling below 15 m.p.h. The small 8-wheeled coaches to which he refers were no doubt of the nineteenth century Natal type, non-corridor, with high, square clerestory roofs, and running quite close coupled. They could have come from many a British railway's stock at that period. The home influence at the time was also shown in the frequent use of prominent roof-boards; but instead of elaborate legends such as 'Paddington, Exeter, Plymouth and Penzance', one saw just plain 'Durban', or 'Maritzburg'.

I have not yet had the pleasure of travelling over this line myself, so am taking the liberty of 'lifting' a contemporary description of the passing scene from J. P. Pearson. He writes,

Beyond Bowker's the curves were amazingly severe, reminding me of some of those on the New Zealand lines, and then, after Northdene, in front on the left, some bare, scrubby mountains came into view. At Pinetown an eight-coupled, bound for Durban, ran through at 10.21 with a load of one large eight-wheeler, six smaller eight-wheelers, and a covered eight-wheeled truck, but what train this was I could not definitely determine. Beyond Palmiet came a splendid valley view, with brown as its prevailing tint, on the right far below us, and then, nearing Wyebank, as my clocking shows, a signal stop was made to let a ten-coupled 'Reid' with a goods train pass us. Very extensive views continued on the right after Wyebank—at first gloriously wooded, with dark trees, but this gave way soon to bare hills, while, on the left, came a very extensive and fine view of brown scrubby hills, with a cup-shaped valley below. Our increasing height above sea was evidently telling on the trees, as, beyond Hill Crest, the hills all around were bare and brown and, nearing Botha's Hill, there was a most magnificent view on the right to flat-topped mountains bounding a tremendous expanse of valley in which other mountains and hills were piled up in a confusion of browns and greens. This was truly a grand sight, and the forerunner of many other of what might be called 'lonely panoramas' which, later, I was to find were, with their flat-topped hills, characteristic of this part of South Africa.

At Alverstone, we passed the down train, due there at 11.17 a.m. which, with Hendrie 'B' class engine No. 303, was just over a quarter of an hour late (it arrived at 11.33) and thus kept us waiting. Its load was five eight-wheeled coaches and three eight-wheeled wagons. Going on from there we curved around, sweeping along at a great height, and then traversing a tunnel and a cutting before attaining Drummond. Beyond Drummond, the line coasts around a valley seen from above, with a view to a stony, flat-topped ridge and to stones of very great size on an adjacent hill. More sweeping curves brings us into Inchanga, near which place the scenery is very fine, or, at any rate, its suggestion of absolute loneliness much impressed me. Wide uplands, with no extensive views, takes us on between Harrison and Cato Ridge, while after the latter station, there was another series of glorious views on the right (recalling that near Botha's Hill) of most tremendous extent. Valleys, mountains rising from the valleys, huge bounding flat-topped mountains, and others farther off still,

137

and higher again still, made a grand sight—all the grander for being bathed in hot sunlight and clear air. Nearing Camperdown, the numerous native kraals on the hill-sides impressed me with the fact that, in a sense, we were in a wild country where the native population forms still by far the greater proportion of the whole.

It was in such a country as this that the giant 'MH' Mallet engines were tested against the first Garratts, as told in Chapter Eleven, and the imagination certainly wanders to picturing how those great engines must have looked, and sounded blazing their way up into this stern countryside.

The 'Orange Express' of today takes the main line from Cape Town to Kimberley, and then, after reversing direction takes the cross-country line from Kimberley to Bloemfontein mentioned in Chapter Five. It is significant of the curves and general obstacles to running encountered on this section that this 106 miles, non-stop, takes as much as 185 minutes. Then the fine road north-eastwards to Kroonstad is followed, again non-stop: 128 miles in 200 minutes. At this point the direction of running changes, not merely that once again the head of the train becomes the tail but that the course lies almost exactly at right angles to that previously followed. The train makes its way across the Orange Free State, still steam-hauled, to Bethlehem, on to Harrismith, and finally to join the electrified main line from Johannesburg at Ladysmith. The boundary between the Orange Free State and Natal is crossed near Van Reenen. There is some very heavy climbing in the reverse direction between Ladysmith and Van Reenen, with a difference of altitude of 2136 ft in 37 miles, and many stretches of 1 in 40, and some short pitches at 1 in 30. J.P.Pearson travelled this way in a stopping train of some 140 tons which was worked unassisted on this severe grade by an old Dübs 4-8-2 tank engine. The 'Orange Express' leaves Cape Town at 3.30 p.m. and reaches Durban at 8.30 on the second morning.

Electric traction has of course completely conquered the difficulties of working on these tremendous inclines in Natal, added of course to the construction of the new line between Durban and Cato Ridge. Even so a bank of 1 in 66 extending for 38 miles is not a thing to be taken lightly in the operation of a corridor sleeping and dining car express of fourteen or fifteen coaches weighing between 500 and 600 tons. With electric traction of course, one can multiply up on the power, and work two, three, or even four locomotives if necessary in multiple unit by a single crew. The deviation which greatly eased the working of heavy trains out of Durban was constructed many years ago; but today the running times between Durban and Ladysmith are being cut substantially by means of the new deviation lines between Ladysmith and Pietermaritzburg. It is not strictly correct to call them 'deviations', because a deviation suggests a detour, and an increased mileage. On these new lines it is a question of building short cuts. The original lines were taken 'round the mountains' to lessen the costs of construction; the new lines are not only built with double tracks, but by extensive tunnelling have reduced the distance between Ladysmith and Pietermaritzburg by 18 miles. The improved running obtained has reduced the overall time between Johannesburg and Durban by a full hour.

The 'Orange Express' and the 'Trans-Natal Express' are made up of modern corridor stock only slightly less luxurious than that of the 'Blue Train'. The coaches are painted in standard colours, and include a number of new all-steel vehicles, with elliptical roofs built in South Africa by the Union Carriage and Wagon Company (Pty) Ltd. of Nigel, in the Transvaal. These named expresses include very attractive lounge cars in their formation. They can indeed form a kind of 'social centre' on these trains which are on the journey for twenty-four hours or more. They are available to both first- and second-class passengers, and provide a pleasant interlude if one desires a change from the privacy of a *coupé*. At one end of the lounge car is a bar, and the rest of the saloon is fitted up like a club lounge with comfortable easy chairs, occasional tables with bowls of flowers, and large windows from which to view the passing scene during the hours of daylight.

CHAPTER THIRTEEN

Electric and diesel locomotives

Among locomotive men, as among non-technical railway enthusiasts, there are extraordinarily strong bonds towards one form of motive power or the other. It may be argued by the most thorough-going modernists that the appeal of steam is purely sentimental, and the result of a primitive expression of emotion; but even in a young country like South Africa I found locomotive men just as devoted to steam as the most diehard members of the 'old guard' at home. Electrical men never disguise their feelings, though sometimes these are so humorously put as to remain '*bon mots*' for all time, in locomotive engineering circles. I shall always remember an occasion some years ago, when steam was still the predominant form of motive power on British Railways, and a paper on problems of fire-box maintenance was read before the Institution of Locomotive Engineers in London. During the subsequent discussion a prominent electrical engineer rose, rather unexpectedly, and said he found the whole thing rather depressing in that such quantities of copper, designed by nature to conduct electricity, should be used to light fires in!

In South Africa the gradual conversion of the main lines to electric traction is proceeding logically, and some very fine locomotives are at work in many parts of the country. The first main line electrification was undertaken in 1925-7 where the heavily graded section of the Natal main line between Pietermaritzburg and Glencoe Junction was equipped on the 3000 volt d.c. system, with overhead current collection. This proved very successful and by subsequent extensions the electrified area was increased to a route mileage of 404 by 1937, covering the whole line from Volkrust to Durban, and the very severe branch line from Ladysmith to Harrismith, over which the 'Orange Express' is routed. Until the year

PLATE 27. Modern Signalling on the Reef

(*above*) Searchlight type colour-light signals and direction indicators, beside gold mines at Driehoek

(*below*) New Canada Junction—main line to Bloemfontein and Port Elizabeth

PLATE 28. Modern Control Panels

(*above*) New Canada Junction—South African Railways

(*below*) C.T.C. Control Panel, Sawmills, Bulawayo–Victoria Falls line,
Rhodesia Railways

1947 the locomotives were of moderate power, being used in multiple where necessary; but at that time the first steps were taken towards the building up of a fleet of powerful modern locomotives to deal with increased traffic on the electrified lines. The '3E' class of 28 locomotives was introduced at the end of 1947, primarily for passenger and heavy freight working in the Reef area. They were built by Robert Stephenson and Hawthorn's Ltd., with electrical equipment by Metropolitan Vickers, and were of 2490 horse power—more than double that of any electric locomotive previously in use in South Africa.

One of the most attractive features of electric traction in a country like South Africa is that the locomotives can be equipped for regenerative braking; when descending a heavy gradient the action of the motors can be reversed, and instead of taking current from the line the motors are switched to act as generators and so feed current back into the line. This causes a powerful braking effect upon the train, and by this electrical braking lessens the wear and tear on the ordinary brake shoes. In the original Natal electrification the 1200 horsepower locomotives were equipped with regenerative braking, an invaluable feature on a line including a bank of 14 miles inclined throughout at 1 in 50. Over this route the giant Beyer–Garratt locomotives of the 'GL' class tackled freight trains of 1000 tons. By using three 'E1' class electric locomotives, coupled in multiple-unit, trains of 1500 tons were handled by a single engine crew. Tests indeed were made with four of these locomotives, though a load of 2000 tons was beyond the range of practical day-to-day operation. A total of 95 of these locomotives was in service up to 1927. The '3E' class, referred to in the previous paragraph, was not fitted with regenerative braking. The lines in the Reef area, for freight working in which the locomotives were primarily intended, are comparatively level. There are none of the lengthy, very steep gradients that characterise the Natal main line for example, and in Natal the new engines were used only on passenger trains.

In steam-locomotive parlance the '3E' class are of the 0–6–6–0 wheel arrangement, having two powered six-wheeled bogies; but the modern notation for electric and diesel locomotives is to use letters for the powered groups of wheels, and figures only for the non-powered wheels. Also the notation uses the former Continental method of designating the wheel arrangement by the number of axles, rather than the number of wheels.

Thus on the Continent a steam 'Pacific', a 4–6–2 in Great Britain, is a '231', or in modern parlance a '2C1'. Thus the South African '3E' class are known as Co + Co. They are powerful locomotives, weighing 120 tons in working order, and having a tractive force of 47,000 lb. on a one-hour rating. In discussing the power of electric locomotives the power output is, within certain limits, dependent upon how much the motors and associated gear can be permitted to heat up. There is an almost unlimited supply of power in the overhead line, and if one 'threw in everything' on the locomotive a very high power output could be obtained briefly; but the overload would immediately cause excessive heating, and consequently the most elaborate safeguarding devices are built into the design to prevent any over-enthusiastic driver from thrashing his locomotive. One cannot therefore 'thrash' an electric locomotive in the same way as an expert driver and fireman can do with steam. So, in stating the power capacity it is usual to refer to 'short term', 'one hour', or even longer ratings. For passenger working the '3E' class were equipped with electrically heated steam boilers for train heating in cold weather. When new these locomotives were painted green, of a shade not unlike the Brunswick green of the Great Western, but rather brighter.

The scene now moves to the main line in the Cape. In May 1954 electrification was completed of the very severe section through the Hex River Pass, with an additional mileage of 149 miles between Bellville and Touws River. At one time it was intended to construct a deviation between De Doorns and New Kleinstraat which would have eliminated the lengthy stretches of 1 in 40 on the original line; but this deviation has not yet been built. Be that as it may, in readiness for the electrification between Bellville and Touws River forty new locomotives of greatly enhanced power were purchased from the North British Locomotive Company, with General Electric Company's electrical equipment. These locomotives, classified '4E' are of the 1–Co–Co–1 type, having a motor horsepower of 3030. They have a total weight in working order of 155 tons, and were designed to handle all traffic passing over the Hex River section, passenger and goods alike, and were equipped with regenerative braking. The designed capabilities were based on the replacement of the existing line by one having a bank of 20 miles continuously inclined at 1 in 66 and the following performance was specified:

142

Passenger Train: 610 tons

Gradient	Required speed (m.p.h.)
Level	56½
1 in 100 up	38
1 in 66 up	34
1 in 66 down	40 to 55

Freight Train: 1070 tons

Gradient	Required speed (m.p.h.)
Level	35
1 in 66 up	24½
1 in 66 down	25 to 40

When the electrified line through the Hex River Pass was brought into operation the line immediately out of Cape Town was still equipped on the 1500 volt d.c. system as installed when the suburban lines were electrified some twenty-five years earlier. All trains had therefore to stop at Bellville to change engines; but by the end of 1954 the 14 miles of suburban line had been converted to the now-standard 3000-volt traction system, and through locomotive working between Cape Town and Touws River commenced. Of the forty locomotives of Class 4E purchased from Great Britain ten were allocated to Natal, and the remaining thirty to the Cape. The continued existence of the formidable original bank between De Doorns and Matroosberg, with its 16 miles of almost continuous 1 in 40 gradient, required two locomotives, though elsewhere over the entire 163 miles between Cape Town and Touws River they were able to handle freight trains of 1200 tons single handed. They were subjected to the most intensive usage, working twenty-four hours a day for three weeks continuously, and receiving only minor attention at terminals, and then spending four hours in the sheds for routine maintenance before going out on a further three weeks of continuous running. Having regard to the very severe conditions in which they were working

143

this was an outstanding performance, and something that was of course completely impossible with steam.

In this connection certain features of the design require special mention. I need not enter upon the highly technical details of the electrical control gear, but two points of general interest are the methods employed for filtering the air intakes and the exclusion of dust, and the protective arrangements against lightning. As regards the former I can only say that early experience was such that so little dust found its way through to the electrical gear even in three weeks of continuous running that it was at one time seriously considered extending the three-weekly spell to four weeks. Although these locomotives were not originally working through the most arid of countryside, such as the Karoo, and the high veldt, the going is hard enough in the rough country north of De Doorns. Lightning surges can be very severe in South Africa, and a constant danger to electrical equipment. On these locomotives, in addition to the conventional double spark gap on the roof, a special surge absorber and auxiliary spark gaps with blowouts are associated with both the power and auxiliary circuits. The introduction of electric traction made possible some considerable accelerations of service, particularly with freight, though naturally the elimination on long passenger runs of stops to take water and clean fires gave electric traction an immediate advantage over steam. My own experience of travel in South Africa would suggest that of a saving of 43 minutes on the previous passenger timing of 270 minutes between Cape Town and Touws River more than half could be attributed to the absence of stops for fuelling and servicing the locomotives en route.

The problem of steam heating passenger trains in electrified areas assumed a new aspect when the intensive working of the new electric locomotives on the Cape main line to Touws River was planned. The locomotives were designed for indiscriminate use in passenger and goods service, and while the ordinary passenger trains scheduled to run between Cape Town and Touws River in 6 hr. 27 min. would require a large water capacity for steam heating, goods service would require nothing at all. So, instead of providing boilers on the locomotives themselves, a design of steam heating tender was worked out, which could be attached to passenger trains, as required. This would save weight on the locomotives, and obviate the need for boilers at all, when freight trains were being hauled. These interesting vehicles, which were built at the

144

PLATE 29. Rhodesia: 12th Class at Work

(*above*) Mixed train from the south nearing Bulawayo

(*below*) Climbing Vakaranga bank on the line from Bulawayo to the south

PLATE 30. Bulawayo

(*above*) Panoramic view of the Station and yards

(*below*) Southbound mail train being hauled by 15th class 4–6–4+4–6–4
Beyer–Garratt locomotive

Durban workshops of the South African Railways, are 40 ft. long and carried on two 4-wheeled bogies. At each end are two large cylindrical water tanks, each with a capacity of 1750 gallons. In the centre is a cab containing the oil-burning steam generator, which has a rated output of 1600 lb. of steam per hour. These tenders are not entirely self-contained. Air is needed for the atomisation of the fuel oil supply to the steam generator, and this is drawn from the air compressor plant of the brake equipment of the locomotive. While the trains on the South African Railways are vacuum braked the electric locomotives themselves are air braked, controlled from a vacuum-air proportional valve. The water pump of the steam heating tender is electrically driven, with current drawn from the locomotive.

A number of other problems in connection with the working of these tenders had to be considered in preparation of their design. In general the winter season in South Africa can be said to last for no more than five months, and therefore the tenders would be laid up for seven months in each year. Attention was therefore given for the provision of a corrosion-resistant internal lining for both water and oil tanks to prevent any deterioration during the time the tenders are out of use. In addition to use on the Cape main line, tenders are also used on the Natal lines, and later on the main lines from Johannesburg to the south, both to Kimberley on the main line to the Cape, and to Kroonstad for the Port Elizabeth and East London trains. When first put into use, in 1954, only two servicing depots were needed, one at Cape Town and one at Pietermaritzburg. There water-treatment plants and bulk storage for oil is provided. The water is chemically treated before being fed to the water tanks of the tender. This not only provides against the risk of corrosion, but also ensures complete uniformity in quality of water supply at the different servicing depots. Enough fuel-oil and water is carried for the longest round trip, to obviate any need for obtaining water or fuel otherwise than through the specially regulated supply at the main servicing station. At the time of their first introduction the longest round trip was on the Natal lines, where one scheduled roster involved a turn of 21 hr. 33 min. away from base. The electric locomotive driver's assistant is responsible for starting and stopping the steam generator. Access to the central cab of the 'tender' is obtained via the end door of the locomotive and an open railed-in walk way beside one of the water tanks. These steam heating tenders have proved very successful, and they were in general use when I was in South Africa in September and October of 1968.

With the extension of the electrified system, to cover the entire main line between Durban and Johannesburg, and main line extensions southward the question of new locomotives was considered. The projected deviation in the Hex River Pass having been postponed the problem of dealing with the 1 in 40 gradient remained. A locomotive of 3000 horsepower being inadequate to deal with such a gradient unassisted on a maximum load train it was decided that the overall provision of new power could best be met by a fleet of locomotives of 2000 horsepower, which when coupled in multiple unit could deal satisfactorily with the De Doorns–Matroosburg bank, and gradients only less severe in Natal. A first order for sixty new locomotives to this general specification was placed with the English Electric Company, and first deliveries were made in 1955. These locomotives, designated Class 5E, are of the Bo + Bo type and are of relatively lightweight construction. Their all-up weight is 83 tons, making an interesting comparison with the '3E' and '4E' classes, thus:

Class	Wheel arrangement	One hour horsepower	Total weight (tons)	Horsepower per ton
3E	Co + Co	2490	120	20·7
4E	1–Co + Co–1	3030	155	19·6
5E	Bo + Bo	2000	83	24·1

Quite apart from the electrical equipment there are some interesting points in the purely mechanical design, including a completely welded underframe and superstructure in one unit, and bogie frames in one-piece steel castings.

These locomotives have a maximum permissible speed of 60 m.p.h. and provide the performance shown opposite.

With the normal loading of the fast passenger, and express trains the use of two locomotives coupled in multiple is necessary, and on the trains in which I travelled, mostly loaded to between 550 and 650 tons a pair was always provided. The '5E' design, however, provided no more than

146

Passenger Train: 340 tons

Gradient	Speed (m.p.h.)
Level	60
1 in 100	42
1 in 50	34

a starting point for a remarkable development, in the '5E1' class, which through successive improvements has seen the one-hour rating increased from 2200 horsepower, first to 2360, and then to 2600. On the trains by which I travelled I noticed it was sometimes the practice to couple a '5E' and a '5E1' together. We had such a combination on the 2 p.m. train out of Johannesburg, with a 16-coach load of about 600 tons, all told. The schedules are not very fast, but provide for numerous slacks and a maximum speed of 60 m.p.h. The 32 miles to Vereeniging are allowed 75 minutes non-stop, with 114 minutes for the ensuing 86 miles on to Kroonstad. On the open sections we were running mostly at 52 to 54 m.p.h. and I noted one maximum of just over 60 m.p.h.

I was able to note only a downhill performance on the mountain section in Cape Province, on the 'Trans-Karoo Express', worked by a pair of '5E1' class, and a 17-coach load. The descent of the 1 in 40 bank between Matroosburg and De Doorns, using regenerative braking was beautifully regulated, with a complete absence of any fluctuation in speed. One just glided steadily down. One felt that the long train was always under perfect control, without any of the heavy brake applications sometimes all too apparent on similar descents elsewhere. The two locomotives got along briskly enough after De Doorns, though of course they were still on a generally descending gradient. It would have been interesting to observe how a pair of them would have taken such a load up the 1 in 40 of the Hex River Pass, but as I have told in an earlier chapter of this book I returned from Cape Town via the Garden Route, and we changed from electric to steam haulage at Worcester. From a study of the performance characteristics I should have expected a speed of around 31 or 32 m.p.h. on the 1 in 40 with two '5E1' class and a train of about 620 tons.

At the time of writing this chapter the news has come through that contracts for 100 new locomotives of considerably increased power have been placed. These will be known as '6E' and they will have a one-hour rating of 3320 horsepower. The main contractors are the Union Carriage and Wagon Company (Pty.) Ltd. of Nigel, Transvaal, but all the electrical equipment will be manufactured in England, some by A.E.I. Traction Ltd., and some by the English Electric Company. The new locomotives will be used on all electrified sections of the South African Railways, and because of their increased power will permit of working some trains with a single locomotive where a pair of '5E' or '5E1' class was previously needed. In outward appearance they will look very similar to a '5E1', but there are many improvements in design, based on the experience gained already. The success of the '5E1' can be judged from the fact that more than 500 of them are now at work, in addition to 158 of the '5E' class.

Diesel traction is being introduced gradually on the South African Railways. The most intensive application so far has been in South West Africa where coal and water for steam locomotives have always been a problem, and where the density of traffic does not justify electrification. For this service a batch of 115 general-purpose locomotives were purchased from the International General Electric Company; these are of well-known 'Universal' type, weighing 106 tons, and having an engine horsepower of 1980. They are designated Class 32. They are now used for all the traffic in South West Africa on passenger and goods, main and branch lines alike. With the exception of a small batch of diesel-hydraulic locomotives purchased from Henschel in 1959 all the diesel locomotives now working on the South African Railways are of American manufacture. At Germiston, for example, a considerable number of the '31' class General Electric Bo + Bo type are now stationed. The latest additions to the stock are the '33' class, also from General Electric, of 2000 horsepower, and although looking very similar to the '31' and '32' classes they include a number of improvements in design. Some of the latest diesels are working in the Transvaal, but I had an opportunity of travelling behind them in the Port Elizabeth area. A pair of them worked the 5.30 p.m. 'fast' for Johannesburg as far as Cradock, 171 miles, with a 19-coach train.

In referring to the power of diesel locomotives, and quoting the figure of 2000 for the General Electric Class 33, the essential difference between a diesel-electric and an ordinary electric locomotive must be appreciated. The 'electric' draws power from the overhead line, and within certain limits can develop a much higher horsepower than its nominal value. At home, on the London Midland Region for example, the 'AL6' type locomotives with a nominal rating of 3500 often develop more than 5000 horsepower, for short periods. A diesel is entirely limited by the capacity of the diesel engine, and taking account of transmission and frictional losses one cannot normally expect to have more than about three-quarters of the engine horsepower available for traction. A pair of Class 33 locomotives coupled in multiple-unit, and having a combined engine horsepower of 4000 could be expected to provide about 3000 horsepower for traction at the drawbar of the second locomotive. While in level running speeds do not generally exceed 55 m.p.h., they would certainly need all that 3000 horsepower to haul a 19-coach train up some of the banks and to accelerate briskly from the numerous intermediate stops. No sustained fast running was made on this journey and I took no detailed notes, other than that we took just over two hours to cover the first 60-odd miles from Port Elizabeth to Alicedale. This is quite typical of the working of these 'fast-passenger' long-distance trains. There was a lot of hard intermediate work to do, and it was smoothly and efficiently done.

CHAPTER FOURTEEN

Northward into Rhodesia

Nowhere in the whole of Southern Africa was the construction of a great trunk line of railway more the outcome of political vicissitudes than in the extension of the Cape Government Railway northward from Vryburg. Cecil Rhodes found the chances of rapid development blocked by political wrangles over the future status of the Bechuanaland Protectorate. He had found great financial interests in the goldfields of the Transvaal, and began seriously to consider abandoning the great project of the Cape to Cairo line, and establishing instead railway communication with Rhodesia not from the south, over the barren, sparsely-populated wastes of Bechuanaland, but from the east coast. The outcome of the Anglo-Portuguese treaty of June 1891 was a decision to construct a railway from the port of Beira to the boundary of what was then termed the British sphere of influence, at Umtali. George Pauling was awarded the contract, but it was for nothing more ambitious than a 2 ft. gauge line. Clearly the original concept was for an entirely independent concern, unconnected with the gradually expanding network of 3 ft. 6 in. gauge lines that was spreading elsewhere over Southern Africa. There were appalling difficulties in construction, from the intense tropical climate, from the attentions of wild animals, and from the difficulties of organising labour. In the two years 1892 and 1893 the official statistics relating to casualties among the staff are barely credible today; they read more like the death roll after some frightful battle than the construction of a railway. But the plain fact remains that in those two terrible years 60 per cent of the staff died on the job; *sixty per cent!*

The unprecedented difficulties being encountered on the Beira–Umtali line were only one factor that caused Cecil Rhodes to change his whole strategy towards the railway approach to Rhodesia. He was engaged in difficult, and sometimes acrimonious, discussions with the home Government on the future administration of the Bechuanaland Protectorate, which he wanted to bring under the management of the British South Africa Company. A telegraph line had been established between Mafeking and Salisbury, and then in the midst of this delicate situation there suddenly broke out the Matabele Rebellion. The country was quickly in a state of confusion. Staff of the Chartered Company were murdered, and the trouble in Matabeleland extended to raids, plundering, and massacre into peaceful Mashonaland. An Imperial force cut off from its main body by a river in spate, was surrounded by Matabele and annihilated, at the Shangani River. Disease rather than military operations brought this first Matabele rebellion to an end, with the death of King Lobengula, and the years 1894 and 1895 were comparatively peaceful. In October 1894 there was an historic dinner party, at which Sir Charles Metcalfe and George Pauling were the guests of Cecil Rhodes. Pauling was invited to build a railway from Vryburg to Mafeking, but at that time the chances of extending the line northward through Bechuanaland were slight. The native chiefs while appreciating the benefits of British protection were not agreeable to having a railway through their territory.

The only alternative to reaching Rhodesia from the south would have been through the Transvaal, and the Transvaal was so hostile to Great Britain at the time that such a project was unthinkable. Then in 1895 came the ill-starred attempt at a *coup d'etat* in the shape of the Jameson Raid, with the temporary eclipse of Rhodes as a power in the land. For a brief period he was prepared to throw in his hand altogether, but tragedy in the north changed the whole picture. Matabeleland and Mashonaland were both in disorder; there was tribal warfare, but worse than this was the catastrophic effect of an outbreak of rinderpest among the cattle. Oxen were used for transport; now none dare be used. The whole country was in despair and the cry went forth, what was Mr. Rhodes going to do about it! Cecil Rhodes himself, humiliated by the revelation of his complicity in the Jameson Raid, and forced to resign from his Premiership of the Cape, never showed his greatness of spirit and character to finer effect than in those terribly anxious months at the end of 1895. He flung himself heart and soul into the task of getting railway communication through to Salisbury from the east and to Bulawayo from the south. George Pauling went to see Rhodes, and told him that given a free hand he would build the 400 miles of line that separated Bulawayo from the then northernmost railhead in 400 days. Rhodes told him to go ahead, and the intrepid contractor started on his 'race' through the rough virgin country of Bechuanaland.

From Vryburg to Mafeking the line runs over the veldt, level and seemingly limitless in every direction for nearly 100 miles, and mostly at an altitude of a little over 4000 ft. It is much the same for many miles north of Mafeking and travellers making the long journey entirely by train have described in glowing terms the effect of sunset on a cloudless evening in this inexpressively quiet countryside. J. P. Pearson, for example writes:

> As the sun set in beautifully quiet fashion the veldt, with its dark bushes, as-sumed to the southwest a curious whitish-green aspect, as if the earth had been sprinkled over with salt. There was a most delicate tint of vermilion just exactly above the point where the orb of the day had disappeared, while elsewhere in the sky, floating in an amber light, were clouds tinted with dark red and heli-trope. Beyond Pitsani, the amber of the sky became richer and deeper, and was bordered, near the horizon, by small clouds of a lovely rich umber-brown colour. These latter disappeared later and the glowing light on the horizon shaded off, as one looked upward, through a red tint into the upper blue, forming a really glorious sky.

Pitsani is some 30 miles north of Mafeking, and just as the line itself runs on a generally straight course for hundreds of miles so the nature of the country changes little, and the altitude not greatly either. It makes a course north-north-eastwards along the fringe of the Kalahari desert, never far from the border of the Transvaal, until, at a point 215 miles from Mafeking it comes to a kind of a half-way house, the little township of Mahalapye. When George Pauling drove the line forward with such vigour to keep the exacting timetable he had promised to Cecil Rhodes Mahalapye scarcely existed; but with the development of the railway it gradually grew into a little railway town with some 300 Europeans at the present time. It is a coaling and watering station, and for many years was a divisional point in the traffic working. Originally the whole section between Vryburg and Bulawayo was operated by the South African Railways. Then from November 1959 the Rhodesia Railways took over the section between Bulawayo and Mahalapye, and some six years later with the Rhodesia Railways taking over the entire working as far south as Mafeking, Mahalapye ceased to be a divisional point.

South African Railways

Four '5E' class electric locomotives at Padarn Eiland depot, Cape Town. Table Mountain in background

North of Mahalapye, and particularly on nearing Seruli, the extreme flatness of the veldt begins to give place to a more wooded landscape, though it is the low scrub, seen in South Africa, rather than the woodlands of Europe. Then however even this begins to give way to thick bush, made up of a tremendous expanse of trees, so close together that one could see nothing else. Between them the single-tracked railway, running straight mile for mile, often has the appearance of a band of red stretching into the distance. The soil is as red as Devon, and it shows bare on either side of the ballasted track. When Pauling blazed the trail I have no doubt there was little ballasting as we know it today, and the road probably looked redder than it does now, when the central portion is finely ballasted with broken stone. Just before reaching Francistown the Tati river is crossed. The original bridge was recently replaced by a fine new one, and the present-day engineers like Pauling in the 1890s had to contend with the peculiarities of river flow that beset all railway engineering in a country of such climatic variations as Southern Africa. When J. P. Pearson travelled this way, in July 1910, the Tati was completely dry. At other times, and particularly at the climax of the rainy season it can sometimes be an almost uncontrollable torrent.

Beyond Francistown the whole character of the line begins to change. There is a steep ascent up from the river crossing, and the long straight stretches of line give place to much curvature as the railway makes its way through the mountain country on the Bechuanaland–Rhodesia border. The line rises 1300 ft. in the 60 miles between Francistown and Plumtree, the first station across the border. At this point the line is 420 miles from Mafeking, and another 60 miles of difficult road remain before Bulawayo is reached. Pearson's account of his journey is most vivid at this stage.

Near the 1289¾ milepost [he writes]—just before reaching Plumtree—there was just a glimpse to the right over an enormous extent of tree-clad veldt, followed closely by another view of the pyramidal hills far away on the same side. We gradually approach these, and near Coldridge in front and on our left there are low hills which, covered with trees for a certain way up their slopes, terminate in stony and rocky summits. Beyond this last mentioned station, the line suddenly enters a very curious region of most gigantic stones, arranged in mounds and poised in such peculiar positions that it seems impossible to imagine that these have not been placed there by artificial means and in such manner as

153

to create wonder by the bizarre nature of their arrangement. These mounds rise either in isolated fashion out of the tree belt or from long ridges. With the line frequently curving, many changes in the aspect of these stony formations become visible. Very large stones are often poised on small ones, while occasionally a huge boulder shaped like an egg, stands on its end above others.

Going on from Marula, [he continues] some further stone heaps of great size now came into view and just before the 1328th post, there was another collection of gigantic boulders. The afternoon—a very hot one—might be described as intensifying the inhospitable, shelterless character of these marvellous stony formations. He then describes how the hot afternoon gave place to a beautiful evening, and then darkness came on swiftly, and it was a rather fine sight, as we approached Bulawayo, to see the long lit-up train rounding the curves, with which the line here abounds.

My wife and I had the good fortune to be taken on a leisurely exploration of the amazing Matopos region by road, and Pearson's description of the formations as seen from the train are subdued, rather than exaggerated. They are quite fantastic. There was however another compelling reason for visiting the Matopos and that was to make pilgrimage to the grave of Cecil Rhodes, high in this strange hill-country with such a prospect in every direction that it has been named 'View of the World'. It was perhaps appropriate that we arrived at the base of the hill towards evening. It was still very hot; storm clouds were gathering, and there was a suggestion of thunder in the far distance. There was something wholly fitting in the rather brooding atmosphere that had developed towards the end of that day. If ever there was a 'stormy petrel' it was Cecil Rhodes, and to visit his grave on some serene, cloudless day would have rather belied the character of the man.

The line was barely thirteen years old when Pearson travelled this way, for the opening to Bulawayo took place on 4 November 1897. Rarely can a pioneer railway have been opened with such rejoicing, and with such manifestations of Imperial significance. Bulawayo lay at the northern end of 483 miles of the slenderest line of communication. Just imagine a single track, with widely spaced passing loops running through country but little removed from plain desert, with sleepers laid in the bare earth, and extending over a distance further than from London to Dundee! Yet tenuous as that line of communication not a voice was raised other than in stoutest optimism for the future. The *Bulawayo Chronicle*, in a

154

leading article headed THE NEW ERA brilliantly summarises popular sentiments of the day.

Today is the parting of the ways for Matabeleland, the relegation of the old method of transport to the past and the beginning of civilization in its entirety. Up to the present we have been living in a kind of semi-civilized state, at times cut off from our fellows, isolated from the seething world outside, but that phase of our history ends when the High Commissioner declares today that the Capetown–Bulawayo railway is open. We remember with what joy we saw the thin iron wire enter Salisbury, and we thought what a link it was with the struggling centres, but the locomotive is a far stronger chain than the telegraph. What differences the railway will make in our life it is difficult to surmise, but that it will make a vast change we are certain. The happy-go-lucky methods, so common in new towns and indeed so necessary in the early days of a settlement will no longer be possible, for we shall have keen business men amongst us, men who are not accustomed, and have no stomach for the pioneering, yet who are quite ready to reap the fruits of the work done by those who bore the heat and burden of the day. In many hearts there will be feelings of regret that the old order of things is passing away, and this regret will be found among the men who have led England's advance into the heart of the Dark Continent and who now realise that they are not suited to the polished life of the town connected by railway with the coast. . . .

We enter the new era with festivities, but we are also called upon to execute the promises we shall make today. Speechifying is not sufficient, though some of our local orators will grow eloquent, but good solid work is to be the watchword of the future.

Speeches there certainly were, and many pages of the *Bulawayo Chronicle* of 11 November 1897 were taken up with verbatim reports. The opening ceremony was performed by Sir Alfred Milner, Governor and Commander in Chief of the Colony of the Cape of Good Hope, and Her Majesty's High Commissioner for South Africa. The scene at the station is vividly described thus:

From an early hour a stream of horsemen and cyclists and pedestrians and vehicles of all sorts was passing to and fro between the town and the temporary buildings at the station, all of which were gay with colour. Just before the opening hour the largest concourse of white people that has ever assembled in Rhodesia was gathered around the roped-in enclosure within which the opening ceremony was to take place. The pavilion in the centre of the enclosure was the

Chef d'œuvre of the decorations. A dais under its roof for His Excellency the High Commissioner was adorned with a handsome canopy, on which the Royal Arms were conspicuous. At one end of the interior of the building was the motto: 'Our two roads to progress; railroads and Cecil Rhodes.' In appropriate portions of the building were shields, bearing the arms of all the South African states and colonies, and the entire pavilion was profusely decorated with drapery of various colours. The telegraph poles, surrounding the enclosure, resembled huge sticks of confectionery, and gay festoons were garlanded between them. Altogether the scene with its brilliant colours, amongst which were many ladies, and the long passenger trains, drawn up close by, made it a picture unique in our history, and one which will not soon be forgotten by those who witnessed it.

The first special train arrived at seven o'clock in the morning, bringing 96 passengers chiefly from Port Elizabeth and East London. The second train came direct from Kimberley, arriving at 7.35 a.m. and conveying 60 passengers. Like the first train it was composed of handsome saloon carriages, and included the celebrated De Beers' coach. This second train carried many Very Important People, including the Bishop of Bloemfontein, the directors and chief officers of the De Beers company, the secretary of the Chartered Company, and certain distinguished newspaper correspondents from the United Kingdom. It was however significant of the haste with which the line had been completed that the third and fourth special trains were so delayed by a derailment that they arrived many hours after the opening ceremony had been concluded. It was the third train that got into trouble when the tender of its engine became derailed three miles to the south of Figtree. This train was conveying guests from Cape Town, Graaff Reinet, and Grahamstown, while the fourth train, which of course was held up further down the line, was conveying guests who had travelled specially from England. When it was clear that the delay due to the derailment was to be a lengthy one it was decided to proceed with the opening ceremony according to schedule, and Sir Alfred Milner duly declared the line open, shortly after noon. The first of the belated trains did not arrive until 3 p.m.

The immense importance attached to the completion of the railway was emphasised in one passage of Sir Alfred Milner's reply to the address of welcome that had been presented to him. Sir Alfred said:

I feel proud to have had the privilege of being here on this auspicious occasion. It is a great day in the history of Bulawayo. It is a great day in the history

156

of South Africa and of the Empire. The importance of it is testified by the presence here of large numbers of visitors not only from all parts of South Africa, but from the Mother Country, but the business, which is first in our proceedings here today, is not confined to being shared by those numerous representatives of South Africa and other countries. It is shared by hundreds of thousands who are watching our proceedings at a distance . . . .

Sir Alfred was of course speaking metaphorically here, though prophetically enough of how such functions are now 'covered' by world-wide television networks. He continued:

The best proof of that fact is that I have been asked to communicate to you a message from Home, a message from one, who by virtue of his official position, speaks for the British Nation on this occasion. [Cries of 'Joe'] and whose high official position gives this message weight. I mean the Secretary of State for the Colonies. [Loud and repeated cheers] The message from Mr. Chamberlain is: 'At the opening of the railway at Bulawayo please say from me, that I am anxious to send a very hearty message to the settlers who are gathered together to celebrate the completion of the railway. I have felt much sympathy in the troubles they have so manfully faced in the past, and it is a source of gratification to think better times are in store for them. I congratulate the inhabitants of Rhodesia, on the rapid and successful completion of the railway to the north, which will afford aid and stimulus to every form of enterprise, and will join north and south together.'

At the conclusion of Sir Alfred Milner's speech the newspaper records that: 'Three stirring cheers were then given for Mr. Rhodes, and three for Capt. Lawley (the Deputy Administrator) and a like number for His Excellency, followed by a further round for Mr. Pauling, the contractor.'

There was nevertheless a certain poignancy in the fact that Cecil Rhodes himself was not present; but the political implications of the disastrous Jameson Raid still clouded a great deal of his public life, and although there were many glowing references to him in the speeches that marked the many functions held in Bulawayo that week—and each reference was immediately greeted with outbursts of the most enthusiastic cheering—one could understand something of why he was not there in person.

Of the railway itself, the newspaper had a somewhat significant item, dated Tuesday 9 November under the heading HAVE PATIENCE:

The accident that occurred on the Railway early on Sunday morning is an object lesson and will serve a good purpose if it brings to the minds of our

157

visitors that all our troubles are not yet over, and that they must not expect too much from us just yet. We have not a London and North Western, or a Midland Railway to work with, but a line which is faulty in many respects owing to the rapidity with which it has been constructed. There is much to be done to it before it can be made a permanent railway. Bridges have to be built, gradients and curves altered and points rectified before the locomotive will run with the smoothness and regularity which are the pride of the English General Manager. Such a consummation could not be expected at this early date, and when the visitors take all the obstacles into consideration it will seem remarkable that the line was constructed at all through miles of country without water or food for man or beast. Water for the engines had to be dragged hundreds of miles, and when Mr. Pauling suggested the speedy completion of the railway many people thought the proposition an incredible one, on account of the country which had to be passed through. Still Pauling Bros. were as good, or rather better than their word and had the line laid before the time they specified.

Despite the sobering effect of carefully worded articles such as the above it was a time of boundless optimism and belief that a gold reef of fabulous extent was waiting to be tapped as surely as was concurrently being done in the Transvaal. Colonel Saunderson who represented the British House of Commons at the various festivities fairly let himself go at the farewell banquet on 10 November. Asked what he would say on return to England he went on, concerning Rhodesia:

They had everything that tended to build up a great people. They had the wealth of the country, they had a magnificent soil, and undoubtedly they had an immense supply of gold, and besides that—and he looked upon this as a most important factor in the prosperity of the country—they were about to make a railway from here to the Victoria Falls, to open up perhaps the greatest coalfields in the whole of Africa. . . .

After much in the vein of ardent Imperialism he added:

They had an Englishman making a railway on the Nile; they had an Englishman building a railway to Bulawayo. He would like to know what force on earth could prevent the two joining hands!

Such was the spirit of the hour, and we can understand the pride and enthusiasm that underlay it; but within two years other circumstances had eventuated in war with the South African Republic, and within a very few weeks of the opening of hostilities Colonel Baden-Powell's

Rhodesian Regiment, as it was called, was besieged in Mafeking, and railway communication between Rhodesia and the Cape was severed. While Baden-Powell's defence of Mafeking for many months of war is one of the epics of British military history the railway to the south remained virtually useless, and it was then that the then unfinished line from Beira to Salisbury assumed the utmost importance. At the outbreak of war the line from Beira to Umtali was only 2 ft. gauge, while the 3 ft. 6 in. gauge line onwards to Salisbury had been opened as recently as May 1899. But to such a man as George Pauling and to his indomitable resident engineer at the Beira end, A. L. Lawley, difficulties like this were a challenge, and how between them they got the men, the horses, and the guns of the force that eventually relieved Mafeking, from Beira to Salisbury and then down the line from Bulawayo, was an epic in itself— not to mention the road transport between Salisbury and Bulawayo! It was not until December 1902 that the railway between the twin cities was established. Despite war conditions Lawley had the Beira–Umtali section converted to 3 ft. 6 in., by August 1900.

I have referred earlier to the appalling climatic conditions under which the labour force worked on the Beira–Umtali section. In his autobiography *Chronicles of a Contractor* George Pauling tells of other hazards:

During the early period of the construction of the Beira Railway, the quantity of game on the Pungue Flats was enormous. It included thousands of buffaloes, zebras, water buck, hartebeeste, wildbeeste, and practically all other kinds of South African game. On one occasion, when Lawley, Mr. Moore, who was the Company's engineer, and I were going back from the Muda River ballast hole to Fontesvilla, the road was in a bad condition and the engine had left the rails three or four times in a distance of a few miles. It behoved us, therefore, to travel very slowly and with extreme caution. There was one truck beyond the engine in which we three were accommodated. We were creeping along at about four miles an hour, taking no particular heed of our surroundings, when suddenly the engine driver discovered ahead a herd of lions, lionesses, and cubs, resting in the side cutting which ran alongside the railway bank. It was an awe-inspiring sight, and the driver was for a moment nonplussed. He knew that he dare not increase speed and run the risk of another derailment. There was not a gun on the train. Few men are valiant in the immediate presence of wild lions, and we three 'passengers' deemed it expedient to scramble out of the truck and on to the side of the engine away from the herd. With a view to making as much noise as possible the driver opened

159

his whistle and cylinder cocks and commenced to creep past the place where the lions were resting. The noise was too much for them, for they all bolted with the exception of one stately old lioness, who stood her ground, and snarled at us as we passed. Had we remained in the truck it is not improbable that she would have made a jump at one of us, but she funked the engine and its steam and noise. Having reached a position of security we counted in all thirty-two lions, lionesses and cubs.

The Muda River was also infested with lions. We had a water tank there for supplying engines, and on one occasion when the pump got out of order we sent up a European fitter from Fontesvilla to repair it. There were only natives pumping and they had built for themselves what is called a scherm, and were accustomed to keep a big fire going in front of it to ward off lions. The fitter was unable to complete his work in one day and, as there was no place for him to sleep in, he got the natives to build him a little pondok, a kind of shelter shaped like a 'V' upside down, with some grass in it for him to lie on. He was a very tall man, so much so that when he lay down his feet protruded from the end of the pondok. During the night he was awakened by something tugging at his foot. He had not taken his boots off, but, luckily, had unlaced them. He let off such a yell that the natives were aroused and they saw that a lion had got hold of him and was trying to pull him out of the pondok. The boys, however, pluckily seized hold of a lot of firebrands and attacked the lion, who made off, taking with him the fitter's boot and part of his heel, which the animal had lacerated with his claws. If his boots had been done up the probability is that he would have lost his life.

I myself had a narrow escape from running over a lion. One morning I left my hut at Chimoio to travel along the line, on a trolley pushed by four boys. At one stage we were going along merrily downhill, all riding on the trolley, when without any warning the boys jumped off, got hold of the trolley and brought us to a standstill. About twenty yards ahead I saw a big lion coming out of the long grass. Quick as lightning I leapt off the trolley, and did my best to secrete my somewhat corpulent figure partly behind, and partly underneath it. The lion, however, after gazing at us for a moment or two in supercilious fashion, evidently concluded that we were unworthy of his attention, or at least would make but an indifferent repast, for he walked across the railway into the long grass on the other side and disappeared. The natives had seen the grass moving and knew it was a lion or some other big animal. If they had not stopped the trolley we should have pitched right into the lion, which would have been bad for either the lion or for the occupants of the trolley.

I resumed my journey and came to a water tank beside which there lived a couple of white men and some natives, employed in keeping the permanent

PLATE 31. Bush Country

(*above*) Rhodesia Railways: diesel-hauled freight for Salisbury near Umtali

(*below*) Kenya–Uganda Railways: a spiral location on the Mombasa–Nairobi main line

South African Railways: '16C' class Pacific of 1919–22 vintage

PLATE 32. Locomotive Miscellany

South Africa Railways: the 'MJ' 2-6-6-0 compound Mallet bank engine of 1917

Kenya–Uganda Railway: the large 2-8-2 class of 1928 built by Robert Stephenson and Co.

Benguela Railway: wood-burning 4-8-0 of 1923

way in order and providing water for the engines. I arrived there about seven in the morning, and was surprised to find nobody about. I therefore shouted, and in response one of the white men emerged timidly from the tent. I spoke severely to him, because the man ought to have been at his work at daybreak. Then I noticed the Kafirs beginning to descend from the water tank. I asked what it meant. It appeared that the noise of my trolley and the shouting of my boys had driven away two lions which had been besieging the men in the tent, and the Kafirs had escaped into the tank to get out of the way. The white men showed me where one of the lions had been sweeping under the tent with one of his paws, trying to reach them. They had been dodging from one part of the tent to another to avoid the lion's claws. The marks were quite plain on the floor of the tent, so I refrained from reprimanding these men for not being at their work as early as they ought to have been under normal conditions.

CHAPTER FIFTEEN

Cape to Cairo line:
Victoria Falls Bridge and the line north

Cecil Rhodes was an extraordinary mixture. There was no more ardent or devoted protagonist of the cause of nineteenth century British imperialism; in hard commerce and political opportunism he had no equal, and yet withal he was a deep sentimentalist. All these characteristics are epitomised in the great single-line railway that runs north from Bulawayo —a major link in the Cape to Cairo project; and not many miles to the north of the vast Wankie coalfield the line built by George Pauling came to the gorge of the River Zambesi. It is remarkable to recall that the Falls, one of nature's greatest wonders of the world, were unknown to civilisation until 1855, when David Livingstone recorded his first impressions: 'creeping with awe to the verge I peered down into a large rent which had been made from bank to bank of the broad Zambesi'. Sixty years later, almost to the day, the first train crossed the gorge.

Rhodes himself never saw the Victoria Falls, but his vivid imagination seized upon the desirability of including so stupendous a spectacle of nature in the route of the Cape to Cairo Railway, and he stipulated that the line should cross the gorge of the Zambesi not only near enough for passengers to see the Falls, but near enough for the trains to be wetted by the spray. Little more than the preliminaries had been arranged when the Boer War broke out and Rhodes himself, through his impetuosity, had travelled to Kimberley and found himself immobilised there for much of the war, during the prolonged siege of that town. It was typical of the enterprise and determination of Rhodes's followers that the surveys for the Victoria Falls bridge continued throughout the war. George Pauling was building the railway northwards from Bulawayo, and although construction was much delayed, his determination saw to it

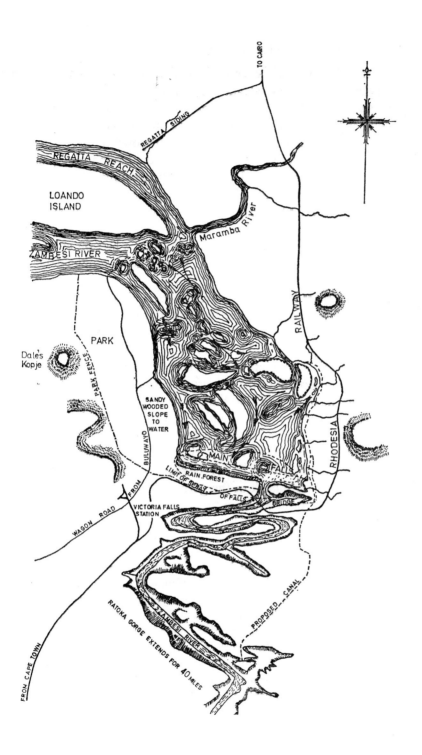

TO CAIRO

REGATTA SIDING

REGATTA REACH

LOANDO
ISLAND

Maramba River

ZAMBESI RIVER

RAILWAY

PARK

Dale's
Kopje

PARK FENCE

SANDY
WOODED
SLOPE
TO
WATER

RHODESIA

MAIN FALLS

RAIN FOREST

LIMIT OF SPRAY

FROM BULUWAYO

OF FALLS

BRIDGE

WAGON ROAD

VICTORIA FALLS
STATION

PROPOSED CANAL

FROM CAPE TOWN

ZAMBESI RIVER

BATOKA GORGE EXTENDS FOR 40 MILES

that communication was never entirely cut off, and in 1901 when the siege of Kimberley was raised, and Rhodes was released, the surveys were sufficiently complete for definite proposals to be laid before him. This was done at his office in London. He was shown sketches of what the bridge would look like, and where it was proposed to cross the gorge. This gave his desired views of the Falls from the passing trains, and certainly came near enough to catch the spray. The accompanying sketch map shows how ingeniously the railway was engineered to do this, though at the same time the site chosen was an eminently practical engineering solution. The gorge extended for 40 miles down-stream from the Falls, and the place selected for the bridge was probably the best on every count. It afforded the minimum distance to be spanned, combined with the soundest foothold obtainable.

One of the most interesting technical descriptions of the bridge was given in a Paper presented to the Institution of Civil Engineers in 1905, by its designer, George Andrew Hobson, a partner in the then-celebrated firm of Civil Engineers, Sir Douglas Fox and Partners; and he gave not only a very detailed description of the engineering features of the bridge but a fascinating account of the conditions prevailing during its construction. The profile of the gorge at the bridge is spectacular, to say the least of it. The width at the top is roughly 650 ft., and the depth from the general level of the ground to water level below is about 400 ft. During flood conditions the water level can rise about 50 ft. above the normal but at such a depth below the line of the railway as not to affect the bridge in any way. The north bank of the gorge, of solid erupted rock, mostly basalt, is almost vertical, while on the south bank there is a shelf, roughly half way up.

Hobson writes:

The rock being very hard, the bridge was designed to fit the profile of the gorge with as little expenditure on excavation as possible; and it would have done so, but for a mistake made by the surveyor in concluding that the rock on both sides was solid. The mistake was perhaps excusable, and was not discovered until the vegetation which thrives in the hot sun and the spray from the falls had been removed, and the work of clearing the ground and the excavation of the rock had proceeded for some time. It was then found that the shelf on the right bank on which it was intended to rest one end of the principal span was covered to a considerable depth with debris. By the time the error had been

164

PLATE 33. Rhodesian Country Stations

(*above*) Norton, near Salisbury

(*below*) Makwiro: Salisbury–Bulawayo line

PLATE 34. Victoria Falls Bridge

The graceful arch

Close-up of the steelwork

discovered, the preparation of the steelwork was too far advanced to permit of any alteration being made in the structure. The difficulty had therefore to be overcome partly by increasing the depth of the concrete foundations, and partly by lowering the level of the entire bridge to the extent of 21 ft.; but both time and money would have been saved had the true facts of the case been recognised at the beginning, the span designed 25 feet longer, and the truss increased in depth at the ends by 20 ft.

Despite the remote and dramatic geographical situation of the great gorge there was no difficulty in deciding upon the type of bridge to be adopted. What is known as a two-hinged spandrel-braced arch was ideal for the situation. It would provide a very handsome bridge, of great rigidity, and was without doubt the most economical design. Furthermore, in a situation where erection was likely to be a major problem, the braced-arch was the simplest that could be devised. It was designed to spring from the rock-walls of the gorge, and to be erected cantilever-wise, member by member, from both sides of the gorge simultaneously. The erection could be done without the necessity of any scaffolding. At the time the design was under consideration all civil engineers concerned with bridges were much exercised with problems of wind pressure, following the revelations of ignorance in this respect in the report of the enquiry into the terrible disaster of the first Tay Bridge, in 1879. The vicinity of the Victoria Falls bridge is not subjected to any extreme winds, and the stresses allowed did not require to be exceptionally high. Of more concern was the variation in temperature, represented by the extreme cold of the African nights in contrast to the maximum day temperatures in summer; and a variation of no less than 60° F. above and below the mean was allowed for. Very ample provision was made for carrying the loads of heavy trains, and Hobson's remit specified a train on each of the two tracks over the bridge, each train double-headed with a total length of motive power of 100 ft. and a uniform weight of $1\frac{3}{4}$ tons per foot. The train following the locomotives was specified as weighing 1.33 tons per foot. This farsighted provision has rendered the bridge capable of carrying the huge Beyer-Garratt engines of today, which have an overall weight of 150 tons.

As designed the centre span of the bridge is 500 ft. long, and together with the short approach girders weighed approximately 1500 tons. The maximum train weight originally provided for was 1820 tons. Of this

165

total weight of 3320 tons only about 280 tons is borne by the outer ends of the 'shore' spans. More than 3000 tons is borne by the four bearings of the principal span. To this load, of dead weight of steelwork, and maximum weight of trains must be added that which arises from variations of temperature, and also from wind pressure, and in all, the calculated 'thrust' which passes through each of the four hinged bearings is about 1600 tons. The design of the bearings was indeed a vital part of the work, and it is very interesting to see how the tragic failure of certain parts of the old Tay Bridge had, unconsciously perhaps, influenced design in this case. In the former case bad design of cast members and atrociously bad workmanship were major factors in leading to the collapse of the bridge. Hobson writes:

The thrust through each bearing being the considerable one of 1600 tons, something of a substantial nature and thoroughly reliable in every way had to be devised. It will be conceived that this purpose could be readily effected by means of a casting, which, indeed, is the method usually adopted. It was felt, however, that the present case was not one in which to run any risk of failure through defective castings; nor was there any necessity to do so. Notwithstanding the great strides which have taken place in steel-foundry practice, there are still risks, if not of honeycombing, then of unequal contraction, and the setting-up of unknown internal stresses in the casting of steel from entirely new patterns. Moreover, the units of construction in this case had to be of a weight convenient not only for transportation to the site but more especially in respect of handling and lowering into positions very difficult of access. A heavy casting was on this account undesirable.

The bearings were in fact formed of steel forgings, contained in a very massive fabricated steel assembly.

Tenders for the construction of the steelwork and its erection on site were invited from a number of leading British, American, and German firms, but the majority were not prepared to quote for more than the first part of the contract. The hazards of erection at the gorge of the Zambesi were certainly daunting to all except the most resolute. In the end only two firms were left. George Pauling who had built the railway was most anxious to get the job, particularly as he had secured the contract for the continuation of the line northwards to the Congo border. But despite all the experience he had gained in the construction of railways in Africa the price he put in was higher than that of the Cleveland

Bridge and Engineering Company, of Darlington, and to the latter firm both parts of the contract were let in May 1903. At that time the railway from Bulawayo had not reached the Falls, and it did not do so until May 1904. It was not until the latter date that delivery of material to the site could begin.

In the meantime arrangements were in progress in England for manufacture of the steelwork, and in the contractor's yard at Darlington, beside the main line of the then North Eastern Railway, passengers by the passing trains saw the bridge beginning to take shape. Many famous bridges have been 'erected' there. In the 1930s I remember vividly the erection of the great Howrah Bridge over the Ganges, and the remarkable 'creeper' cranes used in the work. The actual work of building out the cantilevers of the Victoria Falls bridge in 1903-4 created intense interest, in view of the aura of romance that surrounded this last great project of Cecil Rhodes's adventurous life. He died in 1902, before even the contract was let; otherwise one can be sure he would have insisted on seeing the bridge, perhaps to be taken across it and feel the spray of the Falls even on his death-bed, as Brunel was, across the Royal Albert Bridge at Saltash. The Victoria Falls bridge was one of the first, if not the very first in which the accuracy and completeness of the work done in the bridge-yard was checked by erection on the contractor's premises. It was so effectively done that troubles which would otherwise have been caused at the site were entirely eliminated. When the steelwork was erected across the gorge of the River Zambesi, all the members met accurately together.

It is nevertheless one thing to survey such a site, and then to design a bridge of beauty and technical excellence, but quite another to erect it in a remote part of the world that had been known to white men for little more than fifty years. Little was known for certainty about living conditions, save that there was a strong suspicion of tropical unhealthiness, while the fact that the whole area of the Falls had been shunned by the native population only increased the hazards that any contractor would have to face. It is true that the cantilever principle afforded by far the most efficient method of construction—once the parts for one half of the bridge had been conveyed across that mighty gorge. How was some 750 tons of steelwork to be got across? Three or four miles upstream from the Falls the river was passable, by small boats; but the prospect of conveying all the heavy girders across by this method was dismissed as

167

altogether too costly and tedious. Apart from this, considerable danger to life would have been incurred, because at that time the river was infested with crocodiles and hippopotamuses!

Before even the tenders were invited consultations between the railway authorities and the consulting engineers determined that a massive transporter cable should be thrown across the gorge at the site. The railway company undertook to do this, and moreover to install a cable of such capacity that not only the materials for the bridge, but rails, sleepers and even locomotives for the continuation of the line north of the bridge could be transported. Such was the drive and enthusiasm being put into the extension of the line that it was desired to have a considerable further mileage open for traffic the moment the bridge was completed. Provision was made for conveying across the gorge enough material to lay one mile of track per day on the far side. The capacity of the cable-way was fixed at 10 tons. The conception was regarded with a good deal of suspicion, particularly in respect of the travelling cradle. This was, in effect an overhead travelling crane in which the crane, instead of travelling on rails fixed high along the walls of a workshop, ran on a wire rope. The driver sat in the travelling cab, from which, with electric controls, he regulated the lifting, lowering and travelling movements. The sceptics averred that no man, even for high wages, could be induced to drive the carriage, and to travel backwards and forwards across that tremendous gorge all day long. As it turned out the job proved very popular, and there were always plenty of applicants.

A contractor for the supply and erection of the cableway having been obtained, there was next a question of getting the cable across. The material arrived at the south bank in June 1904, and the first step was to fire a rocket across. To this was attached a small cord, and with this a wire was hauled across. This in turn was used for hauling a small cable, and by this, gradually increasing the strength of the 'wire' across the gorge, sufficient capacity was then available to haul across a small improvised carrier, on which it was possible to transport small items of machinery including a powerful winch. The equipment was now in readiness for hauling the main cable across. This was attached to the 'improvised' carrier, and successfully launched, so much so that in less than two months from the arrival of the material on site the complete cableway with its permanent carrier was installed and in working order. Although there

168

were many incidental troubles in the working of the cable-way the erection of the main steelwork of the bridge went ahead rapidly. A safety net was provided underneath the points where erection was proceeding, but actually no man fell at any time during the erection work. In the contrary way of human nature, the net which was installed for the safety of the workmen, to give them confidence, was objected to, because it made them feel nervous!

Although the whole process of erection had been carefully 'progressed', providing for the arrival at the site of successive loads of steelwork to synchronise with the actual assembly of the members, the work of construction went so smoothly and so rapidly that there were times when the erectors were drawing ahead of their schedule. One interesting feature of the design, which greatly speeded up the work of erection was the use of pins, at the joints of the main members. As each came into place pins were immediately inserted, and erection proceeded further leaving the riveting to be done afterwards. The work of connecting the members could thus proceed some distance in advance of the riveting. It had been hoped to get most of the work done in the dry season of 1904; but because of initial delays a start was not made until October. It continued nevertheless throughout the rainy season, with no interruption during the worst rains of March and April 1905. Then, of course, there was the spray, specified by Cecil Rhodes! In the rainy seasons the columns of spray rise to 3000 ft., but its effect, as Hobson dryly comments, is no worse than rain in Scotland and for five months in the year it does not touch the bridge at all. The heaviest months for the spray are March, April, and May.

Throughout the rainy season the cantilever arms had been extending uniformly from either side of the gorge, and on 1 April 1905, they met in mid-air, and the linking up was made with complete precision. The surveys and design, and manufacture of the members was a triumph of accuracy, that represented a complete abnegation, in Rhodesia at any rate, of the sentiments usually associated with the date on which junction was made. As finished the bridge blends harmoniously with the surroundings, and has added a wonder of engineering to the wonder of nature in the Falls themselves. The construction of the bridge achieved a remarkable sociological change in the district. Hitherto there were no natives living within 60 miles of the Falls, owing to a superstitious dread of the entire locality. Before the bridge was finished a large number of natives were

169

at work on the bridge, painting. There can indeed rarely have been a great engineering work executed with so little in the way of casualties. There were no fatalities at all from fever, sickness, or accident, though two men died in a culpable manner quite unconnected with the nature of the work or the locality. The bridge was officially opened on 12 September 1905.

In the discussion on Mr. Hobson's paper, at the Institution of Civil Engineers several speakers referred to the analogy of the bridge over the Niagara Falls, and asked if consideration had been given at any time to providing a roadway as well as a railway. The author's reply was illuminating:

The provision of a roadway would have added considerably to the weight and cost of the structure. Nor was it desirable, from the railway company's point of view, to provide a roadway: on the contrary, it was to their interest not to allow it. The traffic was mostly long-distance traffic—the local business was practically negligible—and all could be well served by the railway. This great work had been constructed at vast expense, and it would have been foolish to afford facilities to trekkers in a region where control was impossible, or at least prohibitive in cost.

No more than a timber walk-way was provided between the tracks and the parapets of the bridge. This gave rise to some unexpected troubles, for while very careful thought was given to preserving the timber from the rain and spray, and to shield it from the sun, and damage from engine cinders and sparks, the fierce heat of the sun during the winter months distilled creosote covering and allowed the special protective coating to be eroded away. Instructions were given to engine drivers to avoid raking fires, or emitting sparks as far as possible when crossing the bridge, and to ensure there was no damage due to fires a watchman was stationed to examine the bridge after the passage of each train.

This was no more than a temporary expedient, and in any case could not be applied at night. The whole neighbourhood was infested with lions, leopards and many kinds of wild cat, and the bridge had not been open long before these animals found that the timber deck of the walkway provided an excellent way of exploring new pastures, and it was not surprising that no watchman could be persuaded to stay near the bridge alone after dark! As to the natives in general, Hobson remarks:

170

The African native was superstitious and did not usually take risks if he could avoid them, but let the white man give him a lead, and he would go anywhere and attempt almost anything. All the innovations introduced by civilization were to him but the white man's magic, and he accepted the marvels of science and art with calmness and resignation. Some of those employed had come from remote parts of the interior and were quite wild, others were from Nyassa and from the southern colonies and were trained in various degrees. As many as 400 had been employed at one period and the average number was about 200. In addition to assisting skilled whites, of whom about 30 had been employed in erecting steelwork, they had done good service in excavating rock and in painting. Being imitative and patient they became skilful and reliable painters, capable of working in highly dangerous positions and in a very thorough manner. The natives had done no actual rivetting, but all the heating and passing of the rivets had been done by them.

Since the original construction of the bridge the wheel has come full circle, and in the early 1930s, when it had become necessary to renew the decking the provisions were completely changed. Railway traffic did not warrant more than a single track, and so in renewing the decking the layout was altered to provide a full-width highway alongside the single tracked railway. The original contractors, the Cleveland Bridge and Engineering Company, of Darlington were awarded the contract for this new work, and through their courtesy I am able to include some photographs taken while the changeover work was in progress. Now, of course, the famous bridge forms a frontier post between Rhodesia and Zambia. The bridge itself is in the 'no-man's land' between the actual frontier posts on the highway.

It was an afternoon of sweltering heat when my wife and I visited the Victoria Falls. A motor trolley took us down the line from the station to the centre of the bridge, which now marks the international frontier between Rhodesia and Zambia, and from there we saw the Falls, as Cecil Rhodes had stipulated that every traveller should do. After an exceptionally dry winter the volume of water was at a minimum, and the cloud of spray rising from the stupendous cataract did not come anywhere near the railway; but it enabled us to see the Falls themselves to the best advantage. Never surely in the vicinity of a great spectacle has human planning been made to greater effect; for just as the Falls themselves are splendidly seen from a passing train, so the bridge is in the very centre

171

of the majestic picture seen from the gardens and the terrace of the
Victoria Falls Hotel. For some years now, of course, the significance of
the railway and the bridge has been lost on modern tourists, who mostly
come to the Falls by air; but as a freight link of the first importance the
bridge is as vital as ever. Before going out to the bridge on that motor
trolley we had awaited the departure of a northbound goods trains of
some 1700 tons, drawn by one of the huge 20th Class Beyer–Garratt
locomotives.

PLATE 35. Victoria Falls Bridge Modernising

Freight train passing over temporary staging

End view of bridge showing widening in progress

'14A' class 2–6–2 + 2–6–2 for light branch work

The heavy mineral 20th class 4–8–2 + 2–8–4

The express passenger 15th class 4–6–4 + 4–6–4

PLATE 36. Rhodesian Garratts

CHAPTER SIXTEEN

Rhodesian locomotive and train working

The Rhodesia railways of today, in all their constituents, are an outcome of British enterprise originating from the Cape of Good Hope. The ambitions of Cecil Rhodes, and all that those ambitions came eventually to involve run like a continuous thread through chapter after chapter of this book; and it is no more than natural that in the continuation of the Cape Government line through Bechuanaland, and in the enterprising of further railways in Rhodesia itself, that the fledgling administrations in the north should have drawn upon the technical experience and strength of Cape Town. Advice and practical help were freely given, and the Cape locomotives working up through Bechuanaland and maintaining the exiguous first train service between Mafeking and Bulawayo formed the starting point of Rhodesia's own notable locomotive development. At first reliance was placed almost entirely upon locomotives of Cape design, and in 1901 an order was placed with the North British Locomotive Company for twenty 4–8–0s of the Cape Class 7, examples of which were among the old engines still in service that I saw in 1968 at Padarn Eiland, Cape Town. The design dates back to 1892, but it gave outstanding service on the heavy grades of the Cape main line, and it was ideal for the early days of the Rhodesia Railways. The very first locomotive to enter Rhodesia from the south in 1897 was of this class, and a number of them were taken over from the Cape railway to work the Vryburg–Bulawayo line. The last engine of this historic class to remain at work in Rhodesia was No. 43, which was retired from active duty as a shunting engine in Bulawayo Works in August 1964. This engine has now been restored, as near as possible to its original condition, and forms one of the important items scheduled for preservation and inclusion in the Rhodesia Railways museum. Engine No. 43 commenced service on the line in 1904, and thus had an active life of no less than sixty years. The success of the '7' class was as great in Rhodesia as it was in the Cape of Good Hope, and the extreme simplicity of the design was in contrast to some other locomotives purchased from the United Kingdom at about the same time. In mentioning the two engines of the articulated Kitson–Meyer type put into service in 1903 however it is interesting to appreciate that the Rhodesia Railways were very early in the field of articulated locomotives, in view of the extensive use of the Beyer–Garratt type in later years. The Kitson–Meyers were of the 0–6–0+0–6–0 wheel arrangement, and were compounds. The type is basically a tank engine version of the well-known Mallet; but these two Rhodesian examples were so heavy on coal that the bunker at the rear of the cab was totally inadequate, and the engines were soon working with a double bogie tender coupled in rear to provide an extra 4 or 5 tons of coal!

This auxiliary fuel supply did not exactly endear them to the footplate men, when presumably the coal had to be humped from the tender into the bunker before it could be fired. As if this were not enough, the cabs were very enclosed, and got insufferably hot. To crown all, the engines were poor runners, extremely sluggish, and not too steady when they did begin to make some speed. It was hardly surprising that these two engines had a life of barely nine years—a very striking contrast to the splendid longevity of the orthodox Class 7 4–8–0s. Usually it is the boiler that determines the fate of a locomotive, whether it shall be rebuilt, renewed or otherwise repaired—or scrapped. But with the Kitson–Meyers, long before the boilers were worn out the locomotives themselves had been marked down as complete failures, and the boiler of one of them was installed at the laundry of the Victoria Falls Hotel, and as such put in some years of useful service. The result of this experience led to an edict banning the use of articulated locomotives, and while other railways tried Fairlies, Mallets, and some of the earliest Garratts, the Rhodesian Railways stuck resolutely to the orthodox tender types: 4–8–0s, and later 4–8–2s. Of course the speeds were low by any standards, but speed was a secondary consideration. It is the simple fact of having a railway at all that began to revolutionise the social and economic life of Rhodesia.

Engine numbers are not necessarily an indication of the total locomotive stock of a railway; but at the time of their introduction the two Kitson–Meyer engines, Nos. 51 and 52, were actually the fifty-first and fifty-second locomotives to take the road in Rhodesia, just as the preserved 4-8-0 No. 43, was the forty-third. At that time locomotives were rather thin on the ground. By the end of the year 1904 although the line was not opened beyond the Victoria Falls there was, nevertheless, a considerable route mileage of 750 in operation in Rhodesia itself, plus the 203 miles through Portuguese East Africa from Umtali to Beira, for which the Rhodesia administration provided the motive power. From 1900, indeed, the line through from Beira to Salisbury had been combined under the single management of the Beira and Mashonaland Railway (B.M.R.) In those early days, also, Umtali was the headquarters of the system, and the site of the principal workshops for repair and maintenance of the loco-motive stock. So far as actual running was concerned I once read that the 7th class 'was capable of hauling a passenger train at a speed considered quite exceptional in those days.' I can only think that such a statement should have been qualified by addition of the words 'in Rhodesia', be-cause by the summer of 1904 in England the Great Western Railway had made its ever-famous 'record of records' with the Ocean Mail special of 9 May, when the *City of Truro* attained a speed of 100 m.p.h., and the *Duke of Connaught* covered 70.3 miles between Shrivenham and West-bourne Park at an average speed of 80.2 m.p.h. This is not to 'play down' the historic record of the 7th class engines in Rhodesia, which in any case lasted far longer than the spectacular express designs of contemporary vintage on the Great Western Railway.

The Rhodesia Railways certainly had their money's worth out of the 7th class 4-8-0s. The purchase price of these engines was £3153, and by the end of September 1938, after nearly forty years in traffic the preserved engine, No. 43, was valued at £1. Whether any enthusiast prepared to remove her at his own expense could have had her for a pound note is another matter! At that time, of course, the demise of steam was not even on the horizon, and in England at any rate railway relics were going at 'two a penny'. Reverting to the 7th class, however, what with those pur-chased from the Cape Government Railways and those built new by the North British Locomotive Company, the Rhodesia Railways had even-tually a stud of 60 of these engines. So successful and reliable was the 4-8-0 type in general that no other was used for main-line work until the year 1913. The locomotives added to the stock during the intervening years were generally similar to the 7th class, but with larger boilers. These latter were known as the 8th class, and in relation to the severe gradients on many parts of the line the scheduled maximum loads were quite heavy for that period. In recalling these tonnages I should explain that a 'mail' train was one consisting exclusively of passenger vehicles. A 'mixed' train included both passenger and goods vehicles, but the latter were all fitted with the vacuum automatic brake so that there were no complexities in handling on account of the 'mixed' load. The tonnages for the 7th and 8th class 4–8–0s were:

Class	Mail	Mixed	Goods
7th	270	372	480
8th	350	480	620

The train working can be considered in five distinct areas:
1. Portuguese section: Beira to Umtali.
2. Umtali to Salisbury.
3. The heavily worked Salisbury–Bulawayo main line.
4. The Bechuanaland line: Mafeking to Bulawayo.
5. The North Line, Bulawayo-Victoria Falls-Congo border.

Until the year 1949 the whole line between Beira and Salisbury was worked as one, with engine changing at Umtali. Although the first 61 miles from Beira, through the tropical jungle of the coastal belt, are fairly easy from the gradient point of view, there is a tremendous ascent from Vilo Machado, climbing for nearly 50 miles to the top of the escarpment at Gondola, 2033 ft. above sea level. The average gradient is about 1 in 130 throughout, and the ruling gradient 1 in 38. The latter is however compensated for curvature, though it nevertheless presents a very trying section for locomotive working, and it was for this line that engines of the Beyer–Garratt were first introduced in 1926. Even when the crest of the escarpment is reached there is another 85 miles of Portuguese territory to be traversed before the border town of Machipanda is reached and Rhodesia is entered. Umtali lies 7 miles beyond the border. When the whole line from Beira was under the management of the Rhodesia Railways, through-locomotive working was in operation between Vilo Machado and Umtali. The succeeding section of 171 miles on to Salisbury

PLATE 37. Uganda Railway—Nairobi

When the line was first built

PLATE 38. Travel on African Railways

(*above*) An Engineer's inspection motor trolley

(*below*) An obstacle occasionally encountered!

is mainly hilly open country of the veldt type. It reaches the high altitude of 5445 ft. above sea level at Eagles Nest siding, the summit of the line between Beira and Salisbury. As compared with this high altitude, Umtali stands 3552 ft. up, and Salisbury 4825 ft.

The section between Salisbury and Bulawayo, 297 miles, is level on the average, since Bulawayo stands some 4500 ft. above sea level; but there is much hilly country intervening and the ruling gradient is 1 in 80 in both directions of running. It is over this stretch that some of the fastest running ever scheduled in Rhodesia used to be made. In days before air travel completely revolutionised the whole system of inter-continental communications the weekly mail steamer between England and the Cape was of prime importance, and connecting trains ran in many parts of Southern Africa. The Rhodesia Railways saw to it that there was a fast connection with the overnight express from the Cape, and at 10.15 a.m. the 'Rhodesia Express' left Bulawayo for Salisbury each Wednesday morning. In the late 1930s this celebrated train, carrying first- and second-class passengers only, covered the 297 miles in $10\frac{3}{4}$ hours. This may not seem anything wonderful by European standards, but considering that there were a number of intermediate stops, there were many stiff gradients, and that maximum speed did not greatly exceed 45 m.p.h., this was an excellent performance. Mention of this fast daylight service between Bulawayo and Salisbury leads me on to the 4-8-2 engines, the first of which was introduced in 1913.

At that time loads were increasing on the Bechuanaland line, and more powerful engines than the 4-8-0s were needed to work throughout between Bulawayo and Mafeking, 492 miles. The Chief Mechanical Engineer, W. J. Hosgood, specified a 4-8-2 which, while conforming to the limitations of axle load imposed by the weight of rail in use, would permit of the much larger firebox that was desirable on long hard runs. The new engines, seven in the first batch, were designed in detail and built by the North British Locomotive Company, and although their tractive effort of 29,468 lb. showed no more than a moderate increase over the 27,620 lb. of the 8th class 4-8-0s the grate area was 32 sq. ft. against the previous 21.35 sq. ft. and thus rendered them extremely suitable for the long run to the south. The mail train load was fixed at 370 tons, and with this the new 4-8-2s could comfortably maintain 40 to 45 m.p.h. on straight level track. These first Rhodesian 4-8-2s were

M

known as the 10th class, and their success is evident from the purchase of seven more in 1918 and another six as relatively late as 1930. Those working on the long through runs in Bechuanaland were based on Mafeking, and operated by men of the South African Railways. The trains were operated on the caboose system, working in rotation. Engines and men worked the round trip of 984 miles, and in each direction there was a lengthy stop at Mahalapye, 268 miles from Bulawayo, for coaling, watering and firecleaning. The double bogie tenders of these engines carried $8\frac{1}{2}$ tons of coal, and in the hard-slogging service demanded a consumption of 60 to 65 lb. per mile was not excessive.

The 11th and 12th classes on the Rhodesia Railways were both 4–8–2s, the former built in Canada, by the Montreal Locomotive Company, as a wartime expedient in 1917. The 12th class, designed by E. H. Grey, and first introduced in 1926, has proved one of the most successful ever to run the road in Rhodesia. While still conforming to the maximum axle-load of 13 tons imposed on routes laid with 60 lb. rails, a locomotive of 35,450 lb. tractive effort was produced. Just as the 4–8–0s of old had been the maids of all work on the line, running mail, mixed, and goods trains indiscriminately, so the 12th class came to fulfil the same rôle north and east of Bulawayo. Their loads were fixed at 450 tons for mail trains, and 800 tons for goods, and while in the former category they worked the fast daylight expresses between Bulawayo and Salisbury they also worked on the north line, over the Victoria Falls, taking a major share in the heavy coal traffic originating at Wankie. Despite the subsequent introduction of the huge Beyer–Garratt engines the 12th class, eventually 55 strong, are still in regular use north of Bulawayo. In addition to being stationed at headquarters others were shedded at Wankie, Livingstone and Broken Hill, though the recent attainment of independence by Zambia, and the consequent separation of the railway north and south of the Victoria Falls, has brought certain changes in the locomotive working.

At the same time as the first 12th class 4–8–2s were purchased Mr. Grey also arranged for the ordering of the first Garratt engines, specially for working the Vilo Machado–Umtali section. These were of the 2–6–2 +2–6–2 type and had a tractive effort of 39,168 lb. as compared with the 35,450 lb. of the tender engines. It was a fairly early period in the development of the Beyer–Garratt type and in the arduous conditions of service in which the development of maximum tractive effort had to be achieved on a route of exceptional curvature, in extremes of temperature, certain details of these large engines proved troublesome in service. For example, the engines were originally fitted with rotary-cam poppet valves, and the inner radial trucks were of the Cartazzi pattern. The latter were giving excellent service on the high speed main line 'Pacifics' designed by Sir Nigel Gresley for the London and North Eastern Railway, but they gave endless trouble with overheating on the Vilo Machado–Umtali line. Despite these troubles in operation however the general performance of these Garratts, designated 13th class, amply demonstrated the potentialities of the design, and two years later a greatly improved design, the 14th class was put to work on the same line. Such was the success of these latter engines that all future steam locomotives purchased by the Rhodesia Railways were of the Beyer–Garratt type, until 1966 when the administration took over operation of the Bechuanaland line from the South African Railways, and purchased some 4–8–2 tender engines of the S.A.R. '19D' class.

The 14th class, which are also of the 2–6–2+2–6–2 type, were for many years the backbone of the Vilo Machado-Umtali section. In that section of 143 miles the line ascends from 185 to 3552 ft., and the worst gradient, 1 in 50, is uncompensated for curvature and is equivalent to about 1 in 38 on a straight piece of line. In these very severe conditions the 14th class Garratts took a maximum load of 385 tons on the mail trains, and on such gradients the goods train load was not very much more—450 tons. One could hardly expect otherwise. There are sixteen of these notable engines, and although the speed of the trains was naturally low the whole class was averaging about 4000 miles a month per engine, between the years 1936 to 1945. This meant that on an average every engine of the class was doing the gruelling 143 miles between Umtali and Vilo Machado every day, while in actual fact, with the necessary breaks for servicing and repairs, the mileages run by every engine in traffic would have been considerably more. The success of the 14th class Garratts led to the introduction, in 1929, of a much more powerful class, having the wheel arrangement 2–8–2+2–8–2, and known as the 16th class. The eight engines of this class were put to work on the 170-mile section between Salisbury and Umtali, and having a tractive effort of 52,360 lb. were able to handle 520 tons at mail train speed. A further twelve of these engines were purchased in 1938, and with twenty of them available thereafter they handled all the freight traffic between Salisbury and Umtali, but some were available for the north line, crossing the Victoria Falls.

The line northwards from Bulawayo to the Congo border is a difficult one to operate, partly because of the severe gradients, and curvature, and especially on account of the extremely sparse populating of much of the country traversed. The distances and the respective altitudes above sea level give a general idea of the fluctuations of the gradients:

Bulawayo	4500 ft.	0
Sawmills	3505 ft.	58 miles
Dett	3590 ft.	161
Wankie	2448 ft.	212
Livingstone	2977 ft.	287
Zimba	4068 ft.	339
Lusaka	4200 ft.	579

From Bulawayo as far as Dett the conditions are not unduly severe, and for 70 miles approaching Dett the line is dead straight and dead level, even though the track runs through a densely forested region. There is a watering station at Kennedy siding, 26 miles on the Bulawayo side of Dett, and so straight is the intervening track that on a clear night the glare of the headlight of an oncoming train can be first picked out from Dett while the engine is taking water. Conditions become more arduous north of Dett, and when Zambia is entered, after crossing the Victoria Falls bridge the going becomes really tough. It was for working the coal trains from Wankie that the 16th Garratts were introduced on this line, where they were proved capable of taking loads 50 per cent greater than the 12th class 4–8–2 tender engines. In the Bulawayo–Livingstone 'link' the Garratts were not confined to single crews. They were pooled, with re-manning arrangements en-route.

For some reason the class '15th' was left blank between the second batch of the 2–6–2+2–6–2 Garratts, and the 2–8–2+2–8–2 series just described, but the continuity was filled in when a new design of the 4–6–4 +4–6–4 wheel arrangement was introduced in 1940. There were originally four engines of this class, and they were intended for the Cape Town and Johannesburg mail trains between Bulawayo and Mafeking. The weight of those trains was getting more than the very capable 10th and 12th class 4–8–2 tender engines could manage. Some acceleration of service

180

was also envisaged, and the coupled wheel diameter was increased from
the 4 ft. on all previous Rhodesian Garratts to 4 ft. 9 in. The forward
tanks were streamlined at the front end and gave the general impression
of a real express locomotive. They were delivered in Rhodesia in the first
year of World War II, and by that time traffic between Salisbury and
Bulawayo had increased to such an extent that this section claimed priority
for the enhanced engine power and these four splendid new engines,
271, 272, 273, and 274, were all put to work between Salisbury and
Gwelo. The tractive effort is 42,750 lb. and the specified loads were 560
tons for the mail trains and no less than 1050 tons for the goods. Details
of an interesting run made by engine No. 271 with the northbound
Rhodesia Express, indicate the mastery of this class of engine over a
train load considerably in excess of the specified maximum tonnage. The
train was allowed 385 minutes running time to cover the 185½ miles
from Gwelo to Salisbury, with a 550-ton load. On January 29, 1941, the
load was one of no less than 18 bogie coaches, 687 tons, and the sum of ten
start-to-stop runs between intermediate stations added up to 358 minutes,
showing the regaining of 27 minutes on schedule time with 137 tons overload. The running average speed throughout was just over 30 m.p.h.
With a goods train of 1050 tons the same engine made a running average
speed of 19¼ m.p.h. over the same stretch of line.

The general performance of these engines showed a high degree of
reliability; during the war years they were averaging around 6000 miles
per month. After the war was over no fewer than sixty further engines
of this class were ordered, and they took over most of the passenger
workings throughout the line, including the Bulawayo–Mafeking section for which they were originally specified. Even these remarkable
engines did not represent the ultimate in Rhodesian Garratt development
because in 1953 the enormous 20th class was introduced specially for
freight working on the section north of the Victoria Falls. On these
engines the wheel arrangement is 4–8–2+2–8–4, and the tractive effort is
69,330 lb. In post-war years also, improved versions of both the 14th
and 16th class Garratts were put to work. It is interesting at this stage to
trace the gradual development, in size and tractive power of the Beyer–
Garratt type on the Rhodesia Railways, (table shown on next page).

In studying the table it will be appreciated that the 15th class stand
out from the general line of development. All the rest, and particularly

181

Class	Year	Wheel arrangement	Total weight (tons)	Tractive effort at 85% boiler pressure
13th	1926	2–6–2+2–6–2	122·1	39,168 lb.
14th	1928	2–6–2+2–6–2	126	39,168 lb.
16th	1929	2–8–2+2–8–2	150·6	52,360 lb.
15th	1941	4–6–4+4–6–4	179·5	42,750 lb.
14A	1954	2–6–2+2–6–2	131·6	39,170 lb.
16A	1953	2–8–2+2–8–2	167	55,270 lb.
20th	1954	4–8–2+2–8–4	224·8	69,330 lb.

the 16th, 16A, and 20th classes are designed for hard-slogging freight service on the heaviest gradients. The 20th class, for example, were specified to work trains of 1400 tons on the Kafue–Broken Hill section, now part of the Zambia railways. But the 15th class was intended for passenger and mail train working, and although these extremely capable and versatile engines are successfully handling freight trains of 1000 tons, and more, on the more easily graded sections of the line, their principal duties are in passenger service. They proved very free-running, and are generally considered the fastest steam locomotives ever to run in Rhodesia.

Nowadays a gradual transition to diesel operation is taking place, and many new diesel-electric locomotives of both British and American build are in service between Salisbury and Umtali. With the transfer of the Beira–Umtali section to the Moçambique Government in 1949 the Rhodesia Railways were relieved of one of the most difficult sections, though the ability to couple the diesels in multiple-unit means that motive power units of 4000 horsepower can be controlled by a single crew. It is unlikely however that passenger train speeds will be increased as a result of the introduction of the new power. There is no call, for example, for fast daylight expresses between Bulawayo and Salisbury when, for the traveller who is really in a hurry, the journey can be made so immeasurably faster by air. The sleeping car trains are still popular; but there is no need for acceleration during the night when such running would merely result in arrivals either at Bulawayo or Salisbury at uncomfortably early hours.

182

Returning from the Victoria Falls I rode the engine of the mail on the first three hours of its long run through the night to Bulawayo. On another 20th class Garratt we bowled along at 30 to 40 m.p.h. Under a full moon I could see the seemingly endless extent of the African bush-veldt: score after score of miles with nothing but low scrub, scarcely in bud after the long dry winter. The country is nevertheless teeming with wild life, and by night much of it is on the move. Train crews have al-ways to keep a sharp look out for major zoological obstructions, and ahead of us the engine's headlight penetrated far into the night. After Kasibi we were running freely at 45 m.p.h. when the driver gave a shout and pointed to the righthand side of the line; there in the moonlight I saw five elephants. After pounding up the heavy bank from Nashome we were coasting downhill, and I was admiring the way in which the fireman was gradually working down the fire, so as to arrive at Thomp-son Junction, where engines were changed, with the minimum of coal on the bars. We were slowing down to stop at Sambawizi when the driver once again shouted. This time one of the big 'cats'—it was either a lioness or a leopard—was drinking from the small pool at the foot of the water column. When picked up in the engine's headlight she made off quickly enough! Such are some of the incidentals in running the Victoria Falls–Bulawayo mail.

The 20th class Garratt came off at Thompson Junction and was replaced by one of the celebrated 15th class No. 358. During the lengthy booked stop some remarshalling of the train took place, and the load was increased from 430 to 500 tons; there was time to see the signalling control panels, and with a late supper awaiting me in the saloon it was nearly midnight before I turned in, and lay listening for a time to the 'music' of No. 358 hammering away up the banks. In the early hours of the morning she was remanned at Sawmills, for the last 55 miles of the journey to Bula-wayo, and with the sun just coming up as we ran into Igusi, at 5.58 a.m., I logged the rest of the run. It was two hours of hard going, with the line gradually climbing from an altitude of 3780 ft. at Igusi to 4420 ft. at Mpopoma, on the outskirts of Bulawayo. Although there are many short lengths of 1 in 130 gradients the continuous hard work does not commence until Redbank is left, when there is a steady ascent to Pasipas, and an even harder pull from there up to Luveve, continuously up at 1 in 130 for most of the way. The 'log' gives details of our progress and the very excellent start-to-stop average speeds of 33½ m.p.h. from Red-bank to Pasipas, and of 28 m.p.h. from Pasipas to Luveve will be specially noted. On the level stretches between Nyamandhlovu and Redbank we

Station or Siding	Altitude above sea level	Distance station to station	Time taken	Average speeds
	ft.	miles	min.	m.p.h.
Igusi	3780			
—		6·1	11½	32
Deli	3887			
—		8·1	14½	33½
Highfields	3985			
—		6·0	12	30
Nyamandhlovu	3937			
—		5·9	8½	41¾
Morgans	3925			
—		5·0	7¾	39
Redbank	3982			
—		7·3	13	33½
Pasipas	4177			
—		4·9	10½	28
Luveve	4330			
—		5·0	13¾★	—
Mpopoma	4420			

★ Slow running into Mpopoma yards

were certainly making excellent speed, fully maintaining the reputation of 15th class as the greyhounds of the Rhodesia Railways motive power stud. On both sections we just topped 50 m.p.h., running through continuous bush-veldt country. This was indeed a fascinating experience of running on the 'Cape to Cairo' route.

Victoria Falls from the air

A northbound freight hauled by a Beyer-Garratt locomotive, crossing the world-famous bridge

CHAPTER SEVENTEEN

Rhodesia: Traffic control and signalling

The famous slogan of Cecil Rhodes: 'The railway is my right hand, and the telegraph is my voice', has echoed around Southern Africa ever since. Northwards from Vryburg, through Mafeking, along the western frontier of the Transvaal, the line was pioneered through Bechuanaland to reach Bulawayo, and throughout that long line of 480 miles of single track, with widely spaced crossing places, the old telegraph line built by George Pauling in the early 1900s is only now in course of replacement. Whether it was complete in time for Cecil Rhodes to speak over the line before his death, in 1902, I do not know; but there, the spirit of the old pioneers remained, and the trains that ran through between the Cape and Bulawayo were for more than sixty years operated with the aid of the original equipment. There was no signalling in the ordinary sense of the word. All traffic movements were regulated by train orders, and working at stations was by hand signals and hand-operated points. Although this was the original line into Rhodesia, and an essential part of the 'Cape to Cairo' project, it became one of the last sections to receive any attention towards modernisation because of the curiously varying political, and railway administration problems that concerned Bechuanaland, now Botswana. The bulk of the mileage lay in Bechuanaland, and up to 1959 the railway was owned by one foreign country, Rhodesia, and operated by another foreign country, South Africa. The station foremen were all South African Railways staff; so were the train crews. To add to the complication the capital of Bechuanaland, Mafeking, is not in the country at all, but 20 miles over the border, in South Africa!

The gradual take-over of complete control by the Rhodesia Railways began in 1959, when the Vryburg–Mafeking section was sold to the South African Railways, and the Rhodesia Railways assumed responsibility for operating southwards from Bulawayo to Mahalapye—about half-way to Mafeking. In 1966 they took over the whole line to the Botswana–South African border station of Ramatlhabama and for convenience of working were accorded running powers into Mafeking. It was from this time, 1966, that modernisation of the telecommunications system on this historic line began. By then a great deal of experience had been gained on the trunk lines lying entirely within Rhodesia, and decisions could be readily taken as to the best method to apply to the line from Bulawayo to Ramatlhabama. I have opened this chapter in somewhat of a 'cart before horse' manner; but the historic associations of the Vryburg–Bulawayo railway, with both Cecil Rhodes and George Pauling tend to give it a priority that up to now is not justified by the technical nature of its equipment and operation. Until some 20 years ago indeed the equipment of that line was scarcely less primitive than in any other part of the Rhodesia Railways, which had no signalling worthy of the name until some years after the end of World War II. Some tentative moves towards the inception of something less tenuous had been made in the 1930s. A young engineer from England, with experience of Centralised Traffic Control, was appointed as signal engineer; but his approach to the local problems was ahead of the times, and he soon returned home. It was E. W. Dennison, appointed Signal and Telegraph Engineer in 1938, who began to get really to grips with the signalling problems connected with the special operating conditions on the Rhodesia Railways; and although the onset of war in 1939 had the effect of postponing any immediate modernisation plans, the interval enabled him to form a fully comprehensive view of the operating situation as a whole, and when the time came for modernisation he was able to back his proposals with a solid bank of first-hand experience on the line.

Before coming to describe the innovations that Dennison so enthusiastically sponsored, some reference to operating conditions on the two main lines must be made. These were the purely Rhodesian section of the 'Cape to Cairo' line, from Bulawayo to the Victoria Falls, Broken Hill, and Ndola, on the Congo border, and the one time Beira and Mashonaland Railway, coming up from the east coast to Salisbury. Connecting the two, between Bulawayo and Salisbury, was the most heavily worked part of the entire system. Up till 1961 the line was controlled under the so-called Departmental system, with District Offices at Salisbury, Bulawayo, Livingstone (just north of the Victoria Falls), and Broken Hill. Since 1961, with political and other changes the old system has gone, and there are now Area Managers at Bulawayo and Salisbury, the line north of Victoria Falls now lying in Zambia. While the general movement of the traffic was regulated by train orders some primitive installations of mechanical signalling were to be seen at some of the stations. Where there were signal boxes the men were termed signal box attendants, not signalmen, because they had no part in the control of train working.

At some of the larger country stations there would be just one signal for each direction, at varying distances from the outermost facing points. This signal, controlled by a lever at the points, was to keep approaching trains at arms length, so to speak, if any shunting was in progress at the station. The points themselves were thrown by a hand tumbler lever. Big game stories have inevitably punctuated the text of this book; but to operating men in Rhodesia, and farther north they are no joke and no fairy tale. At Zimba, for example, the station foreman cycled down to one end to throw the tumbler lever and admit a train, and found two lions fast asleep beside the lever. The Chief Superintendent of Transportation put in a strong plea to the General Manager asking for signalling, as a means of providing for the safety of the staff. At this, and certain other country stations, double-wire operation of the points was installed, from a central locking frame, with bracket signals sited at appropriate distances on the approach side of the facing points. With the train order system the running of trains was often quite irregular, and trains just as frequently arrived hours *ahead* of time, as hours late! Even at Salisbury and Bulawayo the arrangements were sketchy, to put it mildly. There certainly were locking frames of the old South African Railways type double-wire design; but except for one isolated example, all the signals and ground discs were single wire operated. What was worse, there was no ground detection of points.

D. H. Constable, the Principal Signal Engineer until 1970, gave a vivid picture of working conditions when he joined the railway in 1949, in a paper read to the Institution of Railway Signal Engineers in 1969. Having made a few pithy comments about Salisbury he went on:

Bulawayo was even more frightening than Salisbury. The small standard South African Railways type frame was housed in a signal box, if one could call it that; actually it was more like a gardener's potting shed, situated at ground

187

level, with a shunting track right in front of the window. So, for 90 per cent of the time the Signal Box Attendant (as they were then called) could see nothing.

I was horrified to see 1400-ton coal trains thundering up the heavy gradients from the old North line [from Wankie] into the station yard at 20 to 30 m.p.h. with the home signal off, but no detection of any facing points, and no indications where the train was going!

In Dennison's time a properly interlocked system of mechanical working was devised for intermediate stations on the main line. Approaching a station there was first of all a distance board, acting as a marker. It was not in any way a 'signal', but it warned a driver that he was approaching an interlocked area. Then came the 'outer' signal, with a pointed end as on the South African Railways, followed by a two-arm semaphore preceding the facing points. The upper, and longer of the two arms indicated a road set for the main line, whereas the lower and shorter arm was for the loop. They were interlocked with the points and properly detected. The departure signals at the outgoing ends of each loop were discs, on posts, mounted at about drivers' eye level. They were not lighted at night, but of course could be readily picked in the engine's headlight. The whole outfit, with the facing points each end worked by double wire, needed a 10-lever locking frame. But while this arrangement made the working at stations a good deal safer it did nothing to provide for better regulation of the traffic as a whole, and it was in this respect that Dennison began to wage a more serious battle. The top management, up to the end of World War II, was firmly wedded to conventional methods of working, and the boom in traffic that followed the end of the war led to serious congestion on the critical section between Gwelo and Bulawayo. Previously there had been a general average of seven trains a day in each direction, but in the immediate post-war years there were often 13 or more.

The whole section between Bulawayo and Gwelo, was worked on the telegraphic train order system, and in the 100 miles between the two extremities there were only five intermediate stations: Somabula, Shangani, Heany Junction, Cement and Kumalo. The operating department proposed to open six more stations, and to put in additional crossing places, between these stations. Seeing that every station had got to be manned, and at the intermediate loops the train crews working the points by hand would be subject to the dangers from wild animals, it was proposed to put in Centralised Traffic Control. By bringing the sur-

188

veillance of all train movements under the eye of one office a much better and more up-to-date picture of operation as a whole could be obtained, and by abolishing orders, and directing all train movements by signal indication, an immense amount of time could be saved at the passing places. The effectiveness of C.T.C. in dealing with the kind of situation that beset the management of the Rhodesia Railways had been most strikingly shown during the war in the West, and Middle-West states of America, where lines hitherto worked on the train order system were suddenly called upon to carry double their previous traffic in conveying men and war materials to the Pacific coast for the war against Japan.

Despite this striking object lesson in the U.S.A. the management was not convinced. But certain forward-looking members of the operating department, with Dennison, eventually managed to interest Sir Arthur Griffin, who was General Manager from 1947 to 1953. One very minor concession they had to make however was to rename the system Centralised *Train* Control, instead of Centralised *Traffic* Control; but as the original name was virtually a sales term coined by the two American manufacturers who marketed the rival methods of doing the same job that did not matter in the least. Dennison was half-way towards getting acceptance of the principle of putting in a coded remote control system, whereby all train movements in the section were ordered by signal indication, instead of by pieces of paper handed to the drivers. Eventually Dennison was voted a small sum of money to make a model of his proposed arrangement, and to demonstrate to all concerned how his proposed apparatus would work.

The main argument advanced in its favour was on financial grounds, from two viewpoints. First of all the traffic would be speeded up, and by cutting down the hours of duty for train crews, there would be a considerable reduction in the amount of overtime money paid out—in the majority of cases to crews waiting long hours doing nothing while their trains were held up waiting line clear at the loops. Secondly, the use of station foremen at intermediate stations could be avoided. These intermediate stations served districts that were far from settled towns, and railway housing had to be provided at each, for three station foremen—one to a shift. The proposed installation of C.T.C. would eliminate at least two houses at each station. Furthermore, of course, Dennison's proposal completely obviated the need for having *additional* stations, with all the expenses involved. Dennison substantiated his case to the extent of being authorised to put in a pilot scheme between Bulawayo and Gwelo, but very soon after the order was placed for certain control equipment from England, and plans made for local manufacture of the remainder, the whole scheme was thrown into some disarray, by plans for a re-arrangement of railway facilities in Bulawayo itself. The doubling of the line to Salisbury as far as Cement Station rather cut out the case for C.T.C. right into Bulawayo, and the pilot scheme was shortened to extend only from Cement to Gwelo. Despite all the enthusiasm put into it by the signal department under Dennison's leadership, it was not until the autumn of 1951 that one piece of it from Heany Junction to Shangani was brought into service.

At the start however drivers were chary of going into the section ahead with no order. They had been brought strictly to paper orders, with no running signals at all. At first the paper orders were retained. It was a very big change, and in the early stage the operating officers took great care to train drivers in the new methods. In a very short time it was amply evident that they could do without train orders, and then the operators could not have C.T.C. fast enough! The Signal Engineer was pressed on all sides to get more C.T.C. installed, and having completed the original scheme through to Gwelo, authority was quickly given for an extension to Gatooma, on the main line to Salisbury. The advantages of C.T.C. control were now so very apparent that a survey of operating conditions on the whole line was made, and it was decided that a section of the 'Cape to Cairo' route, between Gwaai and Wankie should be given a higher priority than the Gwelo-Gatooma section, and so the authority was transferred.

When the initial section of C.T.C. was authorised the relatively high cost of some of the equipment was a major consideration, and as the train crews of the Rhodesia Railways knew no other method of working than to operate the points by hand lever this method was retained, with suitable electric interlocking of the hand levers with the C.T.C. controls. This method was used on the Heany Junction–Gwelo section; but the operating staff had now fairly got the bit between their teeth where C.T.C. was concerned, realising that still more time might be saved if hand operation of points was eliminated. Authority was therefore obtained to convert the Heany Junction–Gwelo section to power operation. In the remote districts through the main lines of the Rhodesia Railways run the possibility of a failure of the power supply, for point machine operation, is a factor that must be given the most careful consideration, and although the electric point machines purchased were generally of a type in extensive use in the United Kingdom they included an elaboration not used on the home railways. In the event of power failure the 'home' machines can be cranked over by hand. It entails the insertion, under certain precautionary interlocking measures of a crank something like the hand starting crank of a motor car, and it needs a large number of turns to move a machine from the full normal to the full reverse position. In the kind of emergency when this kind of operation is necessary the little extra time is not of any great importance; but it is quite another matter at an outlying station in Rhodesia.

In the first place the train crew would have to seek authority to obtain the crank from its normally sealed and locked container. Then there would be the procedure for withdrawing it after use, and putting it back in a safe manner, without deranging, or cutting out any of the interlocking. In the United Kingdom use of a hand-crank is made under the direction and supervision of a traffic inspector, but if there were a power failure in the Rhodesian bush the nearest traffic inspector might be 100 miles away. With all this in consideration the Rhodesia Railways decided to use what is termed a dual-control point machine. It is fitted with a change-over gear box, incorporating all the necessary interlocking safeguards, and if it becomes necessary to change over to hand operation a change-gear lever is operated, which completely cuts out the circuit for power operation. The machine is then set for hand operation, and this can be done very simply and quickly by use of a large throw-over lever, in much the same way as with the mechanical throw-over levers of old. These machines proved very successful and have been standardised on the Rhodesia Railways. The news of the success of these dual-control electric point machines spread like wildfire among train crews, and there developed an agitation on the dangers of having to work hand-operated points on the Wankie-Dett section. Constable puts the situation picturesquely:

Here the railway forms the boundary of the Wankie National Park, and there had been several instances of guards going forward to reverse the points for a train to enter or leave a loop and finding a pride of lions or an elephant waiting to help him.

There had been no fatal accidents so far, but no doubt eventually a guard would find an unco-operative or hungry family eagerly awaiting his arrival.

How the installation of C.T.C. was pushed forward, once everyone was convinced of its almost priceless value on a railway of this kind, is shown by statistics for the end of the year 1958. By that time no less than 298 miles were being operated under full C.T.C. control. From a panel in Bulawayo Trains Office there was the Heany Junction–Gwelo section, 93 miles; from Dett, on the 'Cape to Cairo', or North line, there was 116 miles from New Wankie to Gwaai; and from Sawmills a further 89 miles, southwards from Gwaai to Mpopoma, on the outskirts of Bulawayo. This was only a beginning. New installations followed each other as fast as the staff of the Signal Engineer could deal with them, and as fast as the English contractors—three different firms—could supply the specialised equipment. By April 1964 the astonishing situation had been attained that the *entire* main line system of the Rhodesia Railways had been converted to C.T.C. operation with 1200 route miles, with 205 crossing places, controlled from ten control rooms. No more remarkable example of the complete metamorphosis of the operating strategy of a railway could be found anywhere in the world. There were no fewer than three large control panels on the line north of the Victoria Falls, at Monze, Broken Hill, and Ndola, controlling between 374 miles of route; but after July 1967, when the Zambian section was detached, those three panels, and also the one at Livingstone which originally controlled both north and south of the bridge, ceased to be any responsibility of the Rhodesia Railways. Colour light signals are used, to so complete an extent that there is not a semaphore left on the main lines in Rhodesia.

I cannot conclude this account of the truly splendid signalling work that has been done in Rhodesia, in a very short space of time, without mentioning some peculiar problems faced by the engineers, from wild animals. While lions are a constant source of danger to human life other animals and birds cause damage to equipment. I will conclude by once again quoting D. H. Constable:

When C.T.C. was proposed between Gwaai and Wankie we were worried about interference from the vast herds of elephant which roam the Wankie National Park. It was thought that they would scratch their backs against the rail poles supporting the cable routes at the inter-sidings. So we buried the cables.

Uganda Railway 0–6–6–0 compound Mallet

EC2 class 4–8–2 + 2–8–4 'Garratt'

The first-ever 4–8–4 + 4–8–4: the 'EC3' class of 1939

The most powerful metre gauge steam locomotive ever built: the '59'
class 4–8–2+2–8–4

PLATE 39. Kenya & Uganda Articulated Locomotives

PLATE 40. Nakuru New Station

(*above*) General view showing train hauled by '60' class Garratt locomotive

(*below*) The new signal box, with miniature lever interlocking, and tokenless block instruments

To our cost we found the Rhodesian termites love cable covering and consider it a delicacy. After trying various remedies we capitulated and put up one normal overhead route.

At one spot we had quite a lot of trouble with giraffe going down to a water hole and bringing down the overhead telecommunication wires. This was easily overcome by lifting the route on higher poles.

Trouble is also caused in the overhead telephone lines by weaver birds building their nests in them. They build remarkable examples of their art between Wankie and Victoria Falls.

Storks also build huge nests at the top of a telegraph pole, and one can destroy their nests many times before they finally get the message and move to a tree.

When I went to inspect the C.T.C. between Heany Junction and Gwelo I was irresistibly reminded of Sir Noel Coward. For having called in by car at various stations on the way out from Bulawayo and seen the control office and the signal box at Gwelo itself arrangements had been made for me to ride part of the way back on the 12.20 p.m. freight. The thermometer was well into the nineties, and I was to ride a 19th class 4-8-2 for the best part of two hours; 'mad dogs and Englishmen' indeed! But any thoughts of discomfort vanished once I climbed on to the footplate, and listened to the fierce staccato bark from the chimney of that tough mixed-traffic engine as she lifted a heavy train away. The line was busy. At three successive loops we crossed heavy freight trains; but this was primarily a signalling occasion, and it was remarkable to see how well the colour lights showed up, miles ahead in the shimmering noon-day heat. My host was waiting at Shangani with the car, but equally welcome was the sight of a pleasant little 'pub' adjoining the station. I need not say more, after that grilling two hours on the footplate!

CHAPTER EIGHTEEN

Inception of the Uganda Railway

In the year 1890 The British East Africa Company asked the Imperial Government to guarantee the interest on the capital required to build a railway from Mombasa to Lake Victoria Nyanza. A railway was urgently needed to open up a virtually unknown country that lay in the path of Rhodes's project of the 'Cape to Cairo' line. At the western end of the proposed new railway lay the territory of Uganda, which was known to be a hot-bed of the slave trade. The Government of Lord Salisbury, after lengthy consideration, declined to make the necessary guarantee; but in 1895 when the country originally opened up by the chartered company was taken under direct Imperial Administration, and Uganda was made a British Protectorate, the home Government decided to build the railway themselves, and arrangements were made for preliminary surveys.

A vivid account of the conditions existing in the country at the time of the preliminary surveys and the construction of the line was given in the *Railway Magazine* of 1899, by John Partington, a senior British railway officer of the day. He was actually Chief of Audit on the London and North Western, at Euston, but it so happened that a young relative of his was called upon to conduct a caravan of five hundred Swahilis from the existing railhead to Lake Victoria Nyanza, where it was required to set up a base at the inland terminus of the line. This had been decided at a locality named Port Florence, though mere names meant little in Uganda seventy years ago. Inland from the coast of the Indian Ocean there was practically nothing in the way of white settlements. The full length of the line as then projected was about 550 miles, and at the time this young engineer set out, the railhead had advanced no more than 150 miles from the coast at Mombasa. He had, therefore, 400 miles to go, with only a clerk as companion, and the 500 Swahilis, who were to be his labour force in setting up the depot at Port Florence. He set out in December 1898, and was followed—not preceded be it noted—by a Government survey which later presented a report to the House of Commons in June 1899.

Partington's account, published in the *Railway Magazine* is mainly concerned with the adventures of his young and anonymous relative, and the difficulties he had in marshalling his extraordinary party and keeping them together in such a 'trek'; but the report presented to Parliament, contains some extraordinarily penetrating glimpses of what the country itself was like before the railway was constructed. Speaking generally, it says: 'The country actually traversed is in a great measure desert, and as a rule, sparsely populated, waterless, and without resources.' Some areas were covered with almost impenetrable thorny jungle, while elsewhere '. . . in spite of the closeness of the jungle there are no shade trees, and the only effect of the jungle is to shut out any breeze'. Worse than anything perhaps was the lack of good water, and the report contains this grim passage: 'The only water to be obtained in most parts is from filthy pools or water holes. It is either inky black or of a deep brown colour, with a greasy scum on the surface, and is fouled by the animals and men of passing caravans. Even these sources of supply are sometimes wanting.'

Today, when the activities of tourist agencies are much exercised in the organising of trips to the various game reserves it is interesting to read of the kind of conditions the railway pioneers had to deal with, no more than seventy years ago. The Government surveyors' report includes these passages:

'The Athi plains are a great treeless rolling desert teeming with antelope, zebra and other large game.'

And then, 'Progress has been seriously impeded by man-eating lions. 28 men have been killed by lions.'

Beyond the point now marked by the important railway junction of Nakuru the country rises to the Mau escarpment, but the Government surveyor did not proceed thus far. Instead he reported:

'Beyond Mau it is impossible to speak with any certainty as to the details of the country; it is *absolutely unknown*, bare of supplies, and traversed by no definite track; while the cold damp nights at this altitude (8000 ft.) are very severe on man and beast.'

195

What was known, of course, was that in that 'unknown' territory the slave trade was flourishing, and it was into that territory that John Partington's intrepid young relative took his caravan of Swahilis. Imagine a long winding line of natives, many in motley garb, others almost naked, swaying and swinging along on foot each carrying his load and rations; and this caravan was led by a comparative youth with a gun slung over his shoulder, a revolver in his belt, and a hunting knife ready for any emergency. On they pressed, with the pioneer leading the way, pushing aside the jungle branches of trees or elephant grass, clambering over rocks, wading through streams waist deep, and, for three days never to be forgotten, never seeing the sun owing to the dense forest through which they had to pass. When there was an opportunity that young pioneer rode his bicycle, which a porter carried for him when not in use. At one stage on a very narrow pathway there was a rhinoceros blocking the way; he wouldn't move, and it was impossible to make a detour, so the pioneer summoned all of his followers who carried arms, and forming up like a firing squad discharged into the animal. The result was a bonus so far as rations were concerned, and that evening there was a feast. The men were always in high heart after a feast, and would march with a swing, chanting and singing as they went; but when meat supplies were short they became depressed, and the young pioneer had to take the sternest measures to repress laziness and insubordination.

Partington comments upon the many letters he received thus:

This alternation of gaiety and gloom somewhat relieved the monotony of the journey which lasted about six weeks; swamp, forest, rocky rivers, and ravines, elephant grass, desert, and fertile plains were passed intermittently, and at times the beauties of an English landscape appeared, reminding the Pioneer of home and friends far away. The headmen of the villages on the way were mostly peaceably inclined, as they dread a white man, and the exchange of presents such as a few strings of beads, pieces of wire, and coloured cloth for a sheep or two with the customary salaam and a pipe of tobacco, generally ensured safe passage through the adjoining country, and procured a guide to water and the next camping ground.

By such hazardous and toilsome methods they covered the 400 miles from Sultan Mahmoud to Lake Victoria Nyanza, averaging about ten miles a day. Two escarpments were surmounted on the way, first the

PLATE 41. Large Garratts at Work

(*above*) Mail train leaving Nairobi for Mombasa, hauled by 'EC3' class engine
(*below*) Freight train approaching Nairobi

PLATE 42. New Bridge Work

(*above*) New bridge at Magongo Road, near Mombasa, over arterial road location

(*below*) New bridge over the Nile, at the extreme western end of the line at Pakwach

Kikuyu, where the railway now attains its first summit level near Uplands station, and then the Mau. The level near Upland is 8000 ft. above
sea level, and the caravan found the cold at such altitudes at night very
trying after the heat of the day. Between the Kikuyu and Mau escarpments
they had to make their way down into the Great Rift valley, 30 miles
wide, and some 2000 ft. below the summit level. Partington remarks:
'On this rift there are two great extinct volcanoes, Longonot and Suswa—
the crater of one is $2\frac{1}{2}$ miles across—besides many smaller ones. There is
also an immense quantity of lava here, and most of the lakes are obviously
of volcanic origin.' In some of its stark barrenness this country is harsh
enough today. What it must have been like seventy years ago when
white men were first beginning to penetrate into the region takes some
imagining. So eventually they arrived at the lake, and the natives cried
out in amazement 'the big waters'. None of them had ever been there
before.

Having arrived there, and pitched camp there was the matter of communications, and the occasional letter was sent by native runner, carrying
the letter in a cleft stick. Even in such a primitive community, with tribes
constantly at war with one another the 'postman' with the letter in a cleft
stick seemed to enjoy a kind of diplomatic immunity from interference.
He was the emissary of the white man, but being completely illiterate it
was the recognised code of the postmen runners to show the letter they
bore to every European they met, in case he was the addressee. In normal
working these runners would cover about 30 miles a day. After eating the
food they carried from the start, they lived off the countryside as best
they could. Letters despatched this way, from the camp on Lake Victoria
Nyanza, duly arrived in England and one can only admire the fortitude
and sheer 'guts' of men who preceded the full railway working parties
and prepared the camps, often living more than 80 miles from the nearest
white man. Any surveys that had been done previously were of the
sketchiest description. The object was to establish a railhead and port on
the lake, and the original target was fixed at Port Victoria, now Jinja.
Later explorations discovered the deep inlet at the head of which now
stands Kisuma—then called Port Florence—and this saved nearly 100 miles
of construction. The line that now reaches the lake at Kisumu is a branch,
leaving the main line at Nakuru; originally however this was the main line
—in fact the only line. This short cut to the lake, with its terminus at

Port Florence, resulted in the railway never entering Uganda territory at all.

The construction of the line in such a terrain was a tremendous feat of organisation. There were many, with a slight knowledge of Africa, who regarded the enterprise as bordering on the chimerical. The engineering difficulties, while severe, were not overwhelming; but the country itself, as discovered by John Partington's young relative, was almost trackless; one huge expanse of jungle, swamp and desert. The pioneer working parties were warned of the profusion of wild animals, and of even more dangerous savages, and the difficulties experienced from these natural enemies proved that the warnings were mild rather than exaggerated. Not only had the working parties for long periods to be protected by escorts armed to the teeth; night after night the dense jungle surrounding the encampments resounded with the trumpeting of elephants, the roaring of lions and the war-cries and tom-toms of savages, varied by dropping shots and the whizzing of arrows. The days too, had their alarms. Many a brisk skirmish with natives ensued before the working parties could get on with the job. On one occasion two lions 'captured' a train of food wagons, helped themselves liberally, and could not be dislodged for several hours. It was hoped that as the work progressed the natives would be persuaded to work with the white man or trade with him, rather than waste time, energy and life in trying to stop the enterprise. Fewer than 3000 were ever employed at one time, and by far the greater part of the work was done by coolies imported from India.

By the end of 1896 no more than 20 miles of line from the coast had been completed; in another year they had reached milepost 120, and by the end of 1898 mile 250 had been attained. At Christmas 1901 the rails were laid through to the lake, but in the last 100 miles from Nakuru there were many temporary deviations laid in, pending the completion of various bridges and viaducts. There was great anxiety to establish through communication, and these makeshifts were gladly accepted in the spirit of getting the trains through at the earliest possible moment. The gradient profile reproduced herewith, signed by Capt. P. B. Molesworth of the Royal Engineers, is a fascinating document and reveals the vital importance of water supplies on this mountain railway. It shows that when this diagram was prepared the gradients west of Nakuru had been ascertained only by the preliminary reconnaissance. It was then thought
198

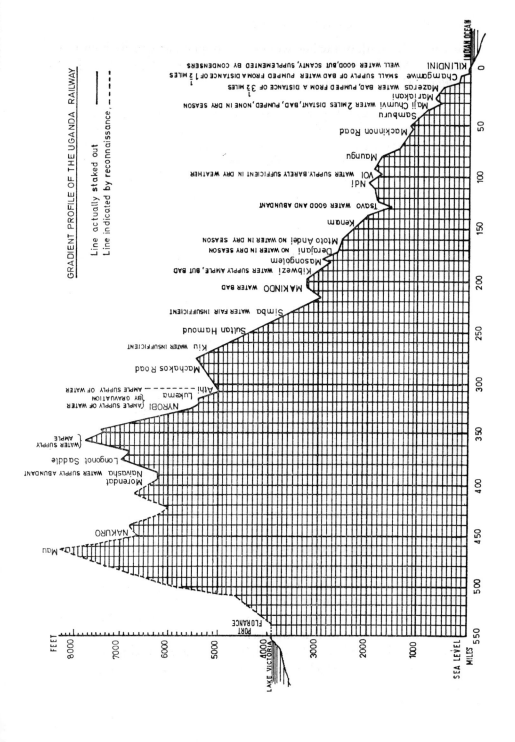

GRADIENT PROFILE OF THE UGANDA RAILWAY

Line actually staked out ————
Line indicated by reconnaissance. - - - -

KILINDINI   WELL WATER GOOD, BUT SCANTY, SUPPLEMENTED BY CONDENSERS
Changamwe   SMALL SUPPLY OF BAD WATER PUMPED FROM A DISTANCE OF 1¾ MILES
Mazeras   WATER BAD, PUMPED FROM A DISTANCE OF 3½ MILES
Mariakani
Samburu   Maji Chumvi WATER 2 MILES DISTANT, BAD, PUMPED, NONE IN DRY SEASON
Mackinnon Road
Maungu
Ndi   VOI WATER SUPPLY, BARELY SUFFICIENT IN DRY WEATHER
Kenani   TSAVO WATER GOOD AND ABUNDANT
             Mtoto Andei NO WATER IN DRY SEASON
             Dergjani NO WATER IN DRY SEASON
             Masongolem
             Kibwezi WATER SUPPLY AMPLE, BUT BAD
MAKINDO WATER BAD
Simba WATER FAIR INSUFFICIENT
Sultan Hamoud
Kiu WATER INSUFFICIENT
Machakos Road
Athi   AMPLE SUPPLY OF WATER
Lukema
NYROBI   AMPLE SUPPLY OF WATER BY GRAVITATION
Morendat   Naivasha WATER SUPPLY ABUNDANT
Longonot Saddle
             WATER SUPPLY AMPLE
NAKURU
Lk. Mau
PORT FLORANCE
LAKE VICTORIA

FEET
8000
7000
6000
5000
4000
3000
2000
1000
SEA LEVEL

MILES 0   50   100   150   200   250   300   350   400   450   500   550

INDIAN OCEAN

that the full length of the line would be 550 miles; as actually built it was 584. On this diagram it is interesting to see the spelling, Nyrobi. The *Railway Magazine* of 1899 reported:

In December 1898 half-year, three trains each way on the average were run at a speed not exceeding 11 miles an hour. A good passenger traffic is springing up, for in December last it amounted to 30,000 rupees, or £2000. Hindoos are opening up bazaars and shops at the principal stations and at Nyrobi, about half-way, which is to be the Crewe or Swindon of the Uganda Railway, probably a town will grow up in a few years; it is 5500 ft. above sea level, and tolerably healthy.

It was no doubt on account of its generally pleasant climate that Nairobi was selected to be the headquarters of the railway with fully equipped workshops for repairs to locomotives, carriages and wagons, and originally also for the machinery of the steamers of Lake Victoria Nyanza. There was another good reason for choosing Nairobi because it lay under the close protection of Fort Smith, which was then strongly fortified and permanently garrisoned. The home Government took an intense interest in the progress of the work, and in December 1902, the then Secretary of State for the Colonies, none other than the great Joseph Chamberlain and his wife, travelled over the line from Mombasa to the 521st mile. Its advanced state, and prospects that its completion opened out, naturally delighted the statesman who for many years had called upon England to 'think Imperially'. In March 1903 the whole line was practically finished, and then, like any new railway at home it was submitted to the inspection of the Board of Trade. This was no formality either, for the officer appointed was none other than Major John Pringle, as he was then, later Colonel Sir John Pringle, and one of the most famous Chief Inspecting Officers of Railways at the Ministry of Transport. The work had been well done, and on 1 October 1903 the line was handed over to the British East Africa Protectorate authorities.

I have written enough of the initial difficulties of prospecting, detailed survey, and construction for there to be an understanding of the country through which the line wriggles its way from the Indian Ocean to the Lake—for very little of it is straight!—and a detailed description of the scenery would fill a book of its own. The general physical features of the countryside may nevertheless be briefly summarised. Thirty miles inland from Mombasa a sandy and waterless desert begins and this continues, while the railway is climbing steeply from Samburn and Mackinnon Road, to the 80th mile. Then there comes some dramatic scenery in the gorges of the Noara Hills, followed by dense jungle until reaching the 250th mile. After that come the Athi Plains, a wide expanse of rolling uncultivated scrub land, which continues almost to Nairobi. By that time the elevation has mounted at most to 5500 ft., and what this means in the way of locomotive work with the heavy trains of today will be apparent in Chapter Twenty of this book. After Nairobi the climbing is continued through a country of a pleasant temperate climate to the summit of the Kikuyu escarpments, at 7700 ft. above sea level. Then comes a most dramatic change, for quite suddenly the line comes out on to the edge of the Great Rift Valley. It is one of those moments in railway travel, that one can never forget the first time of experiencing it.

It is somewhat analogous to that breathtaking first sight of the Rhone Valley from a Lötschberg train descending from Goppenstein, and suddenly emerging from the last of the tunnels and seeing that tremendous cleft in the mountains almost vertically below. A first sight of the Great Rift Valley must have struck dismay into the hearts of those who were literally hacking their way through the jungle to try and reach Lake Victoria Nyanza: a tremendous escarpment at first, and then flattening out to a level valley floor that from this high altitude looks a faint purplish grey. There is nothing of the jungle, nothing of the scrubland of the Athi plains, only an all-pervading 'dead' look. And away on the western skyline the reason for all is clear to see in the gigantic cone of the extinct volcano Longonot. As the line progresses westward several lakes are passed, all due to the volcanic action, and it would seem that earth movements and tremors have not ceased yet. At Naivasha for example the lake is extremely beautiful and recent changes in level are evidenced by the number of dead trees rising from the waters like some petrified forest.

Even before Nakuru is reached the line is climbing steeply to the second great escarpment, the Mau, to attain the highest summit level of the original main line, 8327 ft. at a distance of 489½ miles from Mombasa. From this point it descends towards the lake on very steep gradients, but in complete contrast to the Great Rift Valley it is a country of rich alluvial 'black cotton' soil, and as would be expected luxuriant in dense tropical vegetation. At Port Florence a pier and wharves were constructed, and steamer services on the lake operated from the outset. Early in 1904 the Colonial Office in London received this report:

The Uganda Railway is rapidly revolutionising the conditions of life on this side of the lake; prices of necessaries have fallen, and other articles are being introduced which it was impossible to obtain before. The chiefs are commencing to build houses on European methods, and to fit them with suitable furniture, and to appreciate many of the articles in daily use in England. Trade has increased considerably, and an impetus given to cultivation and agriculture throughout the Protectorate; peace and order have been maintained; there is a marked absence of serious crime, and life and property there today are as safe as in any part of His Majesty's dominions.

Although the railway was originally projected with a view to suppression of the slave trade, by the time the line was through to Port Florence—Kisumu, as it was soon renamed—the slave trade was virtually at an end, and the 'Railway through a Zoo', as it was sometimes called, became a popular tourist attraction among wealthy world travellers. Early passengers included a number of foreign royal families of the pre-1914 era; Winston Churchill made the trip, and a notable account of the line was written by Theodore Roosevelt, the celebrated former President of the United States. Roosevelt wrote:

No such railway journey can be taken on any other line in any other land. At one time we passed a herd of a dozen or so of great giraffes, cows and calves, cantering along through the open woods a couple of hundred yards to the right of the train. Again, still closer, four water-buck cows, their big ears thrown forward, stared at us without moving until we had passed. Hartebeests were everywhere, one herd was on the track, and when the engine whistled they bucked and sprang with ungainly agility and galloped clear of the danger. A long-tailed straw-coloured monkey ran from one tree to another. Huge black ostriches appeared from time to time. Once a troop of impala, close by the track, took fright, and as the beautiful creatures fled we saw now one and now another bound clear over the high bushes. A herd of zebra clattered across a cutting of the line not a hundred yards ahead of the train; the whistle hurried their progress, but only for a moment, and as we passed they were already turning around to gaze. The wild creatures were in their sanctuary, and they knew it. And when once the railway was left behind, the wealth of animal life, of course, became richer still. It was then that the party began its complete odyssey, marching for miles after the day's work was over, resting for the night—now in some friendly bungalow, and now in a rough tent set up in haste by the side of the lion-hunted covert.

There were then four passenger trains a week leaving Mombasa for Nairobi and Kisumu, and the journey took forty-six hours, with stops at all the forty-two stations. The coaches both first and second class included sleeping and lavatory accommodation, but passengers had to bring their own bedding. Refreshments could be obtained only at certain stations, but the majority who essayed such a trip treated it as an expedition on safari, and came with plenty of rations of all kinds. To reach Uganda proper there was a weekly steamer service on Lake Victoria Nyanza. In 1912 however the traffic was growing faster than the limited equipment of the railway could deal with effectively. The rolling stock then consisted of 67 locomotives, 232 passenger carriages and 861 wagons, which was not much on a single-tracked mountain railway strung out over nearly 600 miles of tropical Africa. The Traffic Manager, reporting to the Secretary of State for the Colonies, remarked:

We have been handicapped very much at times for want of good rolling stock and engines. Wagons have sometimes had to stand under load at the coast through want of power to haul trains, and when we are short of rolling stock these delays are most unfortunate, as they decrease the effective use we can make of the stock we have. We have now seventy-five covered goods wagons (20 tons), and twenty open high-sided wagons (20 tons) on order; ten of the latter have just been put into traffic. When these arrive they will very much improve matters, but with our prospects of increased traffic we should most certainly place orders for more now, or the present stress will only be aggravated later on. As all our existing wagons have more or less the same number of years' service, they all tend to fall out at the same time. The necessity for replacing worn out vehicles and the number requiring repairs will increase year by year. Owing to their length of service many will not carry their full load without 'running hot' and this has led to numerous and justifiable complaints of the delay from the public. A start is being made with the introduction of white metal for the bearings; this will no doubt improve matters, and although it is costly, I would urge that the stock generally should be provided with it, as at present wagons are thrown out of service in this way much too often. Two new Mallet engines have arrived and six more are on order, also three shunting engines; as the former will haul double our present loads we shall be well enough off until such times as these have to take their place on the Magadi soda traffic by which time we should have others ready to meet the increase in ordinary traffic.

The passenger stock has been sufficient to meet our requirements, but we must look to losing a certain number from the main line, which will be required for the new branches, and also to more being wanted for local train requirements. The time has now come when our first-class stock should be provided with electric light; the expense would not be large, and would materially add to the comfort of the journey and be much appreciated by the travelling public. It is intended to equip the line from Mombasa to Nairobi with the Tyers Electric Tablet system for working trains, and this system should be in working order before the end of the working year.

In 1912 there had been no extensions to the railway, and its extent was no more than that of the original main line from Nairobi to Kisumu. The Magadi branch, referred to in the report, leaves the main line at Konza 46 miles south east of Nairobi, and runs westward for some 60 miles to the shores of Lake Magadi. With reference to the first branch to be built we have passed beyond the inception stage of the Uganda Railway, and its remarkable subsequent developments are described in the next chapter.

PLATE 43

(*above*) Mail train leaving Nairobi for Mombasa: '60' class Garratt

(*below*) Freight train approaching Naivasha

PLATE 44. Bridge over the Nile at Jinja, with freight train hauled by '90' class diesel-electric locomotive crossing

CHAPTER NINETEEN

Zambesi to the Nile

By the fateful year 1914 the railway map of Africa south of the Nile was still in process of evolution. It was hardly an ordered or consistent process. The phrase 'Cape to Cairo' was still freely bandied about; but in the spheres of influence apportioned to other European powers, and particularly in the two German colonies, railway development was quite unconnected with any overall plan for the continent as a whole. The plain fact, of course, was that in 1914 there was no overall plan. Even Rhodes himself had, in modern slang, been inclined 'to blow hot and cold' over the Cape to Cairo project. He was more concerned that Rhodesia should have more than one outlet to the sea, and having got the line through to Bulawayo from the south, and to Salisbury to the east, it fell to one of Rhodes's most ardent disciples, Robert Williams, to pioneer the line from the west, from the South Atlantic haven of Lobito Bay. The Portuguese were as willing to grant concessions for a line through Angola, as they had been from Beira to Umtali, and so construction of the Benguela Railway started. But progress was very slow, due to difficulties no less severe than those experienced in Beira, or in the early prospecting days of the Uganda Railway, and by 1914 the railway map of the country between the Nile and the Limpopo had a very disjointed appearance. There is no doubt that German colonial policy worked covertly to discourage any attempts at a link-up between the British-sponsored lines in Rhodesia and the Sudan, and the long single-line westwards from Dar-es-Salaam across German East Africa was like George Hudson's thrust of the Midland from Nottingham to Lincoln athwart the proposed main line of the Great Northern from Grantham to Doncaster!

World War I changed everything. Botha, in a brilliant campaign, made short work of German South West Africa. East Africa, because of the terrain, was a more difficult task; but the Germans were gradually driven inland, and although immense damage was done to bridges, track, and rolling stock by the retreating armies the German colony was systematically occupied, and little by little restored to something like order. With both the ex-German colonies confided to British Administration, on behalf of the League of Nations, the British influence over the whole of Africa south of the Nile was virtually complete. The two major lines in Portuguese territory were British-owned, and in the Congo the Belgians, in a completely land-locked colony, were glad enough to co-operate with the Rhodesia Railways, and were ready to welcome with open arms the advance of the Benguela Railway from the west coast. In the meantime considerable interest was displayed in the newly-acquired British responsibility of the line in the former German East Africa. It then consisted of a single main line of 670 miles, without any branches, extending from Dar-es-Salaam to Kigoma, on Lake Tanganyika. In physical features it had much resemblance to the Uganda Railway; it was finely built and heavily ballasted, though the rail section at that time was only 42 lb. per yard.

Principal interest centred around the town of Tabora, 4000 ft. above sea level and 530 miles from Dar-es-Salaam. This was by far the most important intermediate station on the line, and at one time there was doubt as to whether Tabora or Dar-es-Salaam should be the capital of the colony. But it was in respect of the future railway development in Africa that Tabora began at one time to loom so large. It lay at the intersection of several primitive, but nevertheless well-established trade routes, the most important of which was a rough motor road to Mwanza, on Lake Victoria Nyanza. In 1919 the *Railway Magazine* stated that in the near future that primitive motor road would no doubt be supplemented by a railway, and then went on: 'Should this vast country remain in British possession, it is practically certain that the Cape to Cairo Railway will pass through Tabora which will begin to lay claim to the title of "The Clapham Junction of Africa", which has been prophesied for it.' As befitted a line of German origin it was laid to the metre gauge, and in this respect another *Railway Magazine* prophecy of 1919 went awry:

We are not far from the day when connection will be established between those railways in Africa which run roughly east and west of the Cape to Cairo line. This line will be laid to the 3 ft. 6 in. gauge; the railways of the Union of South Africa are 3 ft. 6 in., and so are the Portuguese lines and the Uganda Railway. The metre gauge Central Railway [in the former German East Africa] will have to give way before this vast mileage, and be converted to the slightly wider gauge. As far as structures go this will involve no difficulties, but the steel sleepers are all pierced by rectangular holes to suit the metre gauge, and will have to be punched again or replaced, not a great task, in view of the immense benefits derived. In the great future that lies before this vast country, in whatever hands the future lies, the railway will play a leading part.

As things turned out it was the Uganda Railway and not the Tanganyika that changed its gauge, but much was to happen before that took place.

It is first of all necessary to finish once and for all with the Cape to Cairo project, and in so doing the slow advance of the Benguela Railway must be noted. The optimists who hoped to find in Rhodesia a gold reef richer than that in the Transvaal were sadly disappointed, but in the northern territory and in the Belgian Congo a huge belt of copper was discovered. With a port at Lobito Bay the metal extracted from this area would have 3000 miles fewer to travel to reach Europe. At the end of 1902, less than a year after Rhodes's death, Robert Williams obtained a concession from the Portuguese Government to build a railway right across Angola to the eastern frontier with the Congo. The distance was 830 miles and the terrain was tropical, with all that meant in hardship and disease. Progress was very slow; successive contractors got into difficulties and abandoned the works, and by mid-summer of 1908 the line had been carried no further than 131 miles from Lobito Bay. The progress of the work, and the failure of successive contractors was being closely watched from Berlin. The relative proximity of Benguela and Lobito Bay to the frontier of German South West Africa made Angola a sitting target for the assumption of German influence, and secret representations were made in Lisbon. Fortunately Robert Williams was well aware of these moves, and he succeeded in arranging the necessary finance to enable new contracts to be made with a British firm, none other than the celebrated Paulings Ltd. Through their energetic and experienced methods the line was carried eastwards to the foot of Mount Lepi, 224 miles, by July 1911. Thence, progress was to Nova Lisboa, 265 miles, by September 1912, and to Chinquar, 322 miles, by October 1913.

Immediately war broke out in 1914 all the fears of a German *coup* were intensified, and the railway was put under armed guard. Construction was stopped, but Botha's attack from the south kept the Germans fully occupied, and Angola was unmolested. There was nevertheless a long delay in building the railway, and it was not until August 1928 that the frontier with the Congo was finally reached, and Robert Williams received the honour of a baronetcy. The official opening ceremony took place in June 1929, performed by Senhor Bacelar Bebiano, Portuguese Minister for the Colonies. The Belgians continued the line through the Congo to link up with the Rhodesia Railways at Elizabethville. This momentous event took place in 1931, and with it another objective in the great plan of Cecil Rhodes for the economic development of Southern Africa was attained. The rail link was no sooner completed than the most intense publicity campaign was launched in favour of 'The Shortest Route from Europe to Central Africa and Rhodesia'. A beautifully illustrated brochure gave comparative distances from Southampton to certain business and tourist centres in Southern Africa. Although some of the total distances were not dissimilar, the fact that the sea journey was so much less must have greatly accelerated the total journey time.

Distances from Southampton

Destination	Via Cape Town (miles)		Via Lobito Bay (miles)	
	by sea	by land	by sea	by land
Broken Hill	5987	2015	4889	1602
Victoria Falls	5987	1640	4889	1977
Salisbury	5987	1659	4889	2556
Kimberley	5987	647	4889	2970
Johannesburg	5987	956	4889	2939

What kind of railway connections could be made between Lobito Bay and the South African cities I do not know; but certainly the Benguela put on dining and sleeping car trains in connection with the mail steamers that were the equal of anything then running elsewhere in Southern

PLATE 45. Locomotives on Nairobi Shed

(*above*) '29' class 2-8.2 general service locomotive with Giesl ejector
(*below*) A '90' class diesel-electric, and a '59' class Garratt alongside

PLATE 46. A grandly impressive view of one of the mighty '59' class Garratts at Nairobi sheds.

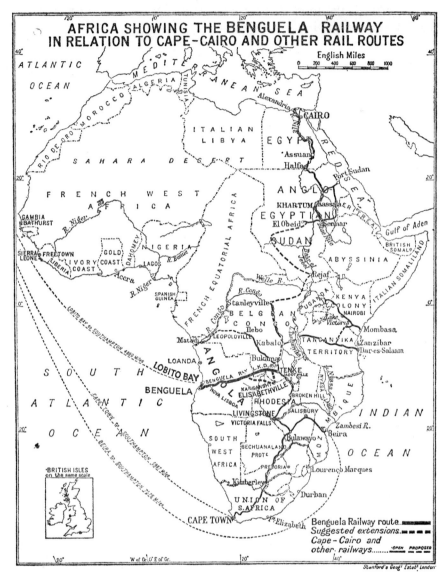

AFRICA SHOWING THE BENGUELA RAILWAY
IN RELATION TO CAPE-CAIRO AND OTHER RAIL ROUTES

Railway map of Africa, 1930, showing route of "Cape to Cairo" line

Africa. Perhaps the most striking savings in distance were in respect of the Katanga district, in the Congo,

Tenke to Southampton

Route	Distance by rail	Distance by sea	Total miles
via Beira	1776	7574	9350
via Cape Town	2463	5987	8450
via Lobito	1168	4889	6057

It is remarkable however that in spite of all that was happening the Cape to Cairo scheme was even yet not dead, and the Benguela Railway, in its brochure issued a map on which the proposed route of this legendary line is actually shown. This map is reproduced herewith, and far from extending northwards through all-British territory it is here shown striking due north through the Belgian Congo to Stanleyville, and then striking east, though skirting Uganda to reach Rejaf in the Sudan. After that it is shown making a very wide detour to the west before joining up with the Sudan Government Railways at El Obeid. Kenya, Uganda, and Tanganyika formed no part of this version of the Cape to Cairo project; still less was there any suggestion of Tabora becoming the 'Clapham Junction of Africa'! The Cape to Cairo project was certainly a long time in dying, but in the meantime the Uganda Railway was rapidly assuming a first-class importance of its own.

Until the 1920s the name of this railway had been a misnomer, in that it did not reach even to the frontier, let alone penetrate into the state of Uganda; but then from Nakuru there was commenced the remarkable extension north-westwards into the mountains that eventually became the main line, and reduced the western end of the original main line between Nakuru and Kisumu to the status of a branch. The aim was of course to reach Kampala, the Capital of Uganda; but the line had to cut through some exceedingly tough country, and on gradients of 1 in 50 uncompensated for curvature it reaches a summit level of 9136 ft. at a few miles from the point where the Equator is crossed. Precisely at the summit is the station of Timboroa, the highest railway station in the British Commonwealth. On this section the railway climbs nearly 3000 ft. in a matter of some 55 miles. Once this summit point is passed an even longer, but equally severe descent follows to Broderick Falls, at 628 miles from Mombasa, and at last on reaching Tororo, 690 miles out, the line does actually enter Uganda. Originally Tororo was a minor junction, serving a branch line 100 miles long to Soroti; but as will be explained it has since become a major focal point of traffic from Western Uganda.

Once into Uganda the line was carried by a rather circuitous route, via Mbulamuti to Jinja, on the right bank of the Nile close to the outflow from Lake Victoria Nyanza. Until the river was successfully bridged at this point Jinja formed a western terminus of the main line, and by the year 1930 there was a twice-weekly mail train between Jinja and Mombasa. The bridge itself, at Ripon Falls, is a very fine one, strikingly similar in its steel arched design to that at Victoria Falls though at a considerably lower elevation above river level. It has a completely separate lower deck for the roadway. The central arch has a span of 260 ft. and the latticed steel approaches on either side are each 100 ft. long. It carries a single line of railway. Once this fine bridge was completed the line was opened to Kampala, in January 1931. From this time onwards a twice-weekly mail train service was operated between Nairobi and Kampala, while over the original main line to Kisumu the mail service was thenceforward once weekly. On the 560-mile run between Nairobi and Kampala engines were changed at Eldoret, 250 miles from Nairobi. When the through-service to Kampala was first introduced ordinary tender engines were employed east of Nairobi. The earliest articulated engines of the Beyer–Garratt type had just been introduced for the mountain sections to the west where axle loads were limited to $10\frac{1}{2}$ tons. The most powerful tender locomotives were the new 2–8–2s, and these were used on the mail trains between Nairobi and Mombasa.

The subsequent extensions of the railway even in the 1950s have a truly pioneering ring about them. It was not enough to reach Kampala. The line had to be extended through what was virtually virgin country right across Uganda to its western frontier, to Kasese, lying at the foot of the Ruwenzori Mountains. The first stretch was from Kampala to Mityana on Lake Wamala, 45 miles completed in 1953. By the year 1955 another 71 miles was opened, taking the line onwards to Kabagole, while the final 93 miles to the present terminus at Kasese were completed only a year later. This latter was a remarkable feat of civil engineering and includes the construction of a causeway across the Lake George swamp, while in difficult mountain country 30 miles short of the terminus a spiral location was necessary to ease the gradient. It is on this stretch of line, between Kampala and Kasese, that the latest light-weight Garratt engines of the '60' class are used. These have the 4-8-2+2-8-4 wheel arrangement, and are, in effect, a modern version of the celebrated K.U.R. 'EC1' class to which reference was made earlier in this chapter. The '60' class was introduced specially in connection with the opening of the Kasese extension, because by that time the 'EC1' engines were almost thirty years old and had reached their full span of life.

Some important improvements and extensions to the line have been made quite recently. The branch from Tororo to Sorote has been extended through north-western Uganda to the Albert Nile, at Pakwach, opening yet another great tract of country, while on the main line the original circuitous route by which Jinja was reached has now been greatly improved by a cut-off line from Busematia, which reduced the distance between Nairobi and Kampala by some 40 miles. Traffic is only just developing on these new routes, but the following figures taken shortly after the opening of the line to Pakwach give a very good impression of the relative densities of traffic on the various sections of the Kenya and Uganda lines.

Annual Estimated Gross Tonnage
in thousands of gross tons

Section	Traffic
Mombasa–Nairobi	9000
Nairobi–Nakuru	6000
Nakuru–Kisumu	2500
Nakuru–Tororo	4000
Tororo–Kampala	3400

The newly-opened, and branch lines are much less busy and the following are naturally only the beginnings of the traffic, namely Kampala–Kasese, 560; Tororo–Sorote, 775; and Soroti–Pakwach 475. The problems involved in working some of the traffics are discussed in a later chapter.

In these days of air travel it might be imagined that first-class passenger

212

business on this railway is relatively small, whereas in actual fact the mail trains are in particular, well patronised between Nairobi and Mombasa. They run during the night, and provide a comfortable and convenient means of transit between the coast and the capital. There are now two trains nightly in each direction. The 'up' passenger leaves Mombasa at 5 p.m. and has booked stops at Changamwe, Voi, Mbololo, Kibwezi, Emali Sultan Hamud, Athi River, and Makadara, reaching Nairobi at 7 a.m. next morning. A total of 14 hours is thus taken for the journey of 332 miles. The up Mail follows at 6.30 p.m. from Mombasa, and has only one publicly booked stop, at Voi. Nairobi is reached at 8 a.m. The down trains arrive and depart at exactly similar times, namely departing from Nairobi at 5 p.m. and 6.30 p.m. with arrivals at Mombasa at 7 and 8 a.m. respectively. The loads, for one of the '90' class diesel-electric locomotives, are 650 tons in the 'up' direction and 680 tons in the 'down'. The maximum speed permitted anywhere with passenger or mail trains is 45 m.p.h.

The rolling stock used on these trains is very fine, and the first-class sleepers can bear comparison with anything operating elsewhere in tropical regions. The loading gauge, as on the South Africa and Rhodesia Railways is very wide and in a saloon, or a dining car with an overall width of 10 ft. one completely loses all sense of travel on a narrow gauge railway. The dining cars in particular are beautifully appointed. I had the opportunity of inspecting a number of carriages of various types in Nairobi station, and was most impressed by their general spaciousness. The livery is now maroon and cream, the body colour blending with that of the locomotives. The line west of Nairobi is operated by mixed trains, including a proportion of both freight and passenger stock; but the entire freight stock is fitted with the Westinghouse brake so that no problems arise through inclusion of freight vehicles in passenger trains.

The scheduled speeds of the mail trains reflect the general tempo of operation on this mountain railway. From the coast, for the first 55 miles where the line is traversing a tropical region of jungle and swamp, speeds are limited to a maximum of 30 m.p.h., in the same way that limitations of speed well below the line maximum have to be imposed on certain important main lines at home. A notable instance that will come to mind is the stretch across the Fens on the East Coast main line between Holme and Yaxley, just south of Peterborough. On the Kenya main line the speed limit is increased to 45 m.p.h. from Taru onwards, and it is from that point that climbing begins in earnest. But because of the restriction on maximum speed in the early stages one has the paradox that the easiest section from the grading point of view has the slowest booked speed. The up mail is booked to cover the 95 miles from Mombasa to Voi in 4 hr. 5 min., an average of only 23 m.p.h., whereas the succeeding section of 45 miles on to Kenani are allowed 94 minutes, an average of 28½ m.p.h. Then comes a short run of 16½ miles on to Mtito Andei, at 27 m.p.h., and leaving there at 1.31 a.m. there is then a 6½-hour non-stop run, to reach Nairobi at 8 a.m. As previously mentioned the only publicly advertised stop is at Voi; the others are for locomotive or crossing purposes.

On the down run, from Nairobi to the coast, the mail has booked stops only at Athi River, and Voi, but there are in addition working stops at Darajani and Mtito Andei. To anyone attempting to record train speeds in detail by the mileposts there could be some confusion, and apparently some unusually high speed on the concluding stretch between Embasaki and the ultimate approach to Nairobi. On that length there are three 'long' miles. Between mile-posts 325 and 326, 326 and 327, and between 327 and 328 the actual distances are 1⅞, 1⅞, and 1⅝ miles. Thus while the milepost distances would suggest that Nairobi Up Yard is 329¾ miles from Mombasa it is actually 332 miles. On the through passenger and freight trains the locomotives are manned on the caboose system. With the mail trains, Mtito Andei is the regular changeover point, and the brief stops at Kenani on the up journey, and Darajani on the down are for the purpose of calling the crew in the caboose, so that they are ready for the changeover at Mtito Andei. This latter station, 165 miles from Mombasa is almost exactly half way to Nairobi.

I have travelled over the line both on the footplate of one of the largest Garratts, and also on a motor inspection trolley, and could not fail to be impressed by the very high standard of the track maintenance, and by the smart upkeep of all the lineside buildings. The nature of the formation naturally varies, in a countryside of such diverse geographical nature. West of Nairobi, for example, the soil is red, as rich as that of South Devon, but the track itself is heavily and deeply ballasted with rock and the riding even on the most severe curves very smooth. On the Athi

214

Plains one sees a different kind of formation, but no less massive rock ballasting of the track, while in the Rift Valley the formation is that of grey volcanic ash. In a developing country all the stations and passing places have been laid out with ample space between tracks, and plenty of room for road vehicles to manoeuvre beside vehicles parked in sidings. Of the actual track layouts I will write in more detail when I come, in a later chapter, to the traffic control methods and signalling.

As might well be imagined in such a country and with steam locomotives of such enormous tractive effort working lengthy turns on heavy gradients, water is a major consideration, and on the 332 miles between Mombasa and Nairobi there are eleven watering stations for up trains, at distances of 8, 42, 85, 103, 134, 165, 197, 210, 230, 269, and 313 miles. Of these, five are provided for up trains only, because in the reverse direction the usage of water, descending towards the coast, is naturally much less. Only one station, Mackinnon Road, provides water for down trains only. The provision of the water itself is a major problem at some stations, where there is no river, or other natural supply of water available. To feed such points a supply of piped water from Mount Kilamanjaro, on which there is perpetual snow, had been provided by the civil engineering department of the railway, and in view of the expense of maintaining such a service it can well be imagined that the advent of diesel traction is welcomed in many quarters in Kenya—much as the magnificent capacity and reliability of the various classes of Beyer–Garratt steam locomotives is appreciated. Mount Kilamanjaro is some 60 miles from the railway at Mtito Andei station.

Nairobi, as befits the Capital City of Kenya, is also the headquarters of the railway which now embraces under one co-ordinated management not only the Kenya and Uganda Railway which was the modern development of the original Uganda Railway, but also the Central line, as it was termed in German colonial days, and later the Tanganyika Railway. The present East Africa Railway system now operates in the three independent states of Kenya, Uganda, and Tanzania with an Assistant General Manager responsible for the working in each of the three countries. To anyone seeing a photograph of Nairobi as it was when the Uganda Railway was first built the metamorphosis is now phenomenal, with a large, well laid-out station, extensive freight sidings, and a big steam locomotive running shed in sight of the platforms.

215

It is nevertheless one thing to have a splendid permanent way that will carry such giant engines as the 59th class Garratts, and to have sheds where they can be serviced; it is another thing to maintain them, and a great tribute must be paid to the workshop facilities that have been built up at Nairobi for maintaining such huge engines in the excellent condition that was evident to me from those I saw at work. In a later chapter I mention how the facilities for maintaining the diesel fleet are being kept entirely separate from steam, and several miles away. It is true that a tremendous amount of design and operating experience has been built into the latest engines of the Beyer–Garratt type, to minimise the amount of monthly servicing they need, and to eliminate, so far as is humanly possible such troubles as hot boxes, big ends, and such like. But the time inevitably comes for major overhaul, and then the Nairobi shops have the task of dealing with boilers, and *lifting* these engines. When these engines, or indeed any steam locomotives of the East African Railways, are turned out after major overhaul not even Crewe, Doncaster, or Swindon in their greatest days could excel the magnificence of turn-out imparted to engines newly out-shopped at Nairobi. The sight of a '59' class Garratt running its first trial trip in the brilliant sunshine of a Kenya morning is worth going half the length of Africa to see!

Even the intense modernity of all present-day railway activity in Nairobi however is not unmindful of certain incidents of its past, and of a time when the Uganda Railway was in its most primeval state. In various parts of this book stories of encounters with big game have been interspersed, and even when these have been exciting enough to the human participants, or have had their humorous sides, the outcome has at any rate been free from casualty. But on the down platform in the modern Nairobi station there is a grim little relic, in the form of an early four-wheeled saloon, mounted on a pedestal. In this vehicle was enacted one of the tragedies of the Uganda Railway, for while up the line one of the early superintendents of the railway was attacked by a man-eating lion, and dragged from the interior of the saloon to a terrible death. It is hard to associate such an incident with the calm, spacious air of the present Nairobi station, and with the finely equipped headquarters of the East African Railways; but then one must be reminded that until some seventy years ago Nairobi scarcely existed, even as a settlement, let alone a dignified capital city.

East African Railways

A '59' class 4-8-2 +2-8-4 Beyer-Garratt locomotive leaving the coastal area with a freight train for Nairobi

CHAPTER TWENTY

Kenya and Uganda motive power: more Garratt country

I shall always remember a remark made to me within the first half-hour I was in the offices of the East African Railways at Nairobi: 'This is a mountain railway'. The gradient profile is certainly spectacular, rising in 329 miles from the coast to Nairobi to 5500 ft. and making a still more dramatic ascent to the crossing of the Equator near Timboroa, at a height of over 9000 ft. Long gradients of 1 in 50, incessant curvature, and a limitation of axle-loading because of light rails combine to accentuate the difficulty of the locomotive designer. In recent years also, traffic has very much increased, and the problems of working a main line nearly 880 miles long, with such physical hindrances, and with infrequent passing loops can be well appreciated. There were times when the number of train movements reached almost to the maximum capacity of the line. It would have been a very expensive process to put in extra passing loops, because a great number would have been needed, and some would have come in the middle of heavy gradients where it would have been most impracticable to stop. The answer instead was to increase the load of the trains, by provision of more powerful locomotives. The history of motive power on the Kenya and Uganda section of the East African Railways has been a continuing struggle between the demands of traffic and the skill of the locomotive designer.

At an early stage in its history the Uganda Railway, as it was originally known, introduced articulated locomotives of the Mallet type as early as the year 1912. The North British Locomotive Company had built some powerful 0-6-6-0s for the very severe gradients of the Lashio line of the Burma Railways, where the maximum axle load permitted was 10 tons.

These proved very successful, and the Uganda Railway purchased some locomotives that were identical in design to the Burmese Mallets except that they were fitted with the Westinghouse instead of the vacuum brake, and that they had taller boiler mountings, taking advantage of the more liberal loading gauge on the African line. Like all the earlier Mallet articulated locomotives they were compounds. The Burmese engines had been specified to haul a load of 260 tons on a 1 in 40 gradient. Those supplied to the Uganda Railway were able to take 300 tons on the 1 in 50 stretches, and as such were a very welcome addition to the rather modest power stud in pre-war (1914) days. At that time, loads of 300 tons were not common, and to some extent the engines were a little advance of their time. As in South Africa and Rhodesia the 4–8–0 tender engine was a generally popular type, and between 1920 and 1930 various British manufacturers between them supplied no less than 68 of the type. The earlier variety, known later as the '22' class, with coupled wheels as small as 3 ft. 7 in., had a tractive effort very little short of that developed by the compound Mallets. They were followed, in 1923, by the much larger 'EB3' class, now known as '24'. They became the standard engine of the line, and 49 of them are still in service today. They are now almost entirely on secondary duties, but they have a long life of hard, reliable service to their credit.

With a tractive effort of 23,000 lb., however, they could not take larger maximum loads than the compound Mallets. There was plenty of work for them on the less heavily used sections of line west of Nairobi, but for the 'key' section, the 329-mile stretch between Nairobi and Mombasa the Beyer–Garratt type was introduced. With the EC1 class, having the 4–8–2+2–8–4 wheel arrangement, the hauling power was practically doubled. As in the non-articulated engines the maximum axle load was limited to 10 tons; but the 'double-engine' principle of the Garratt, fed by the single large boiler produced a locomotive of 40,260 lb. tractive effort. On the long runs to and from the coast a locomotive would be on the road continuously for more than 24 hours, and manning was on a caboose system, with two crews, one relieving the other after the stipulated spell of duty. When first introduced these locomotives were coal fired. There was a number of European drivers, but the majority were Asians, each with two African firemen. These engines were able to take loads of approximately 500 tons on the 1 in 50 gradients, and the speed of ascent, with maximum load was 9 m.p.h. It was mighty hard slogging, but the Garratts did the job remarkably well, and many engines of the 'EC1' and 'EC2' class were put into service between 1928 and 1931.

For the line from Nairobi to the coast, where heavier axle loads were permitted, a class of six very handsome and powerful 2–8–2 tender engines was supplied by Robert Stephenson and Company in 1928. These had axle loads of $17\frac{1}{2}$ tons, and with a large boiler had a tractive effort of 38,000 lb. against the 42,000 lb. of the 'EC1' and 'EC2' Garratts. Although capable of hard work their general performance on this exceedingly arduous railway did not equal that of the Garratts, and no further examples were built. In later years, like all Kenya and Uganda locomotives, they were converted to oil firing, and like all more recent classes they were given names. These six engines became *Mvita*, *Shimanzi*, *Vanga*, *Kilifi*, *Lamu*, and *Malindi*. They have now been scrapped, but only after a hard life of more than thirty years. They were the last orthodox tender engines for the heaviest main-line work introduced by the Kenya and Uganda Railway. All subsequent maximum power engines have been of the Beyer–Garratt type. Since that time three excellent varieties of moderate 2–8–2 have been introduced for secondary and branch line service, but these belong to the period following World War II.

In 1939 the remarkable 'EC3' class Garratts were introduced. They were the first locomotives in the world to have the 4–8–4+4–8–4 wheel arrangement. The total weight was 186 tons, and they were built, not only to work on the metre gauge, but also on those sections of the line laid with nothing heavier than 50 lb. rails. The maximum axle load was $11\frac{3}{4}$ tons, and the tractive effort 46,100 lb. The sheer pulling power of these great engines was shown by tests made against the ordinary 4–8–0s just described, where the Garratt hauled more than double the loads at the same speed. Far more important however was the ability of these 'EC3' Garratts to work very long mileages without any attention other than day-to-day maintenance. On the western end of the line these engines regularly made a round trip from Nairobi to Kampala and back, 1100 miles, with crews working on the caboose system. These engines went into service in wartime, and a typical record is that of No. 87 named *Karamoja*. This engine was put into traffic on 25 February 1941 and ran until 27 April 1944 before entering workshops for heavy repairs. In 38 months it had run 211,630 miles, an average of 5569 miles per month. Having regard to the slow speeds operated on the line this was a remarkable record. Some engines of the class achieved monthly mileages up to 6775, an average of more than 200 miles a day. This indicated that these engines were almost continuously on the run. Even more noteworthy perhaps was that despite the extreme curvature of the main line it was not found necessary to give any attention to the coupled wheels. The wear on the tyre flanges was so small that no intermediate turning was necessary in the whole of the 38 months that the engine No. 87 was continuously in traffic. There were twelve engines of this class, and so ample was their steaming capacity that when another eighteen were added to the stock in 1949–50, the cylinder diameter was slightly increased, to advance the nominal tractive effort to 50,200 lb.—a remarkable figure for a locomotive working on 50 lb. rails.

The line immediately west of Nairobi is the most punishing section of all, climbing very steeply on 1 in 50 gradients, and the curvature is constant and very severe. It is a picturesque section of line, running for much of the way through a cultivated region of rich red soil and pleasant trees, that is quite unlike the open 'bush' country east of Nairobi. When I visited the line most of the workings between Nairobi and Nakuru had been taken over by the English Electric diesels, though steam working predominates west of Nakuru. But whether steam- or diesel-hauled, the sight of a long freight train snaking its way round the curves between Nairobi and Kikuyu is amazing, and I could well imagine what a maximum load train climbing that formidable bank would have looked and *sounded* like when the 'EC3' Garratts were newly on the job. The 'EC3s', or '57' class as they subsequently became, have now all been scrapped; but their successors of the '58' class, with 50,200 lb. of tractive effort, are mostly working between Nakuru and Kampala. In pre-war years the locomotive livery of the Kenya and Uganda Railway was black, as burnished and magnificently kept as the South African locomotives of today; but on the East African Railways a red livery, almost exactly the same as that of the former L.M.S.R., is now standard for all locomotives, steam and diesel alike, right down to the little steam tank engines to be seen on the shed at Nairobi.

The appearance of the '58' class Garratts has been altered considerably in recent years by the fitting of the Giesl oblong ejector, and the efficiency of the locomotives improved in consequence. There are some enthusiasts, I know, who object to the Giesl ejector on aesthetic grounds; but it is important to appreciate just what is behind this ingenious conception. Dr. A. Giesl-Gieslingen, of Vienna, has attacked the problem of locomotive front-end design from first principles. Every nozzle-chimney combination constitutes, in effect, a jet pump in which the exhaust steam from the blastpipe has to entrain the smokebox gases. The kinetic energy of the steam passing through the blastpipe orifice must be adequate to do the necessary pumping and cover the losses incidental to the process. It is perhaps not generally realised that almost two-thirds of the kinetic energy of the exhaust steam is dissipated in what may be termed 'shock' loss due to the difference in speed of the exhaust steam issuing from the blastpipe orifice and exhaust gases in the smokebox. Dr. Giesl has attempted to reduce the 'shock' loss by accelerating the gases before they come in contact with the exhaust steam. To do this required a chimney relatively long in relation to its minimum diameter, and since the height of the chimney is limited by the loading gauge, the only way to secure the desired result was to divide the chimney and the blastpipe nozzles into so many separate units that the necessary proportions can be achieved. Thus the oblong form of the ejector was developed.

On the East African Railways the first applications were so successful that practically all the main line engines have now been equipped, including the new medium-powered 2–8–2 tender engines of the '29' class. The '29' class date from 1951, and from that time until 1955, thirty-one engines of this design were built by the North British Locomotive Company. They are of the same design as the 'River' class of the Nigerian Railways, except that they use oil fuel instead of coal. They are an excellent medium-powered engine for intermediate main line service, and have a tractive effort of 29,835 lb. They work the 'pick-up' goods trains on the main line, and generally act as reserves for the Garratts and the new diesels. They work both west and east of Nairobi, and take heavy trains, though naturally not equal in weight to those of the Garratts. In these engines every consideration has been given to making all parts needing attention readily accessible. This has inevitably resulted in many fittings being hung on outside, and although beneath it one can discern the traditionally handsome outline of a British-designed locomotive, the

221

technique adopted has provided a locomotive remarkably free from incidental troubles, and which has given long-mileage service from end to end of this lengthy railway. All these engines are now named, and they look very smart in the standard red livery.

In Kenya principal interest now centres in the working of the gigantic '59' class Garratts. Improvements in the permanent way between Mombasa and Nairobi having permitted an increase in axle loading to no less than 21 tons, a contract was placed with Beyer, Peacock Ltd. for what is surely one of the most remarkable 'narrow-gauge' engines in the world, and thirty of the new engines were delivered in 1955. They are of the 4-8-2+2-8-4 type, and with the four cylinders having a diameter of $20\frac{1}{2}$ in. and a stroke of 28 in., and an enormous boiler, the tractive effort is no less than 83,350 lb. With a total weight of 252 tons they are the largest and most powerful engines anywhere in the world running on the metre gauge. The boilers are no less than 7 ft. 6 in. diameter, and the overall width is 10 ft., as compared with a rail gauge of 3 ft. $3\frac{3}{8}$ in.! Before giving my own personal impressions of these truly splendid engines it is worth while briefly reviewing the statistical advance in motive power on the Kenya and Uganda Railway since the first intro-duction of articulated locomotives in 1912.

Year	Class	Wheel arrangement	Total weight (tons)	Nom. tractive effort (lb.)
1912	Compound Mallet	0-6-6-0	$89\frac{1}{2}$	22,176
1926	EC1(50)	4-8-2+2-8-4	142	42,600
1949	'58'	4-8-4+4-8-4	$186\frac{1}{4}$	50,200
1955	'59'	4-8-2+2-8-4	252	83,350

The above table provides an impressive record of the advance in motive power on this railway, and while the introduction of the '59' class is in large measure due to the improvements in the track that made such greatly increased axleloads possible, the locomotives themselves are certainly a masterpiece of the locomotive designers' art.

Within 24 hours of leaving my home in the West of England my friends of the East African Railway were taking me round the steam running sheds at Nairobi, and among various tank engines, several '29' class 2–8–2s, and a tough old veteran '24' class 4–8–0 were a number of these huge '59' class Garratts. There I learned how they are the mainstay of the very heavy freight traffic between Nairobi and the coast. There are now nine freights daily in each direction between Mombasa and Nairobi, and as each trip of 329 miles takes a little over 24 hours a total of 27 engines are required to maintain the service. The class comprises a total of 34 engines, and this provides a margin for those units needing attention in shops, or for incidence of minor failures. Since the introduction of the '59' class engines the standard load for all these freight trains has been fixed at 1200 tons, and a serious situation is created if a Garratt is not available, because no other engine on the line could tackle such a tonnage on the 1 in 50 gradient without assistance. In the yard at Nairobi one lost all sense of suggestion that this is a 'narrow gauge' railway. When crossing the line out in the open country, and seeing the permanent way without any of the locomotives and stock it has to carry, the narrowness of the rail gauge is amply apparent; but climb on to the footplate of a '59' class Garratt with a cab 10 ft. wide, and look ahead past a boiler that is 7 ft. 6 in. diameter and any thoughts of a sub-standard scale railway vanishes pretty quickly!

The '59' class Garratts have now been fitted with Giesl ejectors, and this has enabled them to take loads up to 1400 tons when required. This notable increase in capacity of 200 tons per train means virtually another train in each direction between Nairobi and the coast, although generally speaking all the nine trains in the day are not made up to the maximum tonnage of 1200 on every occasion. Nevertheless the capacity is now there, and when I come to a general discussion on the problems of line capacity in a subsequent chapter of this book it will be apparent how valuable an asset this extra locomotive hauling power is. I gathered that when the increase in load for a '59' from 1200 to 1400 tons was first proposed there was some scepticism in Nairobi as to whether it would be possible to *start* such a load from a dead stop on a 1 in 60 gradient. While the stations and passing places have generally been arranged on level, or easier gradients, there is always the possibility of having to stop in section for an obstruction or from some other cause. But Colonel Kenneth Cantlie, who supervised the fitting of the ejectors for Dr. Giesl-Gieslingen, was quite confident, and a demonstration was carried out on a very difficult stretch of line between Athi River and Nairobi, with complete success.

223

While I was in Nairobi the Chief Mechanical Engineer's department arranged for me to see one of these great engines in action. By going eastwards to Athi River, the last watering station on the run up from Mombasa, one of the heavy freight trains could be met; and although this would provide a journey of only 18 miles on the footplate it would include plenty of hard slogging on 1 in 60 gradients, and would be of greatly added interest as showing the general performance of the loco-motive after more than 24 hours of continuous work, during which most of the running would have been of the same character. In the ordinary way steam locomotives are not at their best towards the end of a long continuous run, and I looked forward to a most interesting demon-stration. Shortly after breakfast on a fine spring morning, in mid-September, Senior Locomotive Inspector Baldwin called for me at my hotel in Nairobi and we set off by car for Athi River. Consultation with 'Control' had ascertained that we could conveniently meet train No. 103, booked to leave Mombasa at 3.30 a.m. on the previous morning, and on which the engine would have been at work for about 27 or 28 hours continuously when we joined her.

Leaving Nairobi on a fine open road we quickly left the green vegeta-tion of the district immediately around and to the west of Nairobi, and which is such a pleasant feature of the railway in its climb to the summit at Uplands, and began to descend over bare and uncultivated scrub land. Since my arrival in Kenya my railway friends had not been backward in telling me of their encounters with wild animals, particularly at night, and this open scrub land had certainly not been free of incident. I must say that the prospect of a footplate ride on which one might see some African game, if not necessarily collide with one of them, added some spice to the expedition. Any apprehension I might have had was dispelled by the thought that our mount was to be a 252-ton Garratt, and not a motor trolley in which one of the civil engineers, travelling solo one evening, was paced for some distance by a bull-elephant!! We arrived at Athi River in good time to have a look round to appreciate the spacious track layout at the crossing stations and to observe the arrival of an intermediate class freight train bound for the coast and hauled by one of the '29' class 2–8–2s.

Shortly after this our own train arrived with engine No. 5923. The '59' class are named after mountains, and that bestowed upon this particu-

224

PLATE 47. In Hill Country near Nairobi

(*above*) A '60' class Beyer–Garratt on westbound mixed train

(*below*) Freight train double-headed by one '90' and one '91' diesel-electric locomotive

PLATE 48. A typical scene in Kenya: freight trains crossing at an intermediate loop

lar engine had an added interest for me, *Mount Longonot*. It is the great extinct volcano lying to the west of the Great Rift Valley and I had seen it on the previous day on an inspection trip from Nairobi to Naivasha. With oil-firing even the largest locomotives on the East African Railways now have a crew of only two—on No. 5923 an Asian driver and African fireman. It does not seem to matter where one travels in the world; a footplate pass and a love of locomotives quickly breaks down any barriers of language, colour, or creed, and on No. 5923 at Athi River I was immediately made as welcome as everywhere else on railways, even though the fireman could not speak a word of English. I was soon to see they were a pair of first-class enginemen. The load was not quite up to the maximum registered tonnage, being 1050 tons. Even so, such a train is no plaything to handle on curves and gradients like those of the Kenya 'mountain railway'. After water had been taken and we got the right away, the engine just lifted that big train off the mark, and we were quickly slogging away up a stiff gradient. Although the country hereabouts is quite open, and free from rocky escarpments, the line includes many deviations from the straight, in order to keep the gradients down to a maximum steepness of 1 in 60. To one used to English main lines the curves are exceptionally severe, and more like the West Highlands of Scotland; there were times when the long train was strung out round a complete half-circle. The permanent way is magnificent, heavily ballasted with rock, and maintained in superb condition.

In the meantime the locomotive was climbing splendidly. There was no evidence of 'end of the run' deterioration, and the steaming was very free. With the Giesl ejector the exhaust was not so loud or fierce as with a conventional blast-pipe and single chimney. Even with a train of 1050 tons the locomotive was working some considerable way below her full capacity, and although the regulator was certainly full open the valves were cutting off steam supply to the cylinders after 45 per cent of each piston stroke. On the 1 in 60 gradient we were making a steady speed of 11 to 12 m.p.h., which was excellent in the circumstances. Listening to the working of the engine and watching the expert manipulation of the oil and water feeds I could quite well imagine with what competence a load of 1400 tons had been started on a maximum gradient, and normal running speed subsequently maintained. With a boiler such as fitted to these engines a driver could work with a cut-off of 60 per cent or even

P

more, without 'beating the boiler', as the enginemen's expression goes. The principal hazard, in such maximum conditions of working, is of course slipping, and by this we were scarcely troubled on a fine dry day. There was a moment, after leaving Marimbeti, when the engine was inclined to slip, and the exhausts got out of synchronisation; but this was quickly checked by a brief shortening of the cut-off to 40 per cent. Then the exhausts quickly synchronised again, and we pounded on at a steady 12 m.p.h. It was fascinating work, especially when one looked ahead from that wide spacious cab, and saw the startlingly narrow gauge of the track on which we were running. After all, the cab was just three times as wide as the rail gauge!

I wished that there had been time to see more of the locomotive work in Kenya and Uganda, particularly of the '58' class Garratts west of Nakuru, and of the latest light-weight engines of the type, the '60' class 4-8-2+2-8-4s, of which 30 were put in service in 1954. These latter are mainly used at the far western end of the line, between Kampala and Kasese. The '60' class are fine-looking engines having general proportions similar to those of the original 'EC1' class of 1928 but including all modern improvements in detail design. They are of course designed for working on light-weight rails, and have a maximum axle-load of only 11 tons. Unfortunately, in the spring of 1968 my time in the country was limited, and I had to hurry away to the south of Africa on other business, but I left with the impression of an efficiently organised and well maintained steam power stud. The present tendency is towards the substitution of diesel-electric for steam power; but at the same time the economics of any such tradition are being kept in mind. Since 1950 a total of 184 new steam locomotives have been added to the stock, and when I was in Nairobi in 1968 it was put to me that the railway had got to get its money's worth of ton-mileage out of these engines, and that one could not replace them hurriedly with diesels, for the sake of 'keeping up with the Jones's'.

At the same time the introduction of diesels is proceeding apace, and on a carefully thought out and well organised plan. As in certain other parts of the British Commonwealth diesel-electric traction has not been embarked upon lightly, and while in Nairobi I was able to visit the well-designed maintenance depot at Makadara, about $2\frac{1}{2}$ miles east of Nairobi itself. The first point that I felt was of considerable importance was that all facilities for diesel maintenance were kept well away from the big steam running shed. Diesels certainly moved into the shed yard adjoining Nairobi passenger station, but no servicing or maintenance was done there, in the atmosphere of a steam shed. At Makadara the whole layout was typical of the cleanliness that is needed in dealing with the modern sophisticated equipment of expensive diesel-electric locomotives, and no less with the small shunters that are being introduced in increasing numbers. At Makadara also there is a stationary testing plant on which I saw one of the '90' class main-line diesels running. There are two classes of main line diesel now in service on the East African Railways, the '90' class of 44 locomotives of English Electric design, and the smaller '91' class, also by English Electric, and at the time I was in Kenya in 1968, 10 strong. The former have a maximum engine horsepower of 1840, and the latter, 1100 horsepower.

In referring to the normal power of diesel locomotives it must be appreciated that the power available for traction is considerably less than the engine horsepower. On the heavy freight duties between Nairobi and the coast, for example, two '90' class diesels are needed if one of the '59' class Garratts is not available for a maximum load train. In round terms the power available for traction on diesel-electric locomotives is roughly three-quarters of the engine horsepower, so that the '90' class can be expected to develop about 1300 horsepower at the drawbar. This is admirably suited to the working of the mail trains between Mombasa and Nairobi, and all passenger services are now allocated to the diesels. Diesels are mainly used for both passenger and freight service between Nairobi and Nakuru, and the careful maintenance of the '90' class engines, through the excellent facilities provided at Makadara, is making them capable of consistently reliable service. On the mail trains they are rostered to haul a maximum load of 650 tons, a very substantial one for a diesel of moderate power, over such gradients. The 6.30 p.m. up mail has only one booked stop in the 329-mile run to Nairobi, at Voi, for 15 minutes. The train is due to arrive at Nairobi at 8 a.m., $24\frac{1}{4}$ m.p.h. overall.

One of the most interesting diesel workings, inaugurated in June 1968, was on the through-express tank trains, on which engines are unchanged between Mombasa and Kampala in both directions. To facilitate the turn-round of tank wagons these trains now run at mail-train speed and are worked by a pair of diesels, one '90' class and one '91'. These loco-motives are so designed that they can be coupled in multiple—in other words the two locomotives are connected so that they can be controlled by one man. The combined tractive power of the two is roughly 3000 engine horsepower, and this has been found very suitable for handling this new express freight duty.

CHAPTER TWENTY-ONE

Modern operating and signalling
on the Kenya and Uganda line

The relative traffic density of the various sections of the Kenya and Uganda main line has been mentioned as giving an impression of the differing operating problems involved; but it is now necessary to change from comparisons to the hard facts of moving the traffic. The section between Mombasa and Nairobi certainly provides a classic study of the problems that have developed on many railways built to open up a completely virgin country, and now faced with demands for transportation beyond anything that the most optimistic of the original promoters foresaw. Earlier chapters of this book have told of the heroic endeavours by which the line was surveyed and built. Then the sole object was to establish rail communication, and the track was carried with a minimum of earthworks on the contours of the land. But when things have developed to the extent that nine million gross tons has to be moved over a single-tracked mountain railway every year the operating techniques call for the most modern methods, commensurate with what the economics of the railway budget can withstand. It is in the delicate balance of expenditure on new facilities compared to the profitability of the railway that makes the working and equipment of the Mombasa–Nairobi section such a fascinating study.

It is first and foremost a mountain railway. In the 332 miles there are forty-five intermediate stations, but of these latter nine are unidirectional only—in other words they are not crossing places. In no less than thirteen cases the distance between passing loops is 10 miles, or more. On gradients such as those encountered between Mombasa and Nairobi it takes a considerable time to negotiate these long single-line sections. Length is not entirely the governing factor, and in general operating it is the $8\frac{1}{2}$-mile section between Kiu and Ulu, graded throughout at 1 in 66 that virtually determines the capacity of the line so far as train movement is concerned. This section is booked to be covered start-to-stop in 33 minutes. At the present time the freight traffic between Nairobi and Mombasa requires the conveyance of approximately 10,000 tons of trailing load in each direction daily, and in practical politics this resolves itself into the running of nine trains of around 1100 tons each. In addition to these there are of course the mails and passenger trains together with certain shorter distance mixed workings. It does not need any very complicated mathematics to indicate that with a critical section taking 33 minutes to negotiate there is not much spare capacity on the line.

To ease the problem there are several obvious, but not vey practical remedies: to run faster; to make the trains up to heavier formations, and to put in sufficient extra crossing places to shorten the times of covering the critical sections. So far as faster running is concerned, one does not need to travel far on the footplate, or still more so on a motor inspection trolley, to appreciate the need for a severe overall speed limit. On many sections the curves are incessant and very sharp, and to re-align to permit of faster running would be a fantastically expensive job. But then, even if the speed limit could be raised there is the question of motive power. The freight trains operating between Mombasa and Nairobi are worked by the most powerful steam locomotives running anywhere in the world on metre gauge track. If one of them is not available a pair of diesels has to be substituted to get equivalent power. To get enhanced power a tandem of *three* diesels would be needed, and that would undoubtedly be uneconomic. The capacity of the giant '59' class Beyer–Garratt engines has recently been increased by fitting the Giesl oblong-ejector, enabling the maximum load of freight trains to be increased from 1200 to 1400 tons; but that facility is regarded as a bonus to be taken advantage of in emergency rather than a regular loading. The general operating conditions on the railway as a whole would hardly justify electrification, so that one is bounded by general economics to the retention of present speeds of running, and present loads.

There is next the possibility of putting in additional passing loops, and before discussing the factors that would be involved it is now necessary to review the signalling and working arrangements as a whole. Between Mombasa and Nairobi the working is regulated by the electric tablet system, giving the same degree of safety in operation as on single-line sections on the home railways. There is however an important difference, in that the loops are not equipped with starting signals, and if there happened to be two trains waiting to proceed in the same direction the one to be given priority would have to be advised by word of mouth, at the same time as its driver was handed the tablet for the single line section ahead. Having started away from one of the loop roads, and negotiated the trailing points on to the single-line section, the final 'right-away' to the next crossing place is given by the advanced starting signal, the control of which is electrically interlocked by the electric single-line tablet instruments. One can appreciate that the crossing of two trains at a loop, or the arranging for one train to overtake a slower one running in the same direction can be a slow business.

Supposing a 'down' and an 'up' freight train are to cross at station 'X': the 'down' train arrives first, and its engine crew duly deliver up the tablet for the section they have just traversed. They cannot at once be issued with a tablet for the next section they are to enter, because that section is occupied by the 'up' train they are booked to cross, and they must therefore patiently wait. Eventually the 'up' train arrives, and delivers up its tablet. The stationmaster, if not previously advised by 'Control', has then to decide a matter of priorities: is he to manipulate his tablet instrument to produce a tablet for the 'down' train to proceed, or is he to deal with the 'up' train, giving it authority to depart and keep the down train waiting even longer. Sometimes his decision is simplified by the train second to arrive requiring to take water, to shunt some vehicles, or otherwise to prolong its stop; but eventually, whatever the circumstances, neither train can leave without the appropriate tablet being handed personally to the driver, and when the through freight trains are usually made up to between 50 and 60 vehicles it means a longish walk for the man with the tablet. Of course, if there is no crossing to be made and no station duties to perform the tablets can be exchanged without stopping.

The expedient of putting in extra loops to speed up the working would in the great majority of cases be quite prohibitive in cost. The loops are laid out on much easier gradients, to make easier the starting of heavy trains; re-grading would be very expensive, while the provision of extra loops would bring staff problems. So one comes finally to the one method of attack left, speeding up the actual time spent at the loops. In this re-spect American railway history of some thirty years ago is repeating itself on the Kenya and Uganda line. At the outbreak of war with Japan the great trunk line crossing the Middle-West and Western states of the U.S.A. were suddenly faced with carrying a quite unprecedented volume of extra traffic. They were operated on the train order system, entirely without interlocking—without even any form of single-line token. The driver's authority to proceed was a piece of paper with instructions written on it, handed to him by the 'despatcher'. As in Kenya today it was a verbal authority; the fact that the authority was devoid of any connection with interlocking was immaterial from the viewpoint of efficient operation.

There had to be talk between the train crew and someone on the ground, and it would have been quite contrary to human nature if such conversation had been confined strictly and briefly to railway operating matters! I would not suggest that conversations were prolonged to the extent typical of branch-line working in the west of Ireland, but it did not need a great deal of investigation on the Kenya and Uganda line to show that in speeding up operations at the crossing loops lay one of the cheapest, and most potentially rewarding means of increasing the capacity of the line. It was at this stage that opportunity came to build an entirely new station at the important junction of Nakuru where the original main line to Kisumu diverges from the present main line to Kampala. It is not a very large or busy centre of traffic, but to some extent for prestige purposes the decision was taken to equip the area with modern colour-light signalling, in the most modern British style, with electric point operation, an illuminated track diagram, and a miniature lever all-electric interlocking frame, of the same design as those installed on certain sec-tions of the South African Railways. It was a little show-piece of signalling, but perhaps the most significant feature was not the signalling at Nakuru itself but the means of communication with adjoining stations.

It was, in fact, one of the earliest installations anywhere in the world of the system of tokenless block. It is true that the system of single line working known as Centralised Traffic Control (C.T.C.) does not em-ploy any tokens or tablets; but it requires continuous track circuiting, and usually electric operation of the points. In a country like Kenya, or Uganda, the question of training the staff necessary to maintain it, quite apart from the capital expense involved, would be major considerations. On the other hand the system of tokenless block can be used with mechanical semaphore signalling and very little in the way of additional ancillary equipment. It was installed largely as an experiment, on each side of the new power interlocking at Nakuru, and proved a great success. The instruments themselves were designed in the traditionally massive style of the older types of single-line token instruments, ideally suited to usage in signal boxes where mechanical working predominates. At Nakuru they were placed on the instrument shelf of the miniature-lever interlocking frame. Although quite a pioneer job so far as East Africa was concerned it proved a great success because it demonstrated in no uncertain manner the time that could be saved by the regulation of train movements at passing loops, purely by signal indication, and without any verbal exchanges between the footplate staff and men on the ground.

A study was then made of the busiest part of the main line, between Mombasa and Nairobi, and a decision was taken to install tokenless block of the latest type over a considerable length of the line. One of the dangers of any form of block communication is the risk of interference from stray currents, and in tropical countries from electrical storms; and when tokenless block working was decided upon for the line east of Nairobi the block-controls specified were electronic, which had by lengthy research been proved immune from interference by any known source of stray current. At the same time, as the instruments on this section were intended for installation in the station offices, rather than in the 'rough and tumble' conditions of a mechanical signal box, the actual design of instrument was of a more sophisticated type, with push-button actuation.

The existing equipment of the passing loops needs some consideration. The points at each end are operated on the double-wire system from signal boxes located centrally, and the lie of the points is indicated to ground staff and train crews by discs. These are not disc signals of the conventional type, although they look very similar, but are purely point indicators. The fact that one of these discs is in the 'off' position at the exit of one of the loop lines does not authorise the driver to start away; it merely shows that the points are correctly set. The authority to start is at present given by handing the driver the single-line token. Where tokenless block working is initiated starting signals will have to be used, and the control of these will be electrically interlocked with the circuits regulating the block working.

Writing in plain terms about the details of mechanical equipment, and of ingenious modern electric circuits tends to reduce to drawing board proportions the utter fascination, to a European enthusiast, of a railway running through mountainous regions of Equatorial Africa. The passing loops, and the associated stations may look very similar on a drawing board; but imagine a place like Athi River, an oasis in a treeless plain, at one time infested by big game of all kinds; a few trees on either side of the loop itself, some shacks, a dusty road leading in from the highway, and most important of all a large and capacious water column at either end. Then pass to the west of Nairobi, in to the wooded hills around Limuru: there one would find much the same layout, but set in sylvan surroundings with the intense red soil showing in the cesses on either side of the heavily ballasted track. Trains are due to pass. A crowd of native passengers in the gayest of attire are squatting on the broad station platform. The inner signals for the 'up' line are pulled off, but the first train to arrive is a freight—an enormous one, double-headed with a '58' class Garratt leading and a '29' class 2–8–2 tender engine. Both are smartly turned out in red, and the train, of caravan length, is drawn slowly through to the very end of the loop. With two engines there is no space to spare. Then, from the Uganda end of the line comes a down 'mixed' train, passenger and freight vehicles, and hauled by a '90' class diesel.

For several minutes the scene is highly animated. There is a general scramble for seats in the third-class carriages, until one realises that the majority of people previously on the platform had come to see friends or relations off. Instinctively a visitor from the United Kingdom thinks of the scene at other passing places. Clad in the lightest of tropical clothes I watched from the signal box. I thought of an icy January morning up at Slochd Summit when I was riding the engine of the down mail, and we stopped to cross the 8.30 a.m. from Inverness, and put off our pilot; crossings in the Welsh Marches; or flying through the loops on the Northern Counties Committee section of the L.M.S.R. in Ireland, often at well over 60 m.p.h.! Although the scene below me was so different in its colour, its atmosphere, and its temperature it was all being done in the best traditions of British railroading. The driver of the diesel had the tablet by now. I could see far away at the other end plumes of steam

234

rising from the safety valves of the two engines of the freight train. The 'mixed' moved off towards Nairobi; the driver of our engineer's inspection trolley received the tablet for us to proceed west ahead of the freight, and so we set off again on that lone, fascinating line that leads into the heart of Uganda.

CHAPTER TWENTY-TWO

The lifelines of Southern Africa

It would be the merest platitude to suggest that the times have changed profoundly since Cecil Rhodes coined his memorable phrase 'The railway is my right hand'; but though there have been immense social and political changes in the intervening eighty-odd years, in the economic life of the countries of Southern Africa railways are still the pre-eminent means of transport for freight, and for a surprisingly high proportion of the people as well. This chapter is no mere peroration of the contents of this book. The countries of Southern Africa are still thinking prominently in terms of railways when it comes to developing the remoter areas. They are building new railways; they are setting aside huge sums of money for the improvement of the older ones. It is true that electrification has postponed the tremendous project for improving the line in the Hex River Pass; but there are projects for new extensions in Uganda, there is the great scheme for improvement of the Benguela Railway to ease the gradients and alignments on the very difficult ascent from the coastal regions to the heights of the central plateau, and recently there has been the striking example of the construction of an entirely new railway through Swaziland. This indeed provides yet another example of a commercial lifeline through Africa, and a reference to some of its notable features will aptly conclude this book.

Iron ore in large quantities exists at Ngwenya near Ka Dake on the borders of Swaziland and South Africa, and it was to convey the ore to the coast for shipment from Lourenço Marques that the new railway was built. It is an extremely mountainous and sparsely populated country, and at the very origin of the traffic, the hilltop mine, 5548 ft. above sea level, special plant had to be installed to convey the ore to the loading point at the railway terminus 1000 ft. below. From there the railway journey to the coast begins with a decline fifty-seven miles long, almost continuously at 1 in 50—a nice little operating problem in itself! At the foot of this descent is the depot station of Sidvokodvo, known by the local railwaymen as 'Stergort', and this point is 80 miles from the border of Portuguese East Africa. At present the line is being used entirely for freight, and in view of what I have written in the immediately preceding chapter about methods of maintaining line capacity it is very interesting to study what has been done on this entirely *new* railway.

Train loading is governed by the gradients on the sections of line east and west of Sidvokodvo. The extremely severe conditions on the mountain section leading to Ka Dake makes some limitation of loading necessary, and it is customary for remarshalling to take place at Sidvokodvo into the maximum load formations for the 'easy' sections eastwards to Goba, on which the ruling gradient is 1 in 80. The line is staffed and operated by Portuguese, attached to the Lourenço Marques Railway, and at the present time the motive power is entirely steam, largely made up of ex-Rhodesia Railways 4–8–2 locomotives. Double-heading is customary in order to move maximum tonnage with minimum occupation of the line. I have not travelled over the line personally, though I was associated with the design of some of the special equipment installed. This naturally brings me to the methods of traffic operation. In comparing it with other sections of single-line railway one very important fact must be borne in mind: the management was starting with what could be termed a completely clean sheet of paper. There was no track, no existing communications and no staff!

It is always easy to criticise established railways for their reluctance to adopt modern techniques, and I have the most vivid personal memories of some studies that were made just at the end of World War II towards the equipment of some lengthy stretches of single line in Scotland with centralised traffic control. From the viewpoint of improving traffic operation such projects would have been invaluable; but it is extremely difficult to express such improvements, and the better punctuality resulting, in terms of hard cash savings. And the installation of C.T.C. cannot be done very cheaply. Those Scottish lines were fully equipped with electric token working; the stations were interlocked, and the traffic then existing demanded the attendance of staff 'all round the clock' at most of the passing stations and loops. These could not then be dispensed with, however the signalling might be improved. The outcome of those studies gave a clear-cut answer, that in the conditions then prevailing C.T.C. was not economically justifiable. But it was another matter in a country where one starts from absolutely nothing, and in Swaziland, 140 miles of it is controlled from one central signal box, at Sidvokodvo, with the latest form of electronic remote control of the signals at all the intermediate passing loops. Train movements are regulated entirely by signal indications to the driver. There are no single-line tokens to be given out or exchanged, and no written orders.

The working has been greatly simplified as compared with the more usual single-line practice in Southern Africa, because of the ordered programme of regular freight train movement. At present there is no question of priorities at loops; no arrangements for one train proceeding in the same direction to overtake another. It is thus arranged for all trains to take the left hand turn-out at the entrance to passing loops, passing any opposing train that may be waiting on the right. The points are not worked from the central panel. They are spring-controlled, and lie normally for the left-hand route. The mechanisms are trailable, however, and a train leaving one of the loops, 'trails' the points as it goes, while a hydraulic buffer mechanism together with the spring control restores them to their normal lie after the train has gone. Of course, a train is not allowed to depart from a loop, and so 'trail' the points at the leaving end, until the signal is cleared, giving authority to proceed; and the clearing of the signal is safeguarded by the electronic interlocking from the control panel at Sidvokodvo. These trailable point mechanisms include facing point locks, so that it is quite permissible for passenger trains to be worked over the line when the need arises.

The line was opened towards the end of 1964, and full C.T.C. operation began in March 1965. At first the traffic was almost entirely concerned with the conveyance of iron ore from Ka Dake to the coast but it was not long before a reciprocal traffic in imports began to develop, such as cement, petrol and oil. The initial progress of this finely equipped railway was excellent, so far as financial returns on capital expenditure was concerned, but whether it will ever be used for passenger traffic is another matter. A railwayman friend of mine, now living in retirement in the Cape, has described in glowing terms the magnificent scenery through which the line passes, telling how after leaving Ka Dake the line winds among the hills giving wonderful views of the Usutu forests. As a former railwayman he was well able to appreciate the very heavy civil engineering work involved in the construction of the line, in making horseshoe bends, tunnelling through solid rock, and carrying the track on the brink of fast-flowing rivers. There is some typical low veldt country traversed after the line has turned north from Sidvokodvo, but the final stretches to the Moçambique border are again very spectacular, with heavy engineering works in rocky defiles.

There is talk—only talk so far—of the line becoming a tourist attraction; but at the present time it is connected no more than indirectly with the major railway systems of Southern Africa. Its connection is towards the coast rather than to the Transvaal, although Ka Dake is only 175 miles, as the crow flies from Pretoria. But although it was built in more sophisticated times, with modern machinery, the Swaziland Railway is no whit less a pioneer venture than the Uganda, the Benguela, the Beira, and all the great projects of Cecil Rhodes. As lifelines they were conceived, and as lifelines they continue to function.

INDEX